Cultural Science

Cultural Science

A Natural History of Stories, Demes, Knowledge and Innovation

John Hartley and Jason Potts

B L O O M S B U R Y
LONDON • NEW DELHI • NEW YORK • SYDNEY

Bloomsbury Academic

An imprint of Bloomsbury Publishing Inc

50 Bedford Square
London
WC1B 3DP
UK

1385 Broadway
New York
NY 10018
USA

www.bloomsbury.com

Bloomsbury is a registered trade mark of Bloomsbury Publishing Plc

First published 2014

© John Hartley and Jason Potts, 2014

Library of Congress Cataloging-in-Publication Data
Hartley, John, 1948–
Cultural science : a natural history of stories, demes, knowledge
and innovation/John Hartley and Jason Potts.
pages cm
Includes bibliographical references and index.
ISBN 978-1-84966-602-2 (hardback)
1. Culture–Philosophy. 2. Knowledge, Sociology of. I. Potts, Jason, 1972– II. Title.
HM621.H373 2014
306.01–dc23
2014014855

ISBN: HB: 978-1-8496-6602-2
ePDF: 978-1-8496-6604-6
ePub: 978-1-8496-6603-9

Typeset by Deanta Global Publishing Services, Chennai, India
Printed and bound in Great Britain

Contents

Intro

1

Curiously Parallel

The Nature of Culture

Humankind taken as a whole is becoming a mighty geological force.
Vladimir Vernadsky 1943: 19

How each member ought to act

The study of culture often begins with some notion of individual talent, inspiration, creative activity or expression. But that is not how culture itself emerged. This is how Charles Darwin connected culture and evolution:

> After the power of language had been acquired, and the wishes of the community could be expressed, the common opinion how each member ought to act for the public good, would naturally become in a paramount degree the guide to action. But . . . our regard for the approbation and disapprobation of our fellows depends on sympathy, which . . . forms an essential part of the social instinct, and is indeed its foundation-stone. (Darwin 1871: 99)

The causal sequence is: sympathy (for others) → the social instinct → community → language → common opinion → individual action – in that order. First, evolved traits belonging to the whole population of the species (capacity for sympathy); next, an evolved 'instinct' for sociality and a mechanism for expressing it (language and culture); and only then a capability for individual action, itself steered by group values (dis/approbation of fellows).

Seen this way, individuality – our identity, as much as our actions – is an outcome of sociality, not its causal starting point; and language precedes individual action, rather than arising from it; language is not 'behavioural' in origin. Behaviour arises, in fact, from communication, among a population whose idea of how they ought to act derives from their perception of the 'wishes', 'opinion' and 'approbation' of others, as Darwin put it. On this score, he writes that it is 'hardly possible to exaggerate the importance during rude times of the love of praise and the dread of blame' (1871: 131–2). He goes on to sketch a model of cultural evolution, which he sees as a process through which individual 'moral sense' is slowly developed and generalized as a communal 'standard of morality': 'originating in the social instincts, largely guided by the approbation of our fellow-men, ruled by reason, self-interest, and in later times by deep religious feelings, and confirmed by instruction and habit' (132). In short, culture sets the rules for individual action. This is a view to which evolutionary biology is beginning to return, and we use it as our starting point for cultural science – which is an interdisciplinary attempt to systematize the study of culture in the light of the most recent developments in evolutionary theory and complexity theory.

Darwin argues that any evolutionary advantage that may accrue from developing such a conscience benefits the group rather than the individual:

> It must not be forgotten that although a high standard of morality gives but a slight or no advantage to each individual man and his children over the other men of the same tribe, yet that an increase in the number of well-endowed men and an advancement in the standard of morality will certainly give an immense advantage to one tribe over another. (Darwin 1871: 132)

Darwin views culture as the shared sense of conscience or moral standard arising from sociality, love of praise/fear of blame, reason, self-interest, religion, instruction and habit. Culture confers competitive advantage on the group or tribe (see Chapter 3: 'Demes') in which individuals grow and live. Individual talent, expression, imagination and aspiration are all involved, certainly, but they amount to a talent for sociality, born of 'the love of praise and the dread of blame', through which communities of non-kin learn to cooperate, in conditions of uncertainty and conflict, to ensure survival of the group, not the individual.

Curiously parallel

Darwin saw the relations between nature and culture as 'curiously parallel'. He reckoned that 'languages' (culture) and 'species' (nature) were both evolutionary, by means of the same mechanism of 'natural selection'. In *The Descent of Man* (1871), he wrote:

> The formation of different languages and of distinct species, and the proofs that both have been developed through a gradual process, are curiously

parallel.... The survival or preservation of certain favoured words in the struggle for existence is natural selection. (Darwin 1871: 90–1)

Notice that Darwin describes not only the 'formation' but also the 'proofs' of both kinds of evolution as 'curiously parallel'. In other words, he was claiming not only that culture is evolutionary just as biological species are, but also that the way we can know about this process is the same. He had a hunch that the explanation – the causal mechanism – for changes in languages was the same as the one for changes in species.

He was suggesting that the study of languages, and thence, the study of culture more generally, is an evolutionary science. In this book, we take up the challenge of Darwin's hunch, and call the result 'cultural science'. This is not simply an attempt to apply what is known about the 'origin of species' to culture but, more fundamentally, to rethink culture as an evolutionary process. We do not want to propagate yet more dogma in the field of cultural studies, and we do not claim to know in advance that 'Darwin was right all along', but we do think it is important to start with what Karl Popper calls a 'bold hypothesis', which is that the evolutionary process in question is Darwinian: culture evolves by natural selection, that is, we use the term 'evolution' literally, not metaphorically. We suspect that the *nature of culture* can be explained by examining it in relation to this claim.

An extensive body of published work has sought to explain culture. While anthropology has focused on the culture of traditional societies, cultural studies starts by examining culture in contemporary societies, typically modern, competitive industrial and imperial nations: thus, literary culture; the creative and performing arts. It works towards a definition based on that perception. This long-standing tradition precedes Darwin, especially in Germany (Watson 2010) and Britain (Williams 1960), where the emergence of national literatures – in Germany's case before the establishment of the nation – was accompanied by intensive and passionate theorizing about the nature and role of culture. Thinkers wanted to understand what was unique about particular times and places in the expansive, competitive context of industrialization and the ascendancy of the modern nation-state. Culture was thought to play a crucial role. That line of inquiry persisted into the contemporary period *as literature*, a running conversation among authors who were themselves significant literary figures, from Goethe and Coleridge, via Matthew Arnold, John Ruskin and T. S. Eliot, to Raymond Williams and Richard Hoggart (Hartley 2003).

We see this corpus of literature as pre-Darwinian, an attempt to ascribe *cause* to culture by studying its *effects*. Here, by contrast, we explain culture anew, as a Darwinian concept. We take account of recent progress in the evolutionary and complexity sciences, and seek to produce what E. O. Wilson (1998) calls 'consilience' between them and the work on culture done in the humanities and creative arts. Our ambition is for the study of culture to achieve the kind of 'modern synthesis' that Julian Huxley (1942) achieved for the biosciences. If a 'modern synthesis' can be achieved for it, not only within the social sciences, such as psychology and anthropology, as has already been proposed (Mesoudi 2010, 2011), but right across the disciplinary spectrum, from the arts and humanities, via mathematically based complexity studies, to evolutionary sciences from biology to economics, then cultural science can be established as an evolutionary science.

The systematic study of Darwin's 'curiously parallel' origins of language and species can develop using the armamentarium of contemporary knowledge, rather than relying still on categories derived from German responses to political modernization in the eighteenth century, when the term '*Kultur*' began to be seen as the inner life of imaginative genius or spirit (culture), differentiated from '*Zivilisation*', the outer show of power (politics) and useful productivity (the economy) (Lepenies 2006: 4) – a distinction that was seized upon by literary Romantics and modernists like Coleridge and Arnold to provide for themselves a stick (culture) with which to beat industrializing and democratizing capitalism (civilization), together with its attendant knowledge and social (power) relations.

Culture doesn't arise from that distinction, however passionately one may want to criticize aspects of contemporary productive and associative life. How it does arise has been established in the evolutionary and complexity sciences, using causal sequence, not casuistry, but these insights have not carried across to cultural studies. Nor have the methodological implications of computational scale in data use and analysis been realized, despite widespread interest in the digital media among cultural critics, activists, practitioners and consumers. Pre-Darwinian cultural studies tries to explain culture by critiquing effects and agents, rather than causes and dynamic systems – it's like trying to explain the theory of electricity by asking who switched on the lights. But the means to understand how culture works as an evolutionary system, and how to study that system, are to hand.

Certain favoured words: Social Darwinism?

Darwin did not undertake systematic fieldwork or experimentation in relation to languages as he had in his famous studies of barnacles and Galapagos finches.

Nor did he have access to a well-established body of empirical evidence about the formation and evolution of languages, although he did rely on existing scholarship for his assertions.[1] At that time, linguistics was barely a descriptive discipline, never mind a scientific one. The study of historical changes in languages – known as philology – owed much to its own origins in the exegesis of sacred texts (for religious purposes) and in the investigation of the literary origins of European languages (for nationalistic and imperial purposes). Perhaps that is why the intriguing idea about the 'curiously parallel' evolution of nature and culture was not taken up at the time and has been largely forgotten, at least in the humanities, where Darwin's very name can still cause shivers of revulsion, a hangover from mid-twentieth century rejection of fascist 'social Darwinism' (Hofstadter 1944).

Darwin was a man of his times, using the language of his times, in seeking to explain the 'descent' (evolution) of 'man' (humanity) from 'lowly' (previously evolved) animals. He took for granted not only that humanity was superior, but also that 'savage' (premodern) tribes, such as the natives of Tierra del Fuego ('Fuegians') whom he'd encountered during his voyage on the *Beagle* (Figure 1.1), were 'inferior' (at an earlier stage of material development) to civilized communities such as his own society, with a less well-developed 'moral sense'. Here is part of the concluding passage of *The Descent of Man*:

> The main conclusion arrived at in this work, namely that man is descended from some lowly organised form, will, I regret to think, be highly distasteful to many. But there can hardly be a doubt that we are descended from barbarians. The astonishment which I felt on first seeing a party of Fuegians on a wild and broken shore will never be forgotten by me, for the reflection at once rushed into my mind – such were our ancestors. (Darwin 1871: 618–19)

Lowly . . . distasteful . . . barbarians . . . wild and broken . . . ancestors – the rhetoric seems to require a primitivist and racist interpretation. But Darwin is actually trying to make the opposite point; namely that the behaviour of supposedly 'lowly' animals can be nobler than that of humans. He preferred the idea of descent from a monkey or a baboon compared with,

> . . . a savage who delights to torture his enemies, offers up bloody sacrifices, practises infanticide without remorse, treats his wives like slaves, knows no decency, and is haunted by the grossest superstitions. (Darwin 1871: 618–19)

---

[1] He chiefly credits Charles Lyell's *Principles of Geology*; and of course Alfred Russell Wallace independently discovered the principle of natural selection (*On The Tendency of Varieties to Depart Indefinitely from the Original Type*, 1858), spurring Darwin to publish his own synthesis.

Figure 1.1 'Such were our ancestors'. Fuegian Yapoo Tekeenica at Portrait Cove, as encountered by Charles Darwin during his voyage on the *Beagle*. Frontispiece to Robert Fitzroy's *Narrative of the Surveying Voyages of His Majesty's Ships* Adventure *and* Beagle, Vol II. London: Henry Colburn, 1839. Drawing by Conrad Martens.[2] Note that the portrait shows seven persons (including an infant) and a dog, as well as a dwelling, food, transportation and hunting gear – it depicts a culture or basic demic unit (see Chapter 3), not an individual. Despite this the Fuegian is posed as a kind of Victorian *paterfamilias (manqué)*, the better to highlight his 'barbarian' state.

Darwin was grossly mistaken if he thought that torture, sacrifice, murdering children, enslaving women, indecency and superstition were confined to Fuegians, and were absent in civilized cultures. Since that time, it has become all too clear that the list of atrocities he personifies in the image of 'a savage' from

---

[2] Image is in the Public Domain. Online sources include: www.lindahall.org/events_exhib/exhibit/ exhibits/darwin/48_fitzroy.shtml; and www.sciencephoto.com/media/150851/enlarge.

South America characterizes human behaviour across any known boundary of race or creed, especially in times of war (see Chapter 4 : 'Malvoisine'). But it is clear that Darwin was resisting the temptation to presume that, 'having risen, though not through his own exertions, to the very summit of the organic scale', humanity had escaped its origins:

> We must, however, acknowledge, as it seems to me, that man with all his noble qualities, with sympathy which feels for the most debased, with benevolence which extends not only to other men but to the humblest living creature, with his god-like intellect which has penetrated into the movements and constitution of the solar system – with all these exalted powers – Man still bears in his bodily frame the indelible stamp of his lowly origin. (Darwin 1871: 619)

So closes *The Descent of Man*. Thus, even while freely using the language of 'exalted powers', he rejected the ideas of writers like Herbert Spencer, Thomas Malthus and his own cousin Francis Galton, insofar as these established the tenets of 'social Darwinism'. Note that the last words of the book are 'lowly origin'. Instead, his faith in socially 'impelled' self-improvement led him to posit 'the social instincts' as an antidote to the savage ones:

> The social instincts, which must have been acquired by man in a very rude state, and probably even by his early ape-like progenitors, still give the impulse to some of his best actions; but his actions are in a higher degree determined by the expressed wishes and judgment of his fellow-men, and unfortunately very often by his own strong selfish desires. (Darwin 1871: 109)

The take-out lesson from Darwin's own attempt to subject 'human nature' to evolutionary analysis is that the 'survival of the fittest' did not entail exterminating the supposedly 'unfit' among humans but, on the contrary, it required sympathy with and a judicious ability to learn from others, especially 'lowly' ones. It required a clear-eyed willingness to observe the 'indelible stamp' of evolution as the *condition for* the achievement of the modern, liberal qualities of sympathy, benevolence and intellect. The key evolutionary trait is not selfish competitiveness but what we would now call 'social learning' (Konner 2010: 350–1; 500–17):

> But as love, sympathy and self-command become strengthened by habit, and as the power of reasoning becomes clearer, so that man can value justly the judgements of his fellows, he will feel himself impelled, apart from any transitory pleasure or pain, to certain lines of conduct. (Darwin 1871: 110)

Our only organon[3]

With hindsight, it is evident that Darwin's hunch about the parallelism of natural and cultural evolution was worthy of the 'judgements of his fellows'. But the state of knowledge about culture at the time was simply not ready for such a 'bold conjecture'. So his hunch was not yet capable of 'proofs'. It did, however, qualify as part of what Karl Popper has called 'the logic of scientific discovery':

> Bold ideas, unjustified anticipations, and speculative thought, are our only means for interpreting nature: our only organon, our only instrument, for grasping her. And we must hazard them to win our prize. Those among us who are unwilling to expose their ideas to the hazard of refutation do not take part in the scientific game. (Popper 2002: 279–80)

In his own lifetime, Darwin's theory of evolution by natural selection was marked more by prescience than by 'proofs'. But exposing that theory to the 'hazard of refutation' has indeed enabled the 'advance of science'. Subsequent discoveries (e.g. genes, DNA, the genome code) and a century or more of accelerating growth in knowledge, especially in the biosciences, have tended to confirm his theory in respect of species. It is well past time for culture too to be 'interpreted' by the same means; and for various preceding and existing attempts to do just that to be synthesized into an approach that doesn't just add to cultural studies but reorganizes the field of study.

Darwin did not conduct sustained empirical work into languages. His hunch that they evolved by natural selection could have been ignored for scientific reasons: a 'lack of evidence'. But given the state of scholarship in the period, and its use for sectarian (religious) and partisan (nationalistic) ends, a more likely explanation is that the intellectual soil on which he cast this idea was not fertile enough to sustain it. The problem was not with Darwin or his bold idea; it was with those who studied culture and their ideas.

The claim that culture forms and develops by a gradual process, which may be expressed as a law (of natural selection), turns languages, and thence culture, into a set of systems that behaves, changes and grows according to internal laws and mechanisms. In turn, that conceptualization seems to deny a creative role both to human agency (inspiration, genius, originality) and to spiritual

---

[3] The Greek word 'organon' means instrument, tool, organ. It is the name given to Aristotle's works on logic. Sir Francis Bacon published *The New Organon* in 1620 (http://ebooks.adelaide.edu.au/b/bacon/francis/organon/). Popper writes of 'bold ideas' as 'our only organon' in this tradition.

or metaphysical causation (ideas coming from external sources; supernatural, spiritual or divine).

In some ways the implications of this idea – that meaningfulness evolves by natural selection – were even more provocative than Darwin's work on the origin of species, because it decentred both God and the individual human consciousness from a position of causation in the creation and development of meaning, relationships and identity, and in the growth of knowledge and expression more generally. If the 'survival or preservation of certain favoured words' in a language follows the rule of heritable 'variation, selection, retention', then it would seem to have little or nothing to do with the will or intentions, much less the identity or ideology, of those individuals who utter the words.

Nature versus culture?

In Darwin's day, secular thinkers and spiritual leaders alike saw culture as an expression of something 'higher' than the gradual working out of a struggle for survival. In those days, when they heard the word 'culture', they were likely to reach for their bibles, or for Shakespeare. In other words, they credited the 'fitness' of words to God or Art, not to evolution, during a period when art itself was being sacralized, in opposition to mere 'civilization', that is, industry, modernity, urban life, politics. This approach to culture as a modern substitute for religion caught on among the theorists of 'high' culture, from Matthew Arnold[4] to Kenneth Clark.[5] Culture was 'the best that has been thought and said' – it was not to be confused with worldly getting and gaining, where one might expect to find evidence of the competitive 'survival of the fittest'.

When they thought about nature, as opposed to culture, they were as likely as not to imagine, as Thomas Hardy (1915) did in his poem about the sinking of the *Titanic*, something that is alien and uninterested in humanity's vainglorious creations – something 'grotesque, slimed, dumb, indifferent', in Hardy's words – that was nevertheless implacably hostile to the 'Pride of Life' that motivates human

---

[4] Matthew Arnold is still taken to be the touchstone for the concept of culture in British intellectual discourse. For instance, in a BBC Radio 4 series *The Value of Culture* (2012–13) Melvin Bragg devoted the entire first episode (over 40 minutes of airtime) to Arnold (www.bbc.co.uk/podcasts/series/tvoc).

[5] Kenneth Clark's landmark *Civilisation: A Personal View* (1969) provoked John Berger's influential riposte, *Ways of Seeing* (1972). Clark's series has been reissued: www.telegraph.co.uk/culture/tvandradio/bbc/8311680/Kenneth-Clarks-Civilisation-returns-in-HD.html. For Berger versus Clark, see: www.ejumpcut.org/archive/onlinessays/JC20folder/WaysOfSeeing.html.

individuals and society alike. An adversarial relationship was imagined between an indifferent but hostile nature that needed taming, civilizing, domesticating, and so on – especially the land and peoples of recently acquired colonies in 'wild' Africa, Australasia, the Americas and Asia – as opposed to a divinely or artistically inspired human culture, where the 'struggle' for survival takes the form of philosophical, artistic, or otherwise imaginative endeavour, created by uniquely talented individuals striving for enlightenment and 'perfection' (Arnold 1869).

It wasn't simply that the idea of natural selection painted God out of the picture, but that it dethroned 'the mind' as well. The idea of individual identity, at the heart of Western knowledge since the Renaissance at least, and given wide credence through the notion of the Cartesian ego, was incompatible with the idea of evolution. Evolution and individuals don't mix. Evolution requires populations; individuals and their notions and fancies are but carriers for genes and random vehicles for adaptation. It seemed to culture's first theorists that individuals – with their language, culture, Pride of Life; their meanings, identities, social relationships; their technologies, institutions and networks; their imaginative, descriptive and argumentative expression – cannot be 'known' by evolutionary means. It seemed unthinkable that the 'exalted powers' (social and intellectual) noted by Darwin could have been 'caused' by a mechanism other than the individual mind. Indeed, Darwin's own mentor, the geologist Charles Lyell, posited that culture *halts* evolution. For that idea he coined the popular phrase 'mind over matter':

> It may be said that, so far from having a materialistic tendency, the supposed introduction into the earth at successive geological periods of life – sensation, instinct, the intelligence of the higher mammalia bordering on reason, and lastly, the improvable reason of Man himself – presents us with a picture of the ever-increasing dominion of mind over matter. (Lyell 1863)

Small wonder that Darwin's hint of 'curiously parallel' evolutionary mechanisms for species and for languages fell on stony ground. Folk were having a hard enough time coping with the implications of biological evolution to take on the same idea in culture; asking, as the Bishop of Oxford famously inquired in 1860, whether Darwin claimed descent from a monkey on his grandmother's side or his grandfather's.[6]

---

[6] See *Wikipedia*: Samuel Wilberforce.

Caught knapping

The idea that modern humans had evolved at all took certain individuals among those modern humans by surprise. It took them *aback*. There is a curiously compelling work of art that sums up the moment when all this knowledge began to dawn on the population, not only on scientists. Think of it as the moment of collision among numerous complex systems, and the meaningfulness that was generated when, for the first time in history, this new idea became meaningful to the ordinary person, within the domain of 'ordinary culture' (Williams 1958).

It is William Dyce's painting called *Pegwell Bay, Kent – a Recollection of October 5th 1858* (Figure 1.2; and see cover image). The painting was executed some time between that date and 1860. It was bought 'for the nation' by the Tate Gallery in London in 1894. In 2009 it travelled to the United States as part of an exhibition related to Darwin's bicentenary and the sesquicentenary (150 years)

Figure 1.2 'Eerie beauty ... gnawing anxiety'. *Pegwell Bay, Kent – a Recollection of October 5th 1858*, c. 1858–60, William Dyce (1806–64). © Tate Britain.[7] Used with permission.

---

[7] Tate: www.tate.org.uk/art/artworks/dyce-pegwell-bay-kent-a-recollection-of-october-5th-1858-n01407.

of his *On the Origin of Species.* More recently it was on display again in Tate Britain's exhibition 'Pre-Raphaelites: Victorian Avant-Garde' (2012–13).[8]

It does what art can do: it presents to the spectator, that point of observant intelligibility that is projected out of the painting itself (Lotman and Shukman 1982), an image of some very complex systems coming together into one meaningful experience. The specific place and time given in the title, *Pegwell Bay, Kent* (near Ramsgate, in SE England) and *October 5th 1858* (it was a Tuesday), suggest that a unique event is depicted. It's hard to see in the yellowy sky over the chalk cliffs, but hanging there is Donati's Comet, one of the brightest of such visitors from outer space of the nineteenth century. On this date in 1858 it was nearing its perihelion, or closest point to the sun, and was thus at its brightest. A wandering star, visible in the pervasive glare of an autumn afternoon when no stars should be seen, draws attention to the infinities and scale of the cosmos, and to our ignorance of it, at a time when its enormity was just beginning to be guessed at by the general public.

Despite its portentous presence, the figures in the foreground don't seem to be taking much notice. Instead, they are looking down; checking the wave-cut platform at low tide, as idly curious people are wont to do. But here too, enormity lurked. For Pegwell Bay was a popular source of fossilized sea urchins and other shells, as well as crinoid stems, readily found in the chalk and flint of the cliffs and foreshore, in some places hundreds of feet thick, which are made of fossilized Cretaceous foraminifera and other marine creatures in their countless millions piled upon trillions.

No doubt it was a game for children to find the bigger fossils; but for the artist, William Dyce, it was a dreadful portent. Dyce was a 'High Church Anglican' and an anti-evolutionist (Rothstein 2009), completing this 'recollection' of 1858 during the very year when Darwin's *On the Origin of Species* (1859) was published. Recollecting a moment just prior to this, the artist seems to be depicting a lost innocence, before the true import of fossils – that the earth was millions of years older than biblical accounting imagined – became clear, even to children.

Above them, the comet; below them, the chalk. Observing them, their father, for the figures in the painting are his family – his son, wife and her two sisters (Barringer 1999). At the domestic level, Dyce seems to be doing no more than

---

[8] The exhibition, at the Yale Center for British Art, New Haven, was called 'Endless Forms: Charles Darwin, Natural Science and the Visual Arts': http://britishart.yale.edu/exhibitions/endless-forms-charles-darwin-natural-science-and-visual-arts. For the Tate exhibition see: www.tate.org.uk/whats-on/tate-britain/exhibition/pre-raphaelites-victorian-avant-garde. The painting also featured in a 2005 Tate-BBC exhibition called 'A Picture of Britain': www.tate.org.uk/whats-on/tate-britain/exhibition/picture-britain.

depicting the Victorian craze for visiting seaside resorts: a comforting, middle-class pursuit of leisure and relaxation that brought trainloads of holidaymakers to the Kent coast from teeming London, and a new prosperity to towns like Ramsgate. William Dyce wasn't the only member of the educated classes to make the trip. Augustus Pugin, radical architect and Gothic revivalist, most famous for the interior design of the British Houses of Parliament, had recently been buried in the Abbey he'd built on Ramsgate's clifftop, faced with black and forbidding but beautifully knapped local flint from these cliffs.[9] The town was later a favourite destination for Karl Marx and his own beloved daughters, who made a regular pilgrimage to the Ramsgate sands. Marx's daughter Jenny gave birth to Marx's grandson Edgar in Ramsgate (McLellan 2006).[10]

But Dyce is not comforted by high Victorian prosperity and his status as bourgeois paterfamilias. The attention to pebbly detail in this painting displays the very latest advances in 'scientific precision and imaginative grandeur' that the Tate exhibition associated with the Pre-Raphaelite movement (one of whose luminaries, Dante Gabriel Rossetti, would be buried in nearby Birchington-on-Sea). But his artistic and aesthetic modernism was not matched by his personal belief system. Like the sage Prospero in Shakespeare's swansong *The Tempest*, he is caught between times, staging the very changes that will lead to the supersession of his own knowledge – and his powers.[11] Like Prospero, he seems to be asking his child: 'What seest thou else/ In the dark backward and abysm of time?'[12] Unlike Prospero, Dyce may have dreaded what they would find there – a dethroned ancestry, certainly, but one reaching eons further back than a wronged father, dethroning the deity and humanity as a whole, as its ancestry began to stretch all the way back to the very urchins being prised out of the chalk by the children. Was Dyce painting a picnic, or a premonition of modernism's 'heart of darkness' – 'the horror, the horror'.

It is noteworthy that Dyce has placed the family group in distracted – individualist – isolation; although posed as a group, none seems to be interacting with the others, and they're all looking in different directions, attention caught by different sources of perplexing information in this familiar but alien environment, united only in their style of attire and activity. They are shown as individuals, not

---

[9] But see: www.telegraph.co.uk/culture/art/architecture/8992250/Saving-the-Gothic-master-Pugins-greatest-glory.html.

[10] For Edgar, see: www.canterbury-archaeology.org.uk/#/marx/4557757142.

[11] Once he has achieved the marriage of his daughter, thereby securing the continuation of society, Prospero abjures his magical (scientific) knowledge: 'And deeper than did ever plummet sound/ I'll drown my book'. Shakespeare, *The Tempest* V, i.

[12] Shakespeare, *The Tempest* I, ii (http://shakespeare.mit.edu/tempest/tempest.1.2.html).

yet individualists, hanging somewhere in temporal eternity (with the fossils) and spatial infinity (with the comet), gaining little succour from their own company, but nonetheless forming, with the unseen artist and observer, the basic family unit of a tribe or 'we'-group. Whether he was an anti-evolutionist or not, Dyce has depicted his family *in* nature, with a typically Pre-Raphaelite attention to detail; details that reveal more than the artist knows.

The power of place to condense layers of meaningfulness attends Pegwell Bay itself, for this otherwise unremarkable bit of coast is the legendary landing-place of Hengist and Horsa, reputed Saxon 'conquerors' of Britain. It is also the historical site of the landing of St Augustine, who brought Christianity to the Saxons (there's a commemorative cross in nearby Ebbsfleet).[13] And (thanks to sponsorship by the *Daily Mail*), it is also the permanent home of the replica Viking longship *Hugin*, which was rowed and sailed thither from Denmark in 1949 to celebrate 1,500 years since the Viking invasions. The Romans landed here too. Their earliest 'capital city' was at Richborough (Rutupiæ), opposite Pegwell Bay where the sun is setting in Dyce's painting; they are dimly remembered in Ramsgate's own name ('Romans Gate').[14] In other words, Pegwell Bay is the very gateway through which outside influences have been communicated to the 'English' since time immemorial. It's also where co-author Hartley spent much of his childhood, completing an A-Level Geography project about these very cliffs while soaking up the atmosphere, which was soon noisy, futuristic and bristling with jet-age energy, because a Hoverport was built there to accommodate the giant SRN4 Hovercraft that could get one to France in half an hour.[15]

All of this meaningfulness condenses into the painting (including, for spectators, that which post-dates it). It still has the power to unsettle the thoughtful viewer, because everyone, from the artist to the contemporary observer, knows that this carefully crafted vision has the wrecking ball of Darwinian 'creative destruction' hanging over it:

> The image has an eerie beauty, but it also reflects a gnawing anxiety about the mismatch between the ageless and the temporal, the divine and the mortal, an anxiety not unlike the kind Darwin's theories can still inspire. (Rothstein 2009)

That gnawing anxiety remains today in a continuing 'mismatch' between individual consciousness and the scale of cosmic space-time. The painting

---

[13] The site's connection with St Augustine would not have been lost on 'devout Anglican' Dyce: www.wsws.org/articles/2009/jul2009/darw-j22.shtml

[14] See: www.visitthanet.co.uk/viking/thedms.asp?dms=13&venue=3150257.

[15] It ran from 1969 to 1987: www.britishpathe.com/video/stills/prince-philip-opens-hovercraft-at-ramsgate.

catches the moment when evolution and ordinary culture were linked in 'public thought' for the first time:

> The cliffs and comet and shells allude to the lumbering processes of the ancient earth against which daily experience – the ebb of tides, the attentions of a distracted child in the painting's foreground, the recollections of the artist himself – plays itself out. (Rothstein 2009)

In the following chapters, we shift the long lens of evolutionary analysis from the 'lumbering processes of the ancient earth', observable in cliffs and comet, to the here-and-now of 'daily experience', in an attempt to make the study of culture itself into an evolutionary science.

Part One

Culture Makes Groups

2

Externalism

Identity ('Me' is 'We')

Culture in the broadest objective view appears sub specie evolutionis *as a self-maintaining system or organisation of interconnecting human beings and their products, or if we wish to be a little more precise, of the results of the intercommunication of the minds of human individuals in society.*

Julian Huxley 1955: 11

At the foundation of cultural science is the concept of 'externalism', which is in essence a claim about the cultural nature of the individual; about what they know, how they know it, and who they think they are. Cultural science departs from the long tradition of art history and cultural criticism (to say nothing for the time being about the behavioural sciences) that ascribes creativity and therefore culture to individual talent. During the nineteenth century, when doubts about the divine began to bite socially and politically as well as philosophically, culture provided a get-out for emergent nation-states, whose prosperity was increasingly tied to industrialization and market forces. It decoupled religious expression from causation by supernatural agents, but it retained ritualized practices of reverence towards individual 'inspiration'. It encouraged admiration for artistic genius, as a secularization of the category of the soul (or 'spirit'). It put culture ('perfectibility') in place as a *purpose* for modern nations, replacing the teleological doctrine of the divine Last Judgement or final cause. It was backed up by ever more elaborate cultural institutions (galleries, theatres, opera houses, museums, libraries . . . and, later, broadcasters), as the secularization of the category of the church, whose grandiose architecture and clerical bureaucracy they inherited. Thus, at micro, meso and macro levels (Dopfer and Potts 2008) – at the level of the individual 'soul'; at that of institutional form (where cultural institutions literally replaced medieval cathedrals in both splendour and popular recourse); and at that of macro-societal 'purpose' – culture was captured by religiosity functions, albeit in institutions that disavowed religion itself in favour of doubt, distrust and diversity.

If culture is not a secularized religion, then what is it? Our starting point is that although we accept that culture is distinctively human, at least in the elaborate forms we now observe, it is not of any individual human's making. Culture is a system-generating mechanism that everyone uses but no one invents, the model for which is language. In short, we must look for culture at the level of communicating groups and systems, not individuals; and we must revise our understanding of individuals to explain their 'groupishness'.[1] Because of the sacralization of culture, and its conversion to an individual property right (copyrighted creative talent), the alternative is hard even to grasp. But that is our starting point: that individual talent is an *outcome* of culture, and that culture creates not works of art, talented individuals or even ways of life, but *knowledge-making groups*, which work as complex systems within which individual choice and creativity are produced, such that 'culture makes us' rather than the other way round.

The concept of externalism distinguishes a cultural science approach from other ways of conceptualizing culture (Herrmann-Pillath 2009, 2013). We're not advocating yet another version of the individual-as-cause ('the' brain, 'the' mind, 'the' rational-choice agent, etc.), but seeking the causal agency of the reproduction and growth of the talents that individuals express. We argue that that agent is culture.

Externalism is a simple idea: it is that the individual brain is *constituted* in its networked relationships with other brains and with extra-somatic knowledge (outside the body; e.g. technologically stored). The brain cannot be understood behaviourally (by what it does as an isolated organ), or through methodological individualism (explaining social phenomena by taking individual intentions, choices and actions as their source), or by appeals to individual talent (genius, inspiration, imagination). It can be explained instead as an agent or 'node' in a complex communicative network, which is never as small as 'one' but also not as extensive as 'infinity'. Barring accidents, all humans are raised in a social setting that includes non-kin as well as kin, and from birth they are 'embedded' in mediated sociality via various institutions, the most important

---

[1] The term 'groupishness' has emerged in debates among evolutionary psychologists and others about 'group selection'. A good introduction to the term would be to search it in the debate staged by *The Edge* in 2012, here: http://edge.org/conversation/the-false-allure-of-group-selection (comments by Dennett, Delton, Haidt, Dawkins and Cronin).

of which is language. Thus, the 'linked brain' is formed in childhood across a finite number of real and virtual social relationships, with kin, neighbours, chance and media (see Chapter 8: 'Waste'). Just as starlings mass in millions but each bird only needs to 'shadow' seven of its neighbours to achieve the astonishing synchronicity of a 5-million strong flock,[2] so humans learn how to act synchronously across a culture by attending to a proximate group that we call a 'deme' (see the next chapter). Culture is produced and maintained by the externalized or linked brain acting in concert with others in the deme, and the result – culture – coordinates the actions of millions. In short, individuality is produced by a complex of interacting systems; it is not pregiven by nature.

Self-creation

The concept of externalism can be understood as a species of *autopoiesis* – self-creation. This is the social-systems theorist Niklas Luhmann's name for the process of continuously reproducing identity by filtering meaningfulness from the external environment through communication (Luhmann 1986; after Maturana and Varela 1980), thereby creating a boundary between the self and the other within which selfness can develop. He argues that this is the defining feature of social systems: they *self-organize*, and reproduce themselves, with communication. But Luhmann makes autopoietic organization an attribute of systems, not of life. In fact he makes a 'sharp distinction between *meaning* and *life* as different kinds of autopoietic organization; and meaning-using systems have to be distinguished according to whether they use *consciousness* [psychic systems] or *communication* [social systems] as modes of meaning-based reproduction' (1986: 173; and see Geyer 1994). Thus, for Luhmann, consciousness and communication are not strictly speaking attributes of life but of systems; *meaning* and *life* are not reducible to each other, as the Monty Python crew discovered at about the same time.[3] *Social* systems are based on communication, while *psychic* systems are based on consciousness – and these are not reducible to one another (just as *aggression* is psychic but *violence* is social: Malešević and Ryan 2013). It follows that social systems are not based on individuals, their perceptions or even acts; they are constituted in *communication*.

[2] For starlings in action, see: http://video.pbs.org/video/2365072926/
[3] *Monty Python's The Meaning of Life* was released in 1983. As many readers will know, the plot device used to inquire about the meaning of various stages life is a tank full of philosophically curious fish (in a restaurant) with the faces of the Pythons.

Communication synthesizes information, utterance and understanding; and of course it requires actors to communicate, so individuals are certainly involved, but what Luhmann is getting at is that self-organization and reproduction are functions of systems (populations), not individuals. Individuals use communication to reduce complexity by creating a boundary between themselves and the outside world, and they are constituted through their act of communication with that environment. In so doing, they also construct the outside world through which they know themselves. They are thus self-reflexive – able to observe as well as to act – and Luhmann sees this as a general feature of autopoietic systems, which are cybernetic (self-steering, using feedback loops), not based on testing observations against other, external observations (i.e. rationality). All observations about society are by definition self-observations (Geyer 1994). Self and system are not distinguishable. 'Culture' is a group-scale class of self-creating system.

Communication creates individuals

Using this approach, Luhmann analysed various social systems, such as the economy, the law, science and art.[4] In one of his many books, *Art as a Social System*, he criticizes the Western tradition that relegates 'perception' to a lower status than 'reason', allowing perception to animals but reason only to humans. Luhmann argues the contrary: 'One could argue that a comparison between humans and animals demonstrates the evolutionary, genetic and functional priority of perception over thought' (Luhmann 2000: 5); that is, it is important to distinguish *perception* (as 'the special competence of consciousness') from *communication* (the social system). He goes on:

> A creature endowed with a central nervous system must succeed in externalizing and constructing an outside world before it can begin to articulate self-reference on the basis of its own bodily perceptions as a result of its problems with this world. (Luhmann 2000: 5)

In other words, all creatures (great and small) must establish a *communication system*; it's this that allows them to perceive and thus deal with 'problems' as they arise. That's the origin of knowledge (Figure 2.1).

---

[4] See *Wikipedia*: Niklas Luhmann.

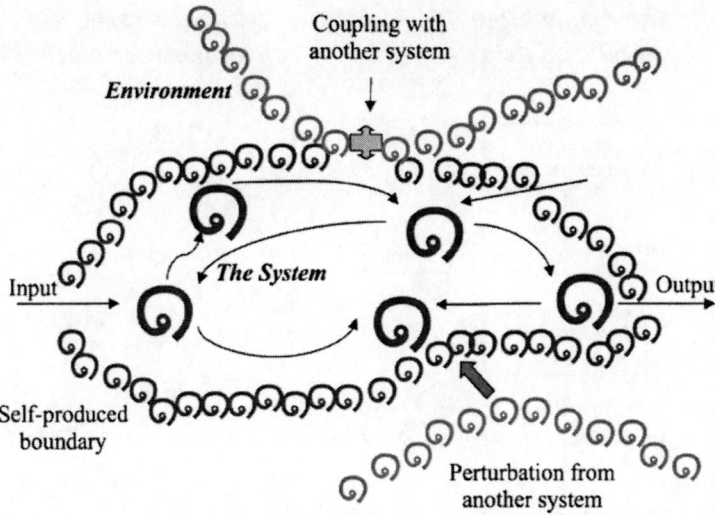

Figure 2.1 Autopoiesis – Inter-system Communication as the Origin of Knowledge (Image: Amanda Gregory 2006).[5] Reproduced from *Management Decision*, 44:7. © Emerald Group Publishing Limited, all rights reserved.

In this apparently remarkable feat, living organisms behave merely as chemicals: for autopoiesis is a chemical process, where the minimal autopoietic system is visualized as shown in Figure 2.2.

Stano and Luisi (2010) comment that their model (Figure 2.2.) 'aims to investigate the minimal requirements for molecular systems in order to display some living properties, while it finds relevance in origins of life studies and in synthetic (constructive) biology'.

This manner of self-organization also can illuminate culture, although human culture has also developed mechanisms and technologies for *externalizing knowledge*, forcing individuals to rely on exosomatic systems, structures and stores for vital, life-preserving know-how and connectivity. These external systems are also 'self-created' by the human organism, but they are not stored within each specimen; rather they link specimens to species to environment. The 'observing consciousness' that makes us think we're the authors of our own thoughts and actions, and that the world is as we perceive it, is in fact the product or outcome of a prior process of external and internal system communication, meaning-filtering, boundary-creation and *thence* perception (the starting point of consciousness) that our species has inherited from much earlier evolutionary systems. In other words, self-organizing systems are 'natural' in the *geological*

---

[5] See: *0010440707001.png*.

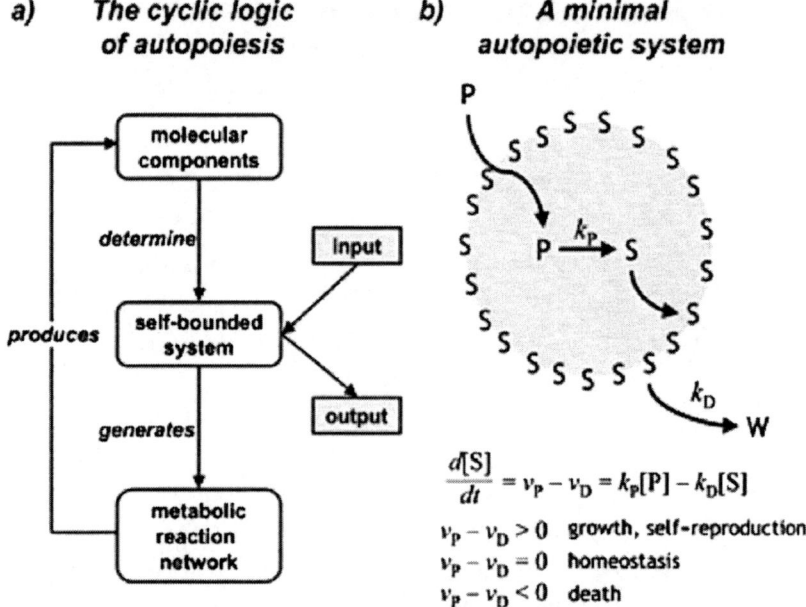

a) The cyclic logic of autopoiesis

b) A minimal autopoietic system

$$\frac{d[S]}{dt} = v_P - v_D = k_P[P] - k_D[S]$$

$v_P - v_D > 0$ growth, self-reproduction
$v_P - v_D = 0$ homeostasis
$v_P - v_D < 0$ death

Figure 2.2 Autopoiesis is Chemistry (Image: Stano and Luisi 2010).[6] Reproduced from *Chemical Communications* (Cambridge), 46:21 with permission of The Royal Society of Chemistry.

sense (Vernadsky 1938, 1943). With Luhmann, we distinguish between psychic and social systems. Culture is the means by which externalized social systems are produced and organized; and that is the mechanism for producing the kind of information that can be shared among humans, namely knowledge.

Conciliating culture and knowledge: The cultural science approach

Since the nineteenth century, the concept of culture has become increasingly restricted to its status as the values-based opposing pole to the material world

---

[6] Source: http://pubs.rsc.org/en/content/articlepdf/2010/cc/b913997d (image at page 3640). The explanatory caption to Stano and Luisi's figure reads: 'Autopoiesis and minimal autopoietic systems. (a) The circular logic of autopoiesis as minimal life. The process of living is seen as cyclic, one in which the internally produced molecular components assemble into the self-bounded functional structure, which generates the microenvironment reaction (metabolic) network, which then produces the molecular components... and so on. The system exchanges energy and matter with the external environment. (b) A minimal autopoietic system is constituted by a self-bounded system, which can uptake a precursor P from the environment, transform it by one or more reaction(s) into the boundary element S, which can also undergo a degradative process to W. Depending on the relative rates of these processes, the autopoietic system can grow, stay in a homeostatic state, or die'.

of industry and science. Yet this sacralizing concept of culture has become a serious impediment to understanding culture in a different way. That is why, in the 1960s and 1970s, Raymond Williams took it on, and argued it to a theoretical standstill. Over a number of important publications (e.g. 1958, 1960, 1977) he challenged 'high' culture (the concept, not individual artworks), by introducing the anthropological concept of culture as 'whole way of life'; or as he put it, 'culture is ordinary'.

Compelling though this work is,[7] backed up by subsequent cultural critics who sought to modernize the concept in order to investigate the culture and media of the modern, urban, industrial and popular classes (and so to invent cultural and media studies), it was only partially successful. That is because the apparatus of public and private patronage, the training institutions of universities and conservatoria, and the market in literature, fine art and serious music, all retain a practical (if not intellectual) commitment to culture as 'the sacred wood' (Eliot 1921). Which government, university, city – or banking corporation – does not have its own fine art collection, sponsored concert hall, or literary prize? That's how you can tell the winners. Thus, these edifices spread all over the world, extending to ambitious emerging countries like China, whose investment in cultural infrastructure since joining the WTO in 2001 and winning the 2008 Olympic Games has been nothing short of staggering; capped off, naturally, by a new French-designed Opera House.[8]

It is not our purpose in this book to fight over the relative merits of high and popular culture (there's plentiful literature on that topic). Rather, we mention the sacralization of culture as an impediment to its reincorporation into the domain of *knowledge*; and thence, within that context, its reconceptualization as an *evolutionary* concept. Here, it is not sufficient simply to change from one horse (culture) to another (evolution) and ride off into the Darwinian sunset in the company of a posse of evolutionary bioscientists, anthropologists, linguists, psychologists and the like, because their conceptualization of culture, while evolutionary, does not carry with it what was important about the 'best that has been thought and said' (Arnold) or 'great tradition' (Leavis) version of culture: namely its commitment to understanding and contributing to the production of meaningfulness, by analysing identity, sociality and humanity's place in a changing world. Thus, a cultural science approach to culture is still interested in 'culture as value', but it asks how that type of meaningfulness has emerged,

---

[7] Hartley (2012: ch. 2) calls Williams' work Cultural Science 1.0.
[8] http://theatrebeijing.com/theatres/national_grand_theatre/

how it changes and, crucially, what it is used for. For this, it isn't necessary to set up art in opposition to evolution – culture versus civilization, or poetry versus science. The history of scientific and artistic endeavour is the same history; the institutionalization of the so-called two cultures stand-off, in C. P. Snow's now venerable but still inaccurate phrase (Edgerton 2006: 197–202), is a problem of bureaucracy, not of knowledge as such.

How, then, may it be possible to reconcile the study of culture as inherited from cultural criticism with that inherited from the sciences? How may we promote consilience in the domain of knowledge, and understand culture's role in its growth? The answer is to attempt a 'history of ideas' approach to culture as well as to science, which will show fairly quickly that the two systems, while very different and aware of their own boundaries, were nonetheless symbiotic and intertwined, such that arts could generate sciences (as Konstantin Tsiolkovsky's invention of rocketry was inspired by Jules Verne), and science could generate art (e.g. the William Dyce painting considered in the opening chapter). More important, both art and science have attempted to solve the same problems of knowledge. In order to shift from 'two cultures' to 'consilience', it will be necessary to do more than dump previous work on culture, as Alex Mesoudi's (2010: 9) 'tree-of-knowledge' diagram of evolutionary approaches to culture seems to do, since 'cultural studies' (or any humanities-based knowledge) is not included in it; or as Bednar and Page (2007: 65–6) appear to do when they dub culture mere 'suboptimal behaviour', falling short of rational choice because of prejudicial customary ideas. What's needed for a true consilience is an approach that recognizes culture as *part* of the growth of knowledge, and adds *meaningfulness* to the sciences' unconvincing reduction of knowledge to 'ideas' or 'information'. Thus, a cultural science approach to the *evolution of meaningfulness* proceeds on the basis of what we might call:

The 10 Recommendments[9]

1. The social production of meaningfulness works through the principle of the *agent as an intentional system* (shorthand: purposeful, performative individual; but not a hypostatized 'soul' or 'mind'), acting with intention. Such agents comprise groups (e.g. firms)[10];

---

[9] We did not coin this odd-looking word. It belongs to the 'wisdom of crowds' as a term to describe what web users would recommend in a given context.

[10] An agent may be a thing, as in Actor-Network Theory (e.g. Latour 2005), which insists on the agency of non-human actors (thus, technology can be an actor). This challenges the notion of

2. Such agents, all of them interconnected to others via various webs of signification and time-based interaction, *produce meaningfulness*: semiosis in any medium that expresses all three dimensions of identity, sociality and meaning at once. That product is not only internal, subjective filtering and processing of information into meanings upon which the agent can base knowledge and actions, but it is also external, objective: it can be 'read', and *'reading meaningfulness'* in others is one of our species' special talents (associated with our big brain, long childhood, care by non-kin, and need to act socially in order to survive).

3. That *productivity – and the ability to 'read' it –* belongs to all of the agents in the system, not just to 'elite' or 'talented' ones: it is productivity at the level of populations, not persons.

4. In turn, productivity, whether it is 'making sense' or 'making money', is *technologically equipped*, operating through 'readable' networks, languages, media, repositories and practices, which themselves are made of combinations of components that include 'artifacts, socifacts and mentifacts' (Huxley 1955: 10).

5. These technologies are both *somatic* (internal to the agent-system; e.g. language) and *extra-somatic* (externalized; e.g. tools; libraries), 'interinanimated' (Richards 1936) like John Donne's lovers' simultaneously embodied and disembodied 'souls' (their 'observing consciousness' in Luhmann's terms, conjoined with their capability for action).

6. The intentions of agents, the productivity of systems and readability of products, together with technologically assisted processes, result, via 'cumulative sequence' of actions, in various more or less generalized *rules or institutions* (which are Huxley's (1955) 'socifacts'), including 'institutions of language'.

7. These rules organize the emergence, assessment, adoption or rejection, and retention or socialization (distribution throughout the population), of *newness*.

8. This, in turn, requires attention to *dynamics, change and choice* as creative processes, where the arrow of time (linear causation) and feedback loops (non-linear causation) intersect at any given point. The process of governing or regulating such dynamics is called 'auto-communication' (Lotman 1990, 2009) – the self-description of systems and cultures that

intentionality, because although non-living systems may be both self-creating and evolutionary (technology, again), they cannot be ascribed intentions in the usual way. Having said that, human agents may act meaningfully without intention (as for instance, when they are *unwitting* agents of some catastrophe), so the 'agency' of intentionality should not be overstated.

makes communication *reflexive, recursive* (building on itself), and able to stabilize.

9. The outcome is that unstable set of arrangements which we call *culture*. Culture is a property of *groups* of meaningfully connected non-kin (which we call 'demes' – see the next chapter).

10. This culture is thence a *knowledge input* into individual agents as intentional systems. Extinction is not the same process in culture as in biology – cultural forms remain available as resources for newness, long after their original use is expired (Lotman 1990).

It will be noted that there is a cascading logic going through the enumeration: you cannot have Recommendment 9 without the previous 8, and 9 is not the end of the process because there is feedback. It is this cascading logic that we want to emphasize here: later in the book we plan to introduce some new terms (note subsequent chapter headings) that further specify culture in relation to groups and the interaction among systems, but at this stage we are simply seeking to 'model' culture as a process for producing *newness* (Chapter 7). This is where we differ from both the 'high' culture approach to culture (which focuses on culture as heritage) and the evolutionary approach to date (which is behavioural rather than knowledge-based). Our concept of culture seeks to account for the emergence of the new, across whole biological subpopulations (demes), and the role that meaningfulness plays in the growth and diversification of knowledge.

Linked brains and externalized knowledge

Where the high-culture approach is interested only in the talented individual, and evolutionary approaches are not interested in individuals at all but only in populations, we seek to solve the problem of the individual by holding purposeful agency and complex system in productive tension. The justification for doing that is the concept of externalism, which explains human 'groupishness', drawing analytic attention away from the individual-as-cause towards a consideration of the system-as-cause. Groupishness involves transmitting what Vedres and Stark (2010: 1152) call 'interwoven lineages' across time (across generations, in fact), through a dynamic process of 'interweaving' that cannot be discerned if individual behaviour alone is studied. Vedres and Stark apply this 'ability to recognize pattern in historical network data' to 'phenomena with low levels of institutionalization such as social movements, emerging industries, or new schools of scientific or literary thought' (2010: 1185). We generalize the idea of interwoven lineages of loosely institutionalized group-made knowledge to encompass *culture as innovation*.

In relation to 'the brain', externalism proposes that it is not the individual brain that produces the network, but the networked brain that produces the individual. The idea comes directly from evolutionary biology (for the brain), combined with complexity theory (for the network). Evolutionary biologist Mark Pagel (2012: 12) calls 'a group of people, somehow organized around an identity', a 'cultural survival vehicle', for which a more familiar term is 'tribe' (our preferred term in this book is 'deme': see next chapter). Pagel notes that the human 'disposition' to form into these groups is a phenomenon that has held throughout our evolutionary history. He comments: 'it can be difficult to shake the habit of thinking we are the main players in evolution rather than our genes, but your body is not replicated in your offspring; rather your genes are'. He goes on to explain that humanity has actually evolved a more complex vehicle even than the body:

> When I use the term cultural survival vehicle, it is to capture the idea that our species evolved to build, in the form of their societies, tribes, or cultures, a second body or vehicle to go along with the vehicle that is their physical body. Like our physical body, this cultural body wraps us in a protective layer, not of muscles and skin but of knowledge and technologies, and . . . it gives us our language, cooperation, and a shared identity. (Pagel 2012: 12–13)

For Pagel, culture is the driving force of human identity; which is the outcome of that process, not its agent. What's more, our identity is carried in phenomena that exist outside of our individual bodies: it's made up out of language, cooperation, knowledge, technology and group relations and interactions, not something bodily that somehow precedes all these. Methodological individualism has it the wrong way round. The rational individual of theory, which Thorstein Veblen wonderfully named the 'self-contained globule of desire' (1898), is no more than a carrier for culture.

Further, once embarked on the road of cultural evolution, much of what evolves is independent of individuals. As Brian Arthur (2009) has compellingly demonstrated, technologies too are 'autopoietic' or self-creating, evolving by combining (or 'interweaving') components of previous technologies into new more complex systems (also Ziman 2000). It takes agents to do that, so his example, the jet engine, has to have its Frank Whittle, but every component in Whittle's invention already existed as an element of something else within the technological repertoire to hand. It is *technology* that evolves, not the genius who invents.

We take seriously the evolution of sociality (the 'instinct' that Darwin saw as founded on 'sympathy'), through which the growth in size and complexity of the human brain – and human groups – occurs as part of that species' adaptation to rapidly changing environments. These adaptations enabled humans (hominins) to able to work together collaboratively, imaginatively and technologically (Dunbar 1998; Boyd and Richerson 2005). Something caused such traits to survive natural selection. That something may be specified by function: evolutionary biologists have pointed to the need for cooperation to permit our extended childhood (itself required to let our big cranium grow, post-partum); to facilitate hunting parties (seven seems to be the magic number); and to allow for the development of our relatively enormous, energy-guzzling brains (Konner 2010; Bowles and Gintis 2011). These giant networks seem acutely attuned to the requirements of sociality – learning, a 'theory of mind' (apprehension of the intentions of others), and language. Through them, that trait which Darwin thought could 'hardly be overestimated' could all the more readily be expressed; namely the 'love of praise and the dread of blame'. That, in turn, is explicable as a mechanism for inculcating sociality in a species where survival required groups, not individuals, to make decisions (get food), and to reproduce (care for infants), using a mode of communication (language) that must carry culturally interwoven knowledge along with individual 'costly signalling' (sexual display), such that 'praise or blame' is bestowed where it is deserved, by a social community whose capacity for scepticism and doubt must exceed the reach of boasting or deceit but not extend so far as to miss out on a promising novelty – a trick that can only be achieved by the externalized brain (knowledge networks) of a group that knows itself and its own meaningful resources.

Mark Pagel (2012: 38) believes that 'social learning' is a key concept. To emphasize its importance, he points not just to our ability to copy the behaviour of others, which humans share with crows (doubtless an underrated species), but also to two more dynamic and impressive abilities: first, our ability to emulate the *new* (we can copy patterns not previously encountered); and second, to *improve* on it ('copying' is creative). When these features are isolated, it's easier to see that 'social learning' is not just a matter of internalizing inherited rules, norms, and so on, but also a playful, creative and competitive process; part curiosity about the world and its changes ('what's new?'); part social one-upmanship ('anything you can do I can do better'); part innovation ('stealing a march'); part Trickster

(Hyde 2008). You don't just copy a tool (better arrow-heads: Mesoudi and O'Brien 2008), a dance move (Gangnam Style),[11] a fashion novelty (this season's 'look') or an idea; you look for angles, and chip away at edges until it's sharper, lighter, more fit for purpose, and more likely to bring you praise and repute among your group (nowadays abstracted and translated into the universal 'language' of price).

The group may also want to hide it from outsiders, especially if it's really good. In culture, aggressive 'borrowing' and defensive secrecy are very common. In economics, the prevention of copying, such as trade secrets and copyright, in order to maximize the profits that one idea or process can yield, is called 'rent seeking'. In both, the secret has a habit of slipping out; copying-and-improving is endemic. It can lead to a stylistic arms race, but that process too is useful (productive) at system level, as competitive experimentation. One individual can 'win all' for the time being (i.e. most players lose most games), but the group adopts and retains the 'New! Improved!' idea as general knowledge. 'Natural selection' (by waste) and 'sexual selection' (by 'costly signalling') *converge* in social learning, for which the beneficiary is the group (firm, deme or culture).

Inevitably, that insight, stressing the importance in decision-making of learning from and copying others in a social network (or 'herd'), has now been taken up in marketing (Earls 2009); and from there re-introduced to cultural and evolutionary theory (Bentley et al. 2011), making marketing one of the first areas of 'applied' cultural science (see also Ormerod 2012).

Hence, cultural science takes evolutionary biology seriously by embracing the concept of 'externalized' identity – an *externalized brain* – for *H. sapiens*. The brain itself evolved to deal with complex interactive communication, not just for cooperative hunting, but also for care for non-kin (given our long childhood), social learning, and the kind of adaptability to new environments that let the species move out of a specialized African niche and into generalized global capabilities. This move saw it eventually occupy very different geographical, ecological and historical sites from those in which it had evolved. None of these can be explained without the concept of externalism, or 'linked brains', that create identity from group knowledge. The human animal cannot live without the core evolutionary cultural unit that we call a deme (a 'meso' phenomenon, in the language of Dopfer and Potts 2008). Culture makes demes (groups of meaningfulness) and demes make knowledge and individuals. In the next chapter we explain how this works.

---

[11] First YouTube video to exceed two billion views: www.youtube.com/watch?v=9bZkp7q19f0.

3

Demes

Universal-Adversarial Groups ('We' vs. 'They')

'Everything is what it is because it got that way'. How it got that way starts not with the Epic of Gilgamesh *but much further back: with our evolving into art-making and storytelling animals.*

Brian Boyd 2008

This chapter is about one of our fundamental claims for cultural science: that *culture is a group-forming mechanism*, being the chief means by which humans create what we are calling 'demes' – a term that we explain and illustrate in this chapter. Our approach is to pursue the conceptual issue of externalized-brain group formation by exploring how it works in a specific instance. *How* does culture work as a group-forming mechanism? To answer that question we focus on one important component: storytelling (Boyd 2009; Boyd et al. 2010). It's not the only way that culture makes groups (the role of children in that process is discussed in Chapter 8: 'Waste'), but it does highlight how language takes specific, organized forms, in this case the kind of storytelling that constitutes a polity – political narrative. These forms carry out a vital cultural function, which is to distinguish 'us' ('we'-communities or demes) from 'them' (external, competitive groups) and to render that distinction meaningful.

Stories

Stories are much more powerful than their commonsensical status as fiction, myth, make believe, fairy tale or entertainment may suggest: stories take people willingly to their deaths, in droves. That is, they act as the glue that binds individuals to purposes that only make sense at the level of the deme; purposes that may prove lethal for the individual, who nevertheless follows those purposes for the sake of the group. Like the Trojan Horse, *some* stories sit in 'our' midst, apparently a gift of wonder but in fact concealing a potentially lethal future for the unwary.

Thus, we pursue the question how 'culture creates the deme' by following one particular narrative thread: namely the celebration of war as the test of national character or, more exactly, the use of political narrative to establish that idea. Our focus is on storytelling rather than on warfare as such. We take a further step towards empirical specificity by looking at these matters via the marginal but innovative form of 'digital storytelling' (Lambert 2006; Meadows and Kidd 2009; Hartley and McWilliam 2009; Lundby 2009; Thumim 2012; Chouliaraki 2012). From that perspective it may be possible to glimpse how apparently wondrous and compelling stories that are told by mainstream storytelling institutions, including historians, educators, the media and the state – stories about our own heroism, character and achievement – may in fact amount to a Trojan Horse in the citadel of culture inside our heads. Our concern is with the use of storytelling for group creation, or what may be called '*user-created citizenship*' (see Chapter 5: 'Citizens'); not simply for self-expression but for the creation of a 'we'-group or deme around civic activism of some kind.

Demes

We borrow the term 'deme' from ancient Greek (the builders of the Trojan Horse), where a deme was a population group within Attica, upon which Athenian citizenship was based (Hornblower and Spawforth 2005). A deme is also a term in bioscience, where it refers to an interbreeding subpopulation of a given species, in this case *H. sapiens*. The word thus links the political 'demos' (and its history) with bio-evolutionary population groups that may found distinct cultures (Liu et al. 2006).

We want to explore the role of stories in *creating human polities*. They do that by organizing groups into symbolic demes or 'we'-groups (hero; protagonist), distinguished from 'they'-groups (villain; adversary), inculcating a sense of 'strong reciprocity' (Gintis et al. 2001; Bowles and Gintis 2011) or group identity among auditors.

From a long-term perspective, stretching back to the earliest evidence we have of group-forming semiosis (about 12,000 years BCE), we argue that the kind of centralized storytelling machines with which contemporary global culture is most familiar, that is, 'mainstream' media based on industrial era command-and-control organizational formats, may in fact constitute a new species of

Trojan Horse. This is because carrying a semiotic form based on local, small-scale demes to global, all-inclusive scale presents serious ambiguities about who 'we' are. Digital storytelling is but one example of a contrary move towards a new kind of microproductivity in culture, in this case opening up storytelling institutions to new kinds of deme-formation in the digital era. Such experiments may serve to challenge incumbent stories, which like that Horse invade our civic headspace with adversarial ideas. The ideas raised in this context may take a while to unfold, which is why this chapter is quite long, as it interweaves the themes of storytelling, deme-formation, scale (a recurrent problem – see also Chapter 4: 'Malvoisine'), and the kind of 'structural folding' (Vedres and Stark 2010) that links them all together in strong reciprocal networks (culture).

We argue that digital storytelling offers a challenge (potential innovation) to the very constitution of polities that are based on 'aggressive parochialism' or 'universal adversarialism' – terms that we explain further later. In order to think through these issues of how the polity is constituted in stories, and how these are competitively communicated within groups, so creating distinct demes, we return more than once to Turkey: from the very earliest (pre-pottery) Neolithic past at Göbekli Tepe, via much more recent (Bronze Age) Troy, to the modern agonistics of World War I at Gallipoli.

The creation of the self

Digital storytelling promotes *self-expression*. The digital storytelling movement is distinguished by the 'facilitated workshop' mode of production, or 'story circle', not simply by the use of digital media for narration, as in computer and video games, which are a mass-media industry rather than part of the 'maker' movement. Digital storytelling is largely organized around the identity, authenticity and experience of the teller. The movement often sets its own work in opposition to the stories told in 'mainstream' media. However, storytelling is also *political*, not in the sense of party-politics and a professionalized political process, but in the older civic sense of 'creating a polity' or what Benedict Anderson (1991) calls an 'imagined community' among those who form its social circle – the audience. Digital storytelling is therefore a kind of 'natural experiment' in localized deme-formation using digital media. It reminds us that social groups of larger scale than kin require a mechanism for *constituting themselves as one group* (a deme or demos), and storytelling is one such mechanism. In that sense, the act of self-expression is part of a 'political' narrative of group formation. Thus 'the audience' comes logically – and historically too, as we hope to show – *before* 'the citizen'; and storytelling *before* the polity. The political narrative we have in mind here is not devoted to winning votes or deciding the issues of the day, but to answering deeper questions of how we know that we are a 'we'; what 'we' are like; and thence, what kind of self *can* be expressed in stories, and what 'we' should do about that.[1]

Stories create meaningful identities for a given 'we'-community by setting the social world into a diegetic story world, rendering social values into character, action and plot. 'We' and 'they' identities are personified into heroes and adversaries. These are tested in action, and at the end are either confirmed (comedy/marriage) or modified (tragedy/death). Semiotic and social structures are mutually constituted (this being the work of culture), which means that stories are necessarily about society as well as the self. The two bonded together are a 'polity' (c.f. Fred Myers 1991: 272 – 'the meeting *is* the polity'). A polity is a social group with a semiotic identity, organized for action and survival under conditions of uncertainty or adversity. This 'we'-community or 'deme' may be as small as a family, 'hunting party' or 'danwei' (单位: 'work unit' in Mao's China), or it may be of societal or global scale. Mediatized or storytelling demes and polities are not coterminous with political governments: institutions of language are not the same as social institutions.

Storytelling can place protagonists and their deme into much smaller units than that of city, province or nation, or much larger ones, right up to species, planet or cosmos. Digital storytelling activities to date seem to be clustered around the small-scale end of this gradient. Broadcast media compete in the middle-to-large scale, typically at the level of the nation, now expanding to global networks. The 'outer limits' are explored by sci-fi (*Star Trek; Dr Who*), fantasy (*Harry Potter; Game of Thrones*), and utopian/dystopian imagination (*Pan's Labyrinth; District 9*). Like stories themselves, groups constituted around 'new media' (Hartley et al. 2013) range from one extreme to the other, such that polities or demes can form around many kinds of affiliation other than traditional ethno-territorial co-presence.

Storytelling as an evolved 'institution of language'

In the field of evolutionary bioscience, 'costly signalling' is a hot topic. The theory goes that for the purposes of sexual reproduction, competing males can

---

[1] 'Storytelling' is loosely defined – the term may incorporate elements of 'show' as well as 'tell' – to include ceremony, dance and song as well as character, plot and action; it is social as well as semiotic, and visual as well as aural/textual.

assure sceptical females of the underlying quality of their genes if they are able to sustain some outward sign – antlers, showy plumage, a Rolex – that clearly costs them dearly in energy and risk, *without possibility of deceit*. Among humans, some evolutionary social scientists think a prime function of language (i.e. an explanation for its evolution) is for monitoring the *honesty of others' utterances*, in order to sustain cooperative groups. This is what brings storytelling (language) and citizenship (large groups of non-kin) together. E. A. Smith (2010: 232) explains the underlying theory thus:

> Language facilitates complex coordination and is essential for establishing norms governing production efforts and distribution of collective goods that motivate people to cooperate voluntarily in large groups. Language also significantly lowers the cost of detecting and punishing 'free riders', thus greatly enhancing the scope and power of standard conditional reciprocity. In addition, symbolic communication encourages new forms of collectively beneficial displays and reputation management.

Herbert Gintis also emphasizes the importance of punishment as a mechanism of large-scale group cooperation or 'strong reciprocity' (Gintis et al. 2001; Bowles and Gintis 2011). But language is itself a duplicitous medium. Anything that can be used to tell the truth can also be used to lie (Eco 1976). Humans have to learn how to tell the difference between truth and 'free-riders' in speech as well as in genes (what economists call 'cheap talk'), and have evolved codes in language and 'institutions of language' to automate the process (e.g. story forms, text conventions, genres, registers, jargon; and also institutional 'languages', e.g. the law, sciences, romance, with specialist functions and features). Thus, language-in-use, as a social system and not just as an abstract set of rules, must develop institutions to 'improve the efficiency and accuracy of communication' (Smith 2010: 242).

Costly scars tell honest stories

One such institution is storytelling. Storytelling shifts 'costly signalling' from the individual level to that of the group or deme. Groups that can build mutual knowledge and trust for solving 'collective action problems' (see Chapter 5: 'Citizens') will prosper compared with others. As Eric Beinhocker has argued, storytelling is how humans think, using inductive reasoning:

> Stories are vital to us because the primary way we process information is through induction. Induction is essentially reasoning by pattern recognition.

... We like stories because they feed our induction thinking machine, they give us material to find patterns in – stories are a way in which we learn. (Beinhocker 2006: 126–7)

Note that this kind of 'thinking machine' is 'external' and social, not a feature of 'the' brain but of *linked* brains, requiring at least two parties, the teller and the told. Stories and storytelling forms are the means by which humans store, distribute and refresh acquired knowledge – they are a kind of oral/ aural library system, promoting social learning in the act of using (which typically includes adapting) the format and its store (Lord 1960; Ong 2012). Selective and competitive pressures would tend to improve the means by which humans determine the trustworthiness of others (non-kin), how they determine causal sequence in phenomena (inductive reasoning; also plot), and how they preserve knowledge across time, distance, generations and even languages (social learning). Such improvements in the efficiency and accuracy of communication, such that communicative duplicity can be detected and punished for the benefit of collective action, explain both the ubiquity and the formalization of storytelling, and its appeal. It is an 'institution of language' not an invention of individuals, and even as we tell stories, stories tell us. So much so that we're reflexively alert to deceit in the stories themselves – we mock the stage villain, stereotypical character or formulaic plot: if we're going to allow a story to teach or thrill us, it must tell *narrative* truth, usually glossed as truth-to-experience. To the extent that a good story, well told, may reveal the underlying qualities of protagonists (which are personifications of demes) as well as the teller, storytelling itself is a form of costly signalling, and may be evolutionarily advantageous:

We show that honest signaling of underlying quality by providing a benefit to group members can be evolutionarily stable, and may proliferate when rare as long as high-quality individuals are neither too common nor too rare, and the cost of signaling is sufficiently greater for low than for high-quality players. (Gintis et al. 2001)

As Gintis and his colleagues assert, not everyone is 'high quality' (some signals are lying); and not every story is trustworthy. To sort the wheat from the chaff, stories carry *within them* signs of 'honest signalling', and such signs are competitively advantageous. Among the most important is that of 'being there' – the eyewitness or participant who can relate the story from first experience. Since scars are hard-to-fake evidence of honesty, the more scarred they are, mentally or physically, in the effort of bringing you the story, the better. Because both tellers and the told can attend only to one narrative at a time, individual stories are also mutually competitive, competing for attention (Lanham 2006).

This results in an evolutionary arms race to improve storytelling as a form, to attract attention to specific tales, and to codify tried and trusted formulae. One important test of truth is authenticity, so that 'authenticity' itself is codified into conventional signs and signals. The authenticity of the observing and narrating self is crucial (unless this is a Trickster's tale (Hyde 2008), in which case the story itself, through genre, poetics and meta-discursive signs, will signal that it is to be 'read' differently). Hearers can discern what it cost a teller, and a protagonist, to bring a particular story to their attention, and humans seem well attuned to the difference between glib assertion and hard-won ('costly') authentic experience – an ability that is exploited equally by con artists and literary artists. Thus the arms race continues. Many fictional characters are visibly damaged by the time they achieve the goal of their story – think of Coleridge's *Ancient Mariner* or Arnold Schwarzenegger's character in *Terminator 2*. The cost to them of telling it seems to guarantee the honesty of their tale.

This means that all stories are also 'about' *storytelling*, carrying with them signs (or 'metadata') that speak to their believability, which is presumably why so many plots are about defeating duplicity, confronting liars and revealing hidden truths. This is why storytelling is a competitive arms race. Cutting through to attract people's attention is not a simple matter; knowledge of how to do it convincingly is encoded in narrative forms and conventions, and even crazy listeners 'know a hawk from a handsaw' (as the saying goes), so scepticism and inattention are built in. The odds are stacked in favour of those who have kept up, so new entrants, for instance amateurs of the kind that the digital storytelling movement encourages, had better watch out. Their real experience may come across as poor storytelling; while media myths may wear the convincing guise of personal authenticity.

Storytelling as leadership

Monitoring the honesty of others' utterances seems to be a prime function of language, said by some (Dunbar 1998; Bowles and Gintis 2011) to be the driver of its early evolution. Language enabled information about others, and what they were up to, to be spread cheaply. The behavioural evolutionists (e.g. Boyd et al. 2003) include language as one of the prime resources for human evolution. The ability to walk upright (bipedalism), to cook, talk and throw (not simply to wield a tool, which crows can do, but to project lethal force over distance), set hominins apart from other apes. Gintis argues that the emergence of lethal weapons in particular precipitated the need for group leadership by some means other than force. The reason for this is that following the adoption of projectiles (sticks and stones) for killing prey, anyone in a group could equally kill others. Leaders could therefore not rely on force alone, because 'dominant males' in a gorilla-like harem-hierarchy could be killed by stealth. So, says Gintis, such hierarchies collapsed and leadership had to be based on other qualities, which were carried *in language*:

> Thus successful hominid social bands came to value individuals who could command prestige by virtue of their persuasive capacities. Persuasion depends on clear logic, analytical abilities, a high degree of social cognition (knowing how to form coalitions and curry the favor of others), and linguistic facility. For this reason, the social structure of hunter-gatherer life favored progressive encephalization and the evolution of the physical and mental prerequisites of effective linguistic and facial communication. In short, two million years of evolution in the presence of lethal weapons gave rise to the particular qualities of *Homo sapiens*. (Gintis 2012: 7)

Language and group coordination co-evolved, converting species-wide attributes (walking, talking, cooking, throwing) into abstract qualities like leadership, prestige, repute and punishment, as well as care for non-kin, in demic groups of up to 600 individuals, 'a size much larger than typical foraging bands and about the size of many ethno-linguistic units in nonagricultural societies' (Boyd et al. 2003). Coordinated collective action benefitted the whole deme: 'increased cognitive and linguistic ability entailed heightened leadership capacities, which fellow group members were very willing to trade for enhanced mating and provisioning privileges' (Gintis 2012: 8).

Furthermore, these enhancements were not limited to in-group privileges, but extended to much wider social networks:

> What is known or can reasonably be inferred about the Late Pleistocene and early Holocene suggests that ancestral humans did not live in small closed groups in which family and self-interest with a long time horizon alone were the cement of society. Rather our ancestors were cosmopolitan, civic-minded, and warlike. They almost certainly benefited from far-flung coinsurance, trading, mating and other social networks, as well as from coalitions and, if successful, warfare with other groups. (Bowles and Gintis 2011: 222)

In our view, these humanizing shifts, from embodied to abstract abilities, from 'brute' force to hegemonic leadership, from kin communication to extensive social networks, and thus from local to representational or abstract knowledge, are all enhanced and stabilized through *storytelling*, as the institutional form of what Gintis calls 'persuasive capacities'. Like other natural abilities, such as the ability to cook or to fight, storytelling talent is a randomly distributed capacity in any population, but it is also *concentrated* by, for and among those who 'command prestige'. Storytelling developed socially as an 'institution of language', where abstract and symbolic values (such as prestige, repute and punishment), could be given a local habitation and a name. Gintis's list of the requisites of leadership – logic, analytical abilities, knowing how to form coalitions and to curry favour – could be attributed to the current boss through the use of flattery. At some point in or following the Late Pleistocene age, a division of labour was established between leaders (politics) and storytellers (poets and priests), where the latter sang the praises of the former. Specialist groups (bards) nurtured, guarded and adapted the skills required to do that (Hartley 2009b). 'Bardic' professionalization of storytelling separated 'persuasive capacities' from the person of the leader, even as it developed rhetorical and discursive expertise (which in turn could be learned and thereby inherited) to overcome listeners' scepticism and hostility or indifference. Ever since, storytelling, rhetoric and 'persuasive capacities' have been part of the apparatus of state power; but they are detachable, and can be used against the very forces that raised them up in the first place.

Power law distribution

As far as a story's reach and impact go, storytelling is distributed along a power law curve, from a 'winner-takes-all' head to the 'long tail' (Anderson 2008). Very few stories catch everyone's attention; many stories catch a few. Clustered around the head are stories about the *polity* (how our group came to be and why it matters) and stories about *religion* (projecting group identity to the supernatural, which can then return in a more terrifying form to punish deceivers and free-riders). Clustered at this extreme too are high-investment social institutions and corporations, especially the media, schooling and the law, all of which legitimate themselves with foundation stories that seem to coincide with those of the nation, polity or deme. They produce the small number of stories that *everyone* knows or sees (sacred texts; law-forming stories; blockbusters).

At the other extreme of the 'long tail', stories tend to be about the *self* (identity in conflict), about *locality* (our place; peasants' tales), or *migration* (the world; sailors' tales) (Buonanno 2005). And here too is where we usually find digital storytelling.

This power law distribution is worthy of mention because stories told by global media corporations are not *opposed* to stories told by persons; they are on a *gradient*. In principle, and over time, stories and players can change places. The difference between them is not antagonistic, because different types of story serve different functions for different scales of group. In short, digital storytelling is not *opposed to* mainstream media narrative; it is on a continuum with it. Thus, it is important not to dismiss storytelling emanating from global corporations, even if it seems – like the Trojan Horse – to outcompete local or individual efforts in terms of investment, airtime, popular attention and even authenticity. It is true that commercial media production is competition for digital storytelling, but that doesn't make it an adversary or 'they' identity. The digital storytelling movement can compete, by mastering the trick of authenticity ('costly signalling'), while attending to the requirements of inductive reasoning and social learning, for the solution of a significant collective action problem, among a specific 'we'-group. Where there may be a conflict or tension between the two extremes of storytelling is not in their structure or form, but in the type of 'we'-community or deme that is imagined within the stories themselves; and in the number of 'followers' willing to join that deme.

Communicative competition

Inevitably, even in advocacy or educational work that may reject commercial or marketing values, *self-expression* is not enough to achieve *communication* with others. To create a 'we'-community, digital storytelling needs to be political and competitive, and open to the logics and potentiality of social networks and 'social network markets' (Potts et al. 2008). Digital storytellers need to know enough about the 'costly signalling' game to be able to use their messages for the 'creation of a polity' around their advocacy. This is not necessarily welcome news for activist agencies, because the strong asymmetry between high-investment commercial media and community-based self-expression is exactly why 'alternative' agencies are active in the first place – they want to take mediation 'back' from industry and relocate it in the community. But the very community they invoke is already suffused with the model of commercial media narration, as a kind of *cultural technology* that contemporary citizens carry around in their heads. 'Everyone knows' how stories work because their forms are reiterated countless times in media, and these models are unselfconsciously rehearsed in everyday talk, play and the like. The arrow of time cannot be reversed: *'we' are mediated selves*. 'Self-expression' needs to compete with the media of which it is a differentiated part. The problem remains, whether competing takes the spontaneous form of informal and untutored popular culture practices such as 'selfies' (Nelson 2013), sexting and so on, where a few randomly probable signals may 'go viral' and produce celebrities while most don't, or whether it is attempted via the more elaborately facilitated and edited forms of digital storytelling. Both storytellers and their audiences live within a semiotic environment where stories must compete to gain attention (Lanham 2006). Hence, those who wish to use stories and digital media for self-expression and community advocacy must go beyond the identity and authenticity of the maker, to embrace communication and outreach, also known as marketing (Bentley et al. 2011).

Stories need some distinctive quality, which digital storytelling needs to teach, because although everyone is familiar with a good story, technique has to be learned – in this case through the 'collective action' of a facilitated workshop. In a competitive environment, 'authenticity' is another ploy, so stories have to outsmart scepticism. Digital storytelling pioneer Daniel Meadows argues:

> If citizens are to make their own TV on the kitchen table – as it were – then it is imperative that Big Media provides them with forms which can be readily learned, elegant forms which allow for an articulate contribution. We should make good Digital Stories, not bad television. . . . Digital Stories are indeed multimedia sonnets from the people but let's not kid ourselves that they grow on trees. (Meadows et al. 2006: 3)

The 'oracle of girl world'

An example of someone who took self-mediation from the blog-in-the-bedroom to global media presence, very much by using 'elegant forms which allow for an articulate contribution', is Tavi Gevinson. Her own 'story' illustrates how authenticity can be combined with communication to powerful effect. Gevinson commenced with a home-based fashion-fan blog at age 11 (*thestylerookie.com*). She went on to use her own story to develop a voice for girls. At 14, she launched a successful online magazine (*Rookiemag.com*), which she edited after school (still using the domestic bedroom as office and factory floor, marshalling the efforts of more than 50 contributors), including two yearbooks. At 15, she gave a high-rating TEDxTeen Talk,[2] and at 16 undertook a national US tour that achieved intense levels of participation among her peers. At 17 she went global; for

---

[2] 'Still figuring it out' (April 2012), had over half a million views at last count: www.youtube.com/watch?v=6osiBvQ-RRg.

example, speaking at the Sydney Opera House and Melbourne Writer's Festival.[3] Small wonder that she was hailed as 'the oracle of girl world' while still a child.[4]

The question her case poses for the digital storytelling movement – for theorists, facilitators and practitioners alike – is this: How come an otherwise anonymous teenager can command global attention in the name of an authentic but critical take on 'girl world', and so help to redefine it, simply by telling her own stories among her own 'demo-graphic'? Tavi Gevinson was not much discussed in the digital storytelling movement. But digital storytelling *as a movement* has much to learn from her ability to combine self-representation with scaled-up digital communication in a good cause. It seems that her success is more than random luck; it attends someone whose talent is authentic, well managed and current, making use of the storytelling institutions and networking technologies to hand, in exactly the same cause – feminism for girls – that many digital storytelling advocacy groups espouse (Şimşek 2012; Vivienne 2013). Here is where copying the mainstream may be seen not as derivative but as part of the process of social learning; a prompt to *innovation*.

Gallipoli – The creation of national character

We turn now from the *communication* element of storytelling to the *political* aspect – the role of storytelling in 'creating the polity'. We argue that this has been a prime function of storytelling since before there were polities; and that it remains an important element of any attempt to create a 'we'-community in the digital era – resulting in a 'digital deme'. As mentioned, the stories that 'constitute the polity' cluster at the head of a long-tail distribution curve of stories circulating in a given society. As a result, they're not the sort of stories that generally crop up in the digital storytelling movement, although as we shall see there are powerful connections between 'polity' and 'personal' that digital storytelling can exploit or be exploited by.

The most important political narrative is the one that constitutes the polity. These stories are common in foundation myths, from Adam and Eve in the Bible's *Genesis* to Romulus and Remus in Virgil's *Aeneid*; from the Trojan War for the Greeks to the Punic Wars for the Romans; from the 'Pilgrim Fathers'

---

[3] Sources: www.drawnandquarterly.com/newsList.php?item=a5230864510be8; http://ideas.sydney operahouse.com/2013/tavi-gevinson-tavis-big-big-world-at-17/ and http://tickets.mwf.com.au/ session2_mwf.asp?s=532.

[4] Michael Schulman (27 July 2012), 'The Oracle of Girl World'. *New York Times*: www.nytimes. com/2012/07/29/fashion/tavi-gevinson-the-oracle-of-girl-world.html.

to *The Outlaw Josey Wales* for America. They supply a reason or cause for the origin of humans in general or of a particular city or nation. Interestingly (for our Turkish connection), an early foundation myth for Britain asserts that it was founded by Brutus of Troy, grandson of Aeneas, and that the British nation descends from Trojans. That story was current throughout the medieval period (e.g. in Chaucer and *Gawain and the Green Knight*). It was still accepted by Shakespeare as historical (via *Holinshed's Chronicles*, 1577).[5]

Despite their own ancient and mythological origins, *etiological* (causation) stories are commonplace still, ascribing reason and meaningfulness to events and places that then explain the character of a nation. Even the US Constitution has one such story, a tale that claims 'natural law' from the supposed natural state of humanity, prior to civilization and government, and therefore taking priority over them. Thus did the Founding Fathers establish as natural (rather than political) the right of individuals to overthrow governments. Causation stories are repeated continuously, achieving thereby the status of law (lore), in school, in journalism and in fiction, all the way from Homer and Virgil to the nightly news and movies, making the polity or 'imagined community' anew each day by recreating the story of who 'we' are.

One prominent genre of etiological stories is associated with national day celebrations. These are staged by both media and public authorities, with high production values and showy symbolic content, especially in modern nation-states born out of popular revolutions (France; Russia; China) or settler-based social experiments (the United States; Australia). Settler nations don't have mythical origins, except among their Indigenous populations, who were typically excluded from their modern constitutions. All the more reason, therefore, to provide themselves with modern myths and legends, and to make these the subject of exorbitant display.

In Australia's case the official national day (26 January), commemorates the landing of the fleet that established the British penal colony at Botany Bay in 1788. As a foundation event, it is contested. It's called 'Invasion Day' among indigenous groups.[6] As a summertime public holiday, it is associated with beach culture rather than constitutional reverence. As the 'Cronulla riots' of 2005 demonstrated, Aussie beach culture can suddenly erupt into political prominence as a stage for conflict about national identity, including racist and

---

[5] See *Wikipedia*: Brutus of Troy.
[6] See for instance: www.australiaday.com.au/studentresources/indigenous.aspx; and: Peter Gebhardt (2013), 'A national day of shame'. *Sydney Morning Herald*, 24 January. Online: www.smh.com.au/federal-politics/society-and-culture/a-national-day-of-shame-20130123-2d7b3.html.

flag-flaunting versions that seek to exclude migrant cultures (Hartley and Green 2006). It is widely ignored by non-English-speaking communities, among whom it has low salience. Constitutionally, moreover, Australia Day is on the 'wrong' day in January. The 'Commonwealth of Australia' was founded in 1901 by Act of Parliament and Royal Proclamation, after referenda in the six colonies, on *1 January* (not 26th).

Small wonder that Australians gain a rather confused and impoverished sense of national origin from Australia Day. In recent years, its significance in this respect is eclipsed by Anzac Day (25 April). Here, a strong sense of a DIY (do-it-yourself) myth of national origin has built up since the 1990s. One popular highlight is the annual 'pilgrimage' to Gallipoli.[7] The destination is a peninsula in Turkey that was unsuccessfully invaded in April 1915 by French and British Empire forces, including Australians, New Zealanders (Anzacs) and Indians, as well as British troops. They withdrew 8 months later with high casualties on all sides, defeated by Ottoman forces under the command of Mustafa Kemal, later Atatürk, founder of the modern Turkish republic.[8]

Over recent decades this unlikely setting has become the place of origin of Australian and New Zealand national consciousness, and Anzac Day the most important day of national memorialization. Just as it is eclipsing Australia Day, so it also eclipses Armistice Day as a memorialization of national war service. Unlike 11 November, Anzac Day is a public holiday, marked by dawn services at war memorials around the country and at Gallipoli.

More popular now than when veterans still lived, these gatherings attract many thousands of attendees of all ages. The trek to Gallipoli is especially popular among backpackers and other young travellers, for whom it seems to function as a place and rite of passage in their own process of self-realization. In that respect, their motivations may not be altogether different from those of the original Anzacs, if contemporary recruiting strategies are anything to go by. The headline 'offer' in a World War I leaflet issued by the State Recruiting Committee for New South Wales was for a *'Free Tour to Britain and Europe – The Chance of a Lifetime'* (reproduced in Larsson 2009: 36–7). In 1914–15 mass 'tourism' meant joining the Australian Imperial Force and going to war. The bar was not set very high: anyone could 'participate in this unique offer' if they were male, aged between 18 and 45, over 5 feet 2 inches tall (1.5 m), and 'able to expand your chest to 33 inches' (84 cm). The only hint of a downside to 'active

---

[7] There was no such thing as an Australian citizen till 1949, only British subjects. Aboriginal people were not citizens until 1967.

[8] See: *www.anzacsite.gov.au*.

service abroad' (war was not mentioned; nor enemies; nor a 'cause') was a table of pensions payable in case of death or incapacity.

Was this 'Free Tour. . . . Chance of a Lifetime' pitch meant to attract the type of crowds who might today head for Bali? If so, then today's Gallipoli pilgrims may be worthy successors. Anzac Cove attracts a music-festival sized crowd, who camp nearby and gather, many flag-clad, for dawn ceremonies. One recent historian, forgetting that this sort of adventure was what the original Anzacs were signed up for, has criticized the event for resembling a 'Big Day Out' – the annual Australian summertime rock concert.[9] He complained that 'official presentations [at the 90th anniversary in 2005] included pop music which inspired dancing and couples were seen canoodling near graves'.[10] He dreaded the 'prospect of a memorial service packed with excitable fans instead of mourners' at the upcoming 2015 centenary.

The explanation for today's popular behaviour (and the squeamishness of experts) is *political narrative* – the story, internalized by many (which the original Anzacs could not have shared as they embarked on their Grand Tour), of how a distinctive national consciousness was forged in the crucible of war. The story triumphs despite the facts: that the campaign was a failed sideshow; that more Australians died at the Western Front[11]; and that nationhood was established in 1901. The narrative (about character) has trumped the realities (military, legal and political),[12] not to mention the enduring cost to 'the human mind and body' (Larsson 2009: 17) that was paid by Anzacs and their families.

Naturally, the Australian news media are eagerly on hand each year, at Gallipoli and elsewhere, disseminating the memorializing story to a wider public and celebrating the purported national character through the apparently self-staged rituals of ordinary people at a widely distributed but simultaneous national corroboree. *The Australian* newspaper plays a prominent role in promoting Anzac Day activities at home and in Turkey. This may be connected with the fact that the proprietor of *The Australian*, Rupert Murdoch, has a family connection with the original events. His father, Keith Murdoch, a young journalist at the time, reported the campaign's failings back to Australian and

---

[9] See: www.bigdayout.com.

[10] King, J. (20 April 2013), 'It's Anzac Day – not the Big Day Out'. *Sydney Morning Herald*: www.smh.com.au/national/its-anzac-day--not-the-big-day-out-20130419-2i5a4.html#ixzz2j9lR6hPO

[11] The Australian War Memorial at Villers-Bretonneux lists 10,000 Australian dead with no known grave: www.dva.gov.au/commems_oawg/OAWG/war_memorials/overseas_memorials/france/Pages/villers%20bretonneux.aspx.

[12] Former Prime Minister Paul Keating, speaking in 2008, criticized this trend, saying: 'we still go on as though the nation was born again, or even redeemed there: An utter and complete nonsense'. www.abc.net.au/news/2008-10-30/anzac-gallipoli-gatherings-misguided-keating-says/188086.

British government officials after a brief visit, despite the efforts of military censorship (Knightley 1975; Fewster 1982). His account established crucial elements of the enduring legend: specifically, the charge of British incompetence (among the general staff) and Aussie heroism (among the diggers). As a recent story in the UK press put it:

> Keith Murdoch's role at Gallipoli is not without controversy, given that the information he smuggled out was mostly second-hand and provided to him by the Daily Telegraph journalist Ellis Ashmead-Bartlett, an arch critic of the campaign. When Murdoch's ruse to smuggle Ashmead-Bartlett's report from the theatre of war was betrayed, he sat down in the office of the Australian High Commissioner in London and dictated his recollection of the report's contents into an 8,000-word letter to Australian Prime Minister Andrew Fisher. 'It was an amazing document, a mixture of error, fact, exaggeration, prejudice, and the most sentimental patriotism, which made highly damaging charges against the British general staff . . . many of them untrue,' said the Australian writer Phillip Knightley. 'But the basis of the charges – that the Gallipoli expedition was in danger of disaster – was correct'.[13]

This version of Gallipoli – Murdoch Senior as brave whistleblowing war correspondent circumventing (British) censorship to tell a new *Australian* truth – is an essential part of its meaning. The other major influence on the creation of the legend was another Australian, Charles Bean (Seal 2004). It was he who first claimed – and through his later monumental histories of World War I he established – that 'the consciousness of Australian nationhood was born' on 25 May 1915.[14] Bean was determined to report what he saw, but what he saw was coloured by what he was looking for. He posed his quest as a question:

> How did this nation, bred in complete peace, largely undisciplined except for a strongly British tradition and the self-discipline necessary for men who grapple with nature . . . react to what still has to be recognized as *the supreme test for fitness to exist?*[15]

The answer was already clear to Bean: 'fitness to exist' was bestowed by '*character*'. He wrote in 1918: 'The big thing in the war for Australia was the *discovery of the character of Australian men*. It was character which rushed the hills at Gallipoli

---

[13] Burrell, I. (16 October 2013), 'BBC unveils the star of its First World War anniversary coverage – Rupert Murdoch'. *The Independent* (UK): www.independent.co.uk/news/uk/home-news/bbc-unveils-the-star-of-its-first-world-war-anniversary-coverage--rupert-murdoch-8884028.html.

[14] C. E. W. Bean, *The Story of Anzac* (1921), cited in the *Australian Dictionary of National Biography* (1979): http://adb.anu.edu.au/biography/bean-charles-edwin-5166; and in in the Australian government's official ANZAC website: www.anzacsite.gov.au/1landing/beanbio.html.

[15] Bean, as previous note; our emphasis.

and held on there'.[16] Bean went on to found the Australian War Memorial, and is himself remembered as the first Australian War Correspondent at Gallipoli and later on at the Western Front.

But it was not Bean who established the meaning of Gallipoli. That honour went to Ellis Ashmead-Bartlett, the *English journalist* who gave the story to Murdoch and first broke it in the British and Australian press.[17] Bean is referring to Ashmead-Bartlett in this passage from his war diary:

> The war correspondent is responsible for most of the ideas of battle which the public possesses. . . . I can't write that it occurred if I know that it did not, even if by painting it that way I can rouse the blood and make the pulse beat faster – and undoubtedly these men here deserve that people's pulses shall beat for them. But War Correspondents have so habitually exaggerated the heroism of battles that people don't realise that real actions are heroic.[18]

Ashmead-Bartlett, who worked for the London *Daily Telegraph*, was the doyen of the Allied press gallery covering the campaign (Fewster 1982; Knightley 1975: 100–3).[19] As well as scooping the story, he also shot the only movie film taken of action in the campaign. Later in the war he toured the United States, Australia and Britain with his story and movie. It seems that the Anzac legend was created by him, as has long been recognized by historians:

> Undoubtedly [the] more important influence that [Ashmead-Bartlett] exerted over the legend is that he probably more than any other person determined how the tale was told. . . . It required gifted observers to pass the story on to the outside world if the landing were to receive the recognition it so richly deserved. . . . The essence of any legend lies as much in the related story as in the events it purports to describe. Ellis Ashmead Bartlett, by his efforts with pen, picture and speech was instrumental in first shaping then institutionalizing a legend which has, and will continue to be passed on for generations. (Fewster 1982: 30)

Australians gathering at Gallipoli have likely never heard of Ashmead-Bartlett, but it is his *story* they come to honour. They won't be the first to feel themselves represented by the story rather than the facts. Even at time, the Anzac soldiers

---

[16] *In Your Hands, Australians* (London, 1918), cited in the *Australian Dictionary of National Biography* (1979): http://adb.anu.edu.au/biography/bean-charles-edwin-5166; our emphasis.

[17] Ashmead-Bartlett's story, as published in the *Sydney Morning Herald*, 8 May 1915, is reproduced in full in Seal (2013), 23–30.

[18] Charles Bean, personal records, 'Ashmead Bartlett and a crisis', item 892, 3DRL/6673, Australian War Memorial 38, cited in: www.anzacsite.gov.au/1landing/beanbio.html.

[19] Knightley's account of Ashmead-Bartlett and Murdoch can be accessed at the Anzac site: www.anzacsite.gov.au/1landing/knightley.html.

themselves recognized Ashmead Bartlett's role as their national 'bard' (Hartley 2009b). One soldier was moved to write in the *Anzac Book* (edited by Bean and published in London in 1916)[20]:

> It is fairly certain that future historians will teach that Australia was discovered not by Captain Cook, explorer, but by Mr. Ashmead Bartlett, war correspondent.[21]

Australian national character may have been tested for fitness in 1915, and this may or may not have revealed its authentic character; but no one would have known anything about it without a narrator. It's the story that carried the knowledge, not the deed; and the communicator who 'creates the polity', not the acts of members of the deme, however authentic or courageous.

Granddads – On not having a story . . .

It took me[22] decades to realize that I had a personal relationship with Gallipoli, not least because it was known as 'the Dardanelles' in the United Kingdom; associated in the popular imagination less with the Anzacs than with the name of Winston Churchill (First Lord of the Admiralty in 1915), whose bold conjecture it had been, and who therefore took the political blame for its eventual failure. My grandfather was there. Of course he wasn't an Anzac – he fought for the 'other side', as it were, the British. He wasn't the type of 'British' that so upset the likes of Ashmead-Bartlett and Murdoch, that is, an incompetent upper-class officer. He was one of the 'other ranks' (a QMS or Quartermaster Sergeant), although later promoted, eventually to Captain, in the tradition of the Army Service Corps. He must have had some connection with the Anzacs, because he kept a 1916 copy of *The Anzac Book*, which I now have.

Josiah Arthur Barnes came from 'the Borough' – Southwark – where Shakespeare's Globe Theatre was situated (and is again). He worked at Mount Pleasant, the biggest postal sorting office in the Empire. Before the war he'd been in the Post Office Rifles (Territorial Army), and afterwards he returned to the Post Office, eventually to become Secretary of the East Central Sorters Branch of the Union of Postal Workers, which was founded in 1919. He was, and

---

[20] 1st edn, edited by C. E. W. Bean, published by Cassell, London, 1916; 2nd edn, published by Sun Books, Melbourne, 1975; 3rd edn, edited and published by the Australian War Memorial: www.awm.gov.au/shop/item/9781742231341/#.UnGrZiRhNdg

[21] 'The Raid on London', by 'Private Pat Riot', 9th Battalion. *The Anzac Book*, 143–5.

[22] This part is narrated in the first person – John Hartley.

remained, solidly working class, of the aspirational and Co-operative type (he read *Reynold's News* to the end of his life) rather than the activist and Socialist. When I became aware of him, in his seventies, he played lawn bowls (I have the cups he won), still drank his tea out of the saucer not the cup ('to cool it'), blew his nose on a military-looking khaki handkerchief, and had an alarming one-eyed Pekinese called Bottle.

To say he 'fought' may give the wrong impression of this latter-day scion of Brutus of Troy, because he served in the Army Service Corps, which was responsible for transport, food supplies, logistics – and the mail. According to a 1914–18 website:

> At peak, the ASC numbered an incredible 10,547 officers and 315,334 men. In addition were tens of thousands of Indian, Egyptian, Chinese and other native labourers, carriers and stores men, under orders of the ASC. Yet this vast, sprawling organisation – so vital to enabling the army to fight – merits just four mentions in the Official History of the war. [23]

It seems there is no 'nation-forming' story attached to the coordination of armies; neither the military itself nor its historians remember the contribution of a third of a million of its soldiers. Although armies can't fight without organization, transport, logistics, food and communications (see Figure 3.2), those who provide them are available to take the blame for what goes wrong. My grandfather kept a copy of the *Final Report of the Dardanelles Commission* (1917–19: 81–2), the official government inquiry into the debacle. I found it forgotten on top of a cupboard long after his death. I wondered why he kept it for so long. Would it reveal something about him?

Looking through it, I found a chapter on 'Postal Arrangements'.[24] After excoriating the 'negligence or stupidity of some postal clerk' (was this him?), the Commissioners mention that 'there was a good deal of looting of parcels' sent via the Army Service Corps Parcel Transit Service (was this him?). Their *Report* relates various scandalous stories of mails damaged, not delivered, delayed or sent astray (p. 81). Noting, however, that the 'amount of letters is stated to have grown to 1,000,000 a week', and the number of parcels up to 90,000 a week, they finally conclude that both the Post Office and Army Service Corps Parcel Transit Service bore responsibility for the 'miscarriages', but that 'we are of the opinion

[23] The Long, Long Trail: www.1914-1918.net/asc.htm. No mention is made of whether the 'men' included women.

[24] www.nla.gov.au/apps/cdview/?pi=nla.aus-vn2035864-s83-e and www.nla.gov.au/apps/cdview/?pi=nla.aus-vn2035864-s84-e.

that, on the whole, no blame attaches to those who had the organisation and conduct of the service' (p. 82).[25]

Doubtless there are some amazing stories here, but the heroes who managed to deliver over 30 million items to troops so far from their various homes in Britain, France, Australia, New Zealand, Egypt and India, not to mention those serving the Turkish army, have remained unsung from that day to this, at least officially, because 'there is no memorial to the Army Service Corps'.[26] But in *The Anzac Book* (1916) it is clear that the fighting men felt very differently:

> Mails, too, are an anodyne. Their arrival eclipses considerations of life and death – of fighting and the landing of rations. The mail-barge coming in somehow looms larger than a barge of supplies. Mails have been arriving weekly for six months, yet no one is callous to them.[27]

The writer singles out letters first: 'they put a man at home for an hour'. Next he mentions the local newspaper, sent from home: 'Intimate associations hang about the reading of the local sheet – domestic and parochial associations almost as powerful as are brought by letters' (*Anzac Book*, 22). Finally, there are parcels, objects of an 'intensity of gloating expectation'. Most prized were tobacco and food, but clothes, toiletries, and writing paper were also mentioned.

Of course, not all the parcels got through, and many that did were damaged. A 'digger's alphabet' gives us some idea of what the troops thought of quartermasters – they were shirkers and looters: 'Q is for . . . the Quarter-bloke, dodging the line'; 'R is for . . . the Rum that the Quarter-bloke pinched' (quoted in Seal 2013: 250–1).

In fact, the only memorabilia I have of my grandfather are the 'spoils of war'. He kept – over the fireplace – a set of murderous looking shells (which I now have), allegedly captured from the Turks and 'proving' that the enemy used 'dum-dum' rounds (lead-tipped, designed to flatten on impact). He also sported a collection of 'trench art', including shell-cases converted into cigarette boxes, powder-puff boxes and so on, some with British silver sixpences (the king's head) let into the base, overlaying the German or Turkish script that indicated whence the shells originated. One such is dated 'APR 15' (Figure 3.1). These bizarre objects are all I have of my grandfather; a clutter of memorabilia-without-memories. He died while I was away at the orphanage. My mother wrote and told me to pray for

---

[25] 'Those who had the organisation and conduct of the service' means 'officers'. Effectively, although not explicitly, the *Report* 'closes ranks', as it were; it protects the officer class by putting any blame on (anonymous) 'other ranks'.

[26] *The Long, Long Trail*: www.1914-1918.net/asc.htm.

[27] 'Glimpses of Anzac', by Hector Dinning, Aust. ASC. *The Anzac Book*, 17–23.

Figure 3.1 Trench art – A cigarette box made of two German shell-cases dated April 1915, with a Turkish fuse as knob; a George V sixpence is let into the base (Photo: J. Hartley).

him – a tricky task, for he was Church of England and a Freemason, my mother was a Catholic convert, and I was at a Protestant orphanage. Would praying for him in the wrong religion be OK? Evidently my mother didn't think it mattered, for she buried him in the same grave as my non-religious father, both of them in the Catholic bit of the vast, windswept municipal cemetery.

I barely knew him as a person. I can't remember much affection on either side. The only present I remember having from him was a parcel that mysteriously but excitingly arrived at the orphanage 1 year when I was about 10. It proved to contain a pair of boxing gloves. Instinctively I read the 'present' as a rebuke. He was encouraging me to make a man of myself (a sure sign that I had already failed in that endeavour). As the only surviving male in the family I was always going to inherit the memorabilia of war – and his masonic apron. I don't like them much but can't chuck them out, so there they stay, souvenirs of an unknown life, transmitted through time without any story attached to them, and almost completely meaningless, certainly to my daughters, who will no doubt have to decide what to do with them one day.

Neither my mother nor grandmother told stories about him after he died. We (my two sisters and I) discovered decades later that he had two sisters. Who knew? What did he do in the war? No one knew, beyond pictures of him on a camel by the Great Pyramid and wearing his officer's uniform so proudly. Was he brave? Did he perform herculean service? Was he on the take? Was his a war of 'negligence and stupidity'? We'll never know, although I don't think so, because he called every house he lived in to the end of his life 'Rafa', referring to the city of that name in Palestine, where his war took him after the Dardanelles and Egypt. I don't know if he was at the Battle of Rafa in January 1917, which prominently featured the Anzacs and Chauvel's Light Horsemen. It was a difficult battle, plagued by ammunition shortages, so quartermasters certainly played a role, and it marked the entry of the Empire Expeditionary Forces into Palestine, which he called the Holy Land. Maybe that was the time of his life. But none of his family knows, because there's no story.[28]

I could make all this into a digital story.[29] That's its structural place in this chapter, but such an indeterminate tale would go against the grain of the genre. The story would be telling you that there is no story. My grandfather's tale may express something about the British 'national character' (class differentiation; 'a nation of shopkeepers') but not in ways that follow the accepted script (killing; death), which doesn't associate glory with complex systems and logistics, or making sure that bread and letters from home got through (Figure 3.2).

There are many digital stories about Anzacs, and they generally do follow the script. Some are made by school students, doing oral history projects about veterans from their locality. Others are made by veterans themselves, or their widows or descendants. None that I can find has been made by the backpacking pilgrims to Gallipoli's Dawn Service. From my research,[30] it does seem that when it comes to digital storytelling about Gallipoli, there is a *pre-scripted story* that

---

[28] Stories *were* told. Here's one, featuring the British (Scottish), the Anzacs, and some 'hot and blasphemous Quartermaster-Sergeants' (here, victims not perpetrators of looting), outside Rafa in 1917: 'The Australian light horseman has the bump of acquisitiveness even better developed than the Lowland infantryman, and having a horse on which he can hang his trophies he can give this penchant greater scope. But when he is going into action – or believes himself to be – he unhesitatingly sacrifices all that will incommode him in the serious business of war. In consequence the ground recently vacated [by the Australian cavalry departing to attack Rafa] appeared at dawn to our astonished eyes covered with a litter of discarded possessions. . . . We were on mobile rations, bully, biscuit, milk and jam. Vegetables and the "wee piece ham" had disappeared. Surely Australians did not live like that. Nor were we disappointed. Foraging parties returned laden with sides of bacon, cheese, bread, Maconochies, sacks of onions and desiccated vegetables, enough to make us quite certain of a full meal on Christmas Day, so long as we did not move in the interval. Nor was this all. Folding benches and tables, matting and bivouac poles, frying pans and canvas buckets, books and tobacco, a watch and even a real live horse were discovered – all the things which stand for wealth among such a primitive tribe as we then were. It is rumoured that hot and blasphemous Australian Quartermaster-Sergeants rode back that evening to retrieve some of their property. Well, they did not find it all. People who like bacon shouldn't leave it lying in deserts in front of hungry Scotchmen'. (From *Highland Light Infantry in the War 1914–1918*, by Officers of the Battalion. Glasgow, 1921: www.gutenberg.org/files/20250/20250-h/20250-h.htm).

[29] Here's one that I made earlier: www.youtube.com/watch?v=fIxu33F8r2w.

[30] See, for instance: http://museumvictoria.com.au/discoverycentre/websites/making-history/student-uploads/;www.dpc.vic.gov.au/index.php/veterans/victorian-veterans-virtual-museum/digital-stories-in-our-words; https://open.abc.net.au/openregions/qld-tropical-north-93gv1ap/posts/remembering-billy-26wn8wx; http://generator.acmi.net.au/gallery/category/conflict-australians-war; https://www.raiseaglass.com.au/ (click on 'Your Stories'); www.au.dk/en/about/news/single/artikel/cultural-memory-more-relevant-than-ever/.

EACH ONE DOING HIS BIT
Drawn by W. OTHO HEWETT

Figure 3.2 'Each one doing his bit'. Drawing by W. Otho Hewett. *The Anzac Book* (1916) p. 167. The item arrowed at the end of the 'long tail' of the line is 'Bread'.

people differentially populate with their own identities, experiences and families. The individual experience may be unique but the template is copied. I can't tell you my granddad's Gallipoli story because it's the other way round; the individual was commonplace but there is no template for this story. On the evidence of Gallipoli stories, it's the copy that wins the day; people want their story to fit in with the meanings that have already been scripted; it's a kind of votary offering to the ancestors. What they actually did or what they thought about it may be of less significance than what their descendants need for them to mean. That certainly seems to be the case for Jason's granddad, as the next section reveals.

The last patriarch

When John told his granddad story, I realized that I had one as well,[31] although here the story begins in World War II, on the airfields of southeast England,

---

[31] This part is narrated in the first person – Jason Potts.

with a volunteer serviceman from New Zealand flying de Havilland Mosquito bombers. Fortunately, Owen Ward Potts arrived towards the end of the war and never saw action. But he did meet a young Welsh lass, and in the compressed time that runs hot through war, they were soon married and she was with child, although probably not in that order. Thus my father was born at the close of the war in the Rhondda valley in Wales. The three of them soon shipped out to the family farm in New Zealand; she a war bride who returned home only once, 40 years later, and my grandfather, who settled into the role of family patriarch, his apparently natural and destined position for the next 52 years.

Apart from a certain fondness for patriotic teaspoons, there was little evidence of Welsh ancestry in the family home in Balfour (in the deep south in New Zealand) where I grew up, nor of war service, nor of any time before that. Duty was done, and life returned to its bucolic rhythms in which a new story was created about the enterprise of a hard-working family of boys on the land. That was the story I was born into – although there was also one daughter: my father's sister Carolyn, who was not destined, through family politics and personal choice, to be part of this rural idyll. She trained in art, became a journalist, moved to the city; just as I was later to leave that same farm, train in economics, become an academic, move to Australia.

A few years ago, 20 years after Owen Potts died, that same Aunt Carolyn – a professional storyteller – decided to write a book on him, which I have only just read. This story, based in archival records and research, has a very different colour from the one I received as a child. There is less derring-do war hero, and a great deal more struggle and luck. But it also presents my grandfather as a very different person from the one I had always imagined. It turned out that he needed to fight extremely hard to *get into* the war, to get posted overseas, specifically in the Royal Air Force. He had a great gift for technical details and organizational leadership; he was the sort of person who may well have sought to escape life in backwater rural New Zealand.

Not so his boys, however, including my father. They were naturalized farmers who couldn't imagine a better place to be, and so the story went down that path with them. The *national* story of the sacrifice of servicemen and the safe return to the hearth to raise good families became *our* story.

But I'm not so sure that this is really what happened. My grandfather was awarded a clutch of medals for his effort, but he never picked them up. They stayed in London. My aunt discovered them in the course of her research (Figure 3.3). Why would he leave them there? On one hand, it's consistent with

Figure 3.3 Left in London – Story Surplus. Long-lost medals of a World War II RAF Officer (Photo: Jason Potts).

the duty and sacrifice story: job done; go home, no fuss. Yet maybe he didn't want to go home, but now, with a young family to look after, he had no choice. So he *lost the life* that those medals represented; it was a kind of 'story surplus' after the war. The medals had no meaning in the new story.

It is also interesting to find how easy it was to remake the story among the children of that newly established deme, and how hard it was to find the real story, or even to want to find it. The story my grandfather created, the one that I was raised in, was consistent with that of a ruling patriarch – a proper paterfamilias. The complex back-story and other possible stories were erased, and instead a 'foundation myth' took root in which 'we' were always from here, always farmers, and always would be. 'They' were those arrayed against the interests of farmers – journalists and academics surely among them.

As the generations have unfolded, it turned out he was the first and last patriarch in our family. The complexity of evolving global produce markets, new technologies and outside opportunities overwhelmed this simple lineage. The family farm is now run by my sister and her young family. A new story is being crafted about the rise of the first *matriarch*, securing the place for her young children.

It seems that families, like nations, need to tell stories *about* themselves *to* themselves that may bear very little relation to reality. The stories serve a different, deme-building purpose, in the interests of local integration and identity. Small wonder that my grandfather's medals struggle, as he did, to *mean* anything other than what others need them to mean, which may be why he let them go, to mean nothing at all.[32]

Original stories seem to require a higher level of narrative investment than digital storytelling typically commands, and in our experience families are not reliable sources of any alternative. On the contrary, the stories that are passed down the generations seem more likely to reproduce national or demic myths with grandparents' faces.

Despite our desire to know what really happened to our own ancestors, and despite the potential of digital technologies to make alternative accounts more widely known, it seems likely that new or revisionist stories will continue to be created at the national and corporate end of the spectrum, by professional storytellers with a critical point of view. What will the new story be? It's a pretty safe bet that it won't include our granddads; but mythic ancestors may figure prominently (as we shall see).

Göbekli Tepe – V. Gordon Childe and revolution

Unbeknownst to the thousands gathering annually at Gallipoli's Lone Pine memorial, there is another lonely hill in Turkey where a much deeper myth of human political origin is beginning to be undermined and reordered. The place is Göbekli Tepe (Potbelly Hill), site of impressive ancient stone monuments that were erected before human settlement and before farming, predating Stonehenge and the Egyptian pyramids by *7,000 years*.

The deeper 'myth' that its discovery challenges is the accepted story of the 'Neolithic Revolution'. That theory was first synthesized by an Australian archaeologist, V. Gordon Childe (1925, 1936). His theory states that human civilization 'dawned' with the invention of farming, which required hunter-gatherers to settle and thus enabled the development of cities. In other words, after a rapid domesticating 'revolution', the economy (agriculture) and politics

---

[32] We return here to the co-authorial 'we'.

(cities) determined culture (civilization).[33] It is a strongly Marxist political narrative, following the base/superstructure model of economic determination (Williams 1973), which is not surprising as Childe was a convinced Marxist, political activist, and lifelong supporter of Stalin.[34]

Vere Gordon Childe is widely forgotten in his native Australia, except by John Doyle (a.k.a. Rampaging Roy Slaven, half of the Roy and H. G. comedy duo), whose 2013 play *Vere [Faith]* was inspired by playwright Doyle's discovery of his existence.[35] But Childe ranks as one of the most important archaeologists of the twentieth century: if not Indiana Jones, then certainly his teacher.[36] He was reputed to loathe archaeological digs (he was no Aussie 'digger' in this respect), although he excavated the important site of Skara Brae in the Orkney Islands. His strength was synthesis. He performed for archaeology the 'modern synthesis' that Julian Huxley achieved for the biosciences, at about the same time. He was able to gather piecemeal discoveries and sites across Eurasia into a coherent story: the story of the Neolithic Revolution. As Egyptologist John Romer has put it:

> The 'Neolithic Revolution' ... that most useful phrase, was concocted by the Australian archaeologist Vere Gordon Childe in the 1920s ... specifically to combat the then current climate of ethnic stereotyping in European archaeology. ... Not surprisingly, perhaps, given the contemporary climate, Childe's newly invented Neolithic Revolution, a two-word adventure story in itself, soon became part of Western history. (Romer 2012: 32)

The *story* of the Neolithic Revolution (if not the science) has held sway ever since, diffusing ever further into global common sense. For instance, in a 2013–14 exhibition about *Anatolian Civilisation* touring China in 2013–14,[37] the Neolithic period (12,000–5,500 BCE) is introduced with a label that reads as shown in Figure 3.4.

Note the chain of causation proffered by this story: hunter-gatherers and nomads settled and became productive because of farming and herding (food

[33] But, for a contrary view, see: www.telegraph.co.uk/science/science-news/5604296/Is-farming-the-root-of-all-evil.html.
[34] The *Wikipedia* entry on V. Gordon Childe is a good place to get a flavour of the man, his times, his work and its impact.
[35] Story at: www.sydneytheatre.com.au/magazine/posts/2012/september/feature-vere-gordon-childe.aspx.
[36] Childe is mentioned as such in one of the Indiana Jones films: http://indianajones.wikia.com/wiki/Vere_Gordon_Childe.
[37] Information plaque, *Anatolian Civilizations: From the Neolithic Age to the Ottoman Empire*. Shanghai Museum (2013–14): www.shanghaimuseum.net/en/special/special_readmore.jsp?id=214

新石器时代（公元前 12000-5500年）
NEOLITHIC AGE (12000-5500 BCE)

新石器时代见证了人类由狩猎-采集到生产，从游牧至定居的生活方式的转变。定居生活促进了建筑的建造。人类开始种植谷物、驯养动物、制作陶器。定居生活以及多余的产品推动了社会阶级的形成和专业化，为村庄和城市的出现奠定了基础。在这一时期，生产力的发展取决于宗教部门，形成了"庙宇经济"体系。目前在土耳其发现了近400处新石器时代的遗址。

The Neolithic Age saw the transformation of hunter-gatherer and nomads way of living to a more settled and productive one. A new architectural practice emerged as a result of living in permanent settlements. Food supply was enriched with grain and animals in the process of domestication. Pottery appeared in human history. Localized dwellings and surplus products brought about the emergence of social classes and specialization, and led to foundation of villages and cities. As the production activities developed depending on religious institutions during the period, "temple economy" was formed. The Neolithic Age is represented in Turkey so far with nearly 400 settlements.

Figure 3.4 The 'Neolithic Revolution' lives on. Shanghai 2013 (Photo: J. Hartley).

supply 'enriched with grain and animals in the process of domestication'). This generated 'localized dwelling' and surplus, which in turn caused social classes to emerge, thence cities, and finally a 'temple economy'. The assumed arrow of causation is clear:

Transformation in the mode of production
→ Surplus and Settlement
→ Civilisation and Cities
→ Belief systems (Religion and Culture)

Reversing the arrow of causation

The only problem with this, as the Turkish Ministry of Culture and Tourism (who co-organized the exhibition) ought to have known, given the location of the counter-evidence, is that the arrow of causation may be *exactly the wrong way round*. Recent archaeological work in Turkey itself has revealed that the first 'temple architecture' was produced by nomadic hunter-gatherers, not by settled agriculturalists. To accomplish this feat, they needed to *organize* food and settlement for those engaged in making the singing-and-dancing place. Settlement and farming followed. In short, *culture* – the creation and representation in stone and ceremony of a 'we'-community or deme – *preceded* both *economy* (farming; herding) and the *polity* (cities).

But Childe's materialist, or economic-determinist story – that 'material prosperity . . . brought social and artistic progress in its wake', as Romer (2012) summarizes it – exerted its own powerful influence on scientific thought.[38] The science may be 'tricked out with fashionable neo-evolutionary economics', but as Romer points out, 'the very language of the inquiry' determines what will be found: the story precedes and determines or *scripts* the evidence, which is largely a work of the imagination, ascribing causal sequence to 'the relics of the past'. Thus, for many decades there has been no need to argue that economics was primary and culture was dragged along 'in its wake' until the discoveries at Göbekli Tepe. Now, it seems, the flow of causation is reversed, because the monument builders themselves were hunter-gatherers, who neither farmed nor settled. It turns out that symbolic ritual, including gathering, dancing, feasting and possibly worship, was staged in massive, elaborate stone-built circles that have no economic or residential function. The tallest monoliths there may resemble ancestors, who may be gathered in a ceremonial (story) circle, perhaps linking the living and the dead.[39]

Storytelling, not 'worship'

Storytelling creates the polity: literally. These feats of construction both organized and represented what can be described as the earliest known political narrative. They predated and likely precipitated both farming and settlement. Klaus Schmidt, lead excavator of the Göbekli Tepe site, has concluded:

> The evolution of modern humanity involved a fundamental change from small-scale, mobile hunter-gatherer bands to large, permanently co-resident

[38] V. I. Vernadsky (1938) cites Childe in his account of the transition from biosphere to noösphere: see next chapter.

[39] 'Pillars at the temple of Göbekli Tepe – 11,600 years old and up to 18 feet tall – may represent priestly dancers at a gathering'. *National Geographic*:http://ngm.nationalgeographic.com/2011/06/gobekli-tepe/musi-photography

communities. The factor that allowed the formation of large, permanent communities was the facility to use symbolic culture, a kind of pre-literate capacity for producing and 'reading' symbolic material culture, that enabled communities to formulate their shared identities, and their cosmos. (Schmidt 2010: 253–4)

What Schmidt calls 'shared identity' was *performed* here: in the monuments themselves, in the work needed to make them, and in the attendant ceremonies. Göbekli Tepe was an improbably early site of *mediation*. Schmidt has been reporting this finding in scholarly publications and to the general public for years – via the *Smithsonian Magazine*, and *Archaeology*, for instance, as well as the *National Geographic* – but the ingrained script has proven resistant to change.

Indeed, as soon as it got wind of the discovery, Western journalism immediately turned it into different story: about 'the birth of religion'. For instance, Schmidt is reported in the *Smithsonian Magazine* (2008) as arguing for 'upending' the Childe thesis:

To Schmidt and others, these new findings suggest a novel theory of civilization. Scholars have long believed that only after people learned to farm and live in settled communities did they have the time, organization and resources to construct temples and support complicated social structures. But Schmidt argues it was the other way around: the extensive, coordinated effort to build the monoliths literally laid the groundwork for the development of complex societies.[40]

But the article is headlined 'The World's First Temple?' *Archaeology* didn't bother with the question mark.[41] It's the same story in the *National Geographic*, whose *reporter* was excited by the revision of Childe's theory. Schmidt is quoted: 'Twenty years ago everyone believed civilization was driven by ecological forces. I think what we are learning is that civilization is a product of the human mind'.[42] But the *magazine* wanted this high-prestige cover story to be about the 'birth of *religion*', headlining Göbekli Tepe 'the world's oldest temple'.

---

[40] Curry, A. (November 2008), 'Göbekli Tepe: The World's First Temple? ... Turkey's stunning Göbekli Tepe upends the conventional view of the rise of civilization'. *Smithsonian Magazine*: www.smithsonianmag.com/history/gobekli-tepe-the-worlds-first-temple-83613665/?page=2.

[41] Scham, S. (November 2008), 'The World's First Temple'. *Archaeology* 61(6): http://archive.archaeology.org/0811/

[42] Mann, C. (June 2011), 'The Birth of Religion'. *National Geographic*: http://ngm.nationalgeographic.com/print/2011/06/gobekli-tepe/mann-text.

Klaus Schmidt himself is not so sure about that: 'we can not say with certitude if concepts of god existed at this time' (2010: 254). So there is no need to follow the *National Geographic* in its own 'political narrative':

> We used to think agriculture gave rise to cities and later to writing, art, and religion. Now the world's oldest temple suggests the urge to worship sparked civilization. (*NG*, June 2011)

Göbekli Tepe certainly challenges the notion of the Neolithic Revolution, but 'the urge to worship' is not needed as a causal mechanism. 'Worship', 'religion' and 'temple' are loaded terms, saying more about now than then, and the excavator himself draws no such conclusion. Occam's razor should be applied to such interpretations.

Singing the deme – the world's first mass medium

Thanks to the painstaking work of Klaus Schmidt and his colleagues, stunning monuments of almost unthinkable antiquity – and beauty – have been rediscovered. What these abstract human figures, realistic animal carvings, stone circles and structures *meant* to their makers is not preserved. However, whatever else they were used for, they do appear to have served 'demic' purposes – calling together the members of a non-kin (cultural) group of considerable size for construction and ceremony, staging among the stones an all-dancing, all-singing expression of the deme's identity and its boundaries of place and time (here and now vs. death and the ancestors).

Perhaps the edifice also signalled the power of *this* deme in comparison to others ('they' communities). For Göbekli Tepe was not alone, nor even the first such stone structure in the region. The French archaeologist Danielle Stordeur reported news of a site at Jerf el Ahmar in Syria, since inundated by an irrigation dam-lake, in 1999. She wrote:

> This type of structure has never been recovered for this period. As a building intended for specific communal activities, it seems to have several points in common with structures found at Hallan Çemi, and it anticipates the early PPNB Anatolian 'sanctuaries' of this period, such as Nevali-Çori and Göbekli, some 100 km from Jerf el Ahmar'. (Stordeur 1999: 3)

It seems that the logic of a 'costly signalling' competition in communal/ritual buildings and symbolism among pre-pottery Neolithic (PPN) demes in the Fertile Crescent – 'anything you can do we can do better' – was well under way by the time Göbekli was built. That these structures represent a cultural (rather than economic or civic) story doesn't seem to be in doubt. They externalize and perform the identity and knowledge of their demes at an unprecedented level of ambition and complexity. It does seem reasonable to assume that the builders told each other a motivating story as to their intentions when they built it: they were working to a purposeful 'script'. The monument itself may be regarded as a 'media platform' or 'institution of language' – the first ever 'mass medium' if you like – for storytelling on the grand scale.

So our proposition is that Göbekli Tepe is a relic of *political narrative* – a story that called together a deme to common purpose, distinguished it from others nearby, and so constituted the polity that needed to support that giant enterprise by inventing agriculture, husbandry and settlement. We suggest that 'demic diffusion' (Ammerman and Cavalli-Sforza 1984; see Sokal et al. 1991) required a prior moment of *demic concentration* (our term) as the trigger of the 'Neolithic Revolution'.

Stonehenge – not one deme, but two

Something along the lines of a story that brings a deme together to overcome unknown adversaries, uncertainty and death, may explain the findings at Göbekli Tepe. If so, then the form – the 'media platform' – in which that ambitious act of wish-fulfilment was 'published', using charismatic megalithic circles, persisted along with the stories. About 7,000 years after Göbekli Tepe (and unconnected with it), the (currently) much more famous stone circle at Stonehenge may tell a similar story. According to its most recent excavator, Mike Parker Pearson (2012: 342–3), the monument itself, considered with others in the surrounding landscape, represents a 'place of the dead' (cremation, excarnation, burial) in stone, contrasting with monuments located nearby (Durrington Walls and Woodhenge), which signified a 'place of the living' in timber (feasting, residence). As for the 'place of the dead' itself, Parker Pearson believes that the bluestone megaliths, which were brought from the Preseli hills in far-off Wales, represent ancestors, who were also, significantly, among the first farmers in Britain (2012: 288):

> The link between Preseli and Stonehenge . . . involved a powerful polity within the Nevern valley [West Wales], a people whose earliest Neolithic ancestors had brought the tradition of megalith construction to this part of Britain. Perhaps they had celebrated their power and their ancestry by erecting one or more stone circles with monoliths taken from a range of nearby quarries.

The quarries have been located, but not the bluestones taken from them. Parker Pearson concludes that, 'later, for one reason or another, the momentous decision was taken to dismantle these circles and move them over 180 miles to Stonehenge' (288). Once there, these bluestones stood for 500 years (3,000–2,500 BCE) before being repositioned when the much larger and locally sourced sarsen stones were first erected. The sequence of events and placement of stones suggest to Parker Pearson that Stonehenge as we now see it was built not only to venerate the ancestors (in the form of the bluestone monoliths) but also to perform a strictly political ceremony, where the plan of the sarsens – including the familiar circle with lintels and the internal horseshoe arrangement of trilithons – 'copied' timber enclosures and 'D-shaped meeting houses' (Parker Pearson 2012: 334), such that:

> The stones with Welsh origins were now contained within arrangements of stones brought mostly from the Marlborough Downs [20 miles N. of Stonehenge]. This raises the possibility that Stonehenge's identity, as expressed through the stones' origins, represented a union of two groups with geographically diverse ancestries – the people of the bluestones and the people of the sarsens. (2012: 338)

In our terminology, then, Stonehenge is a 'mass medium' that broadcasts to all and sundry – perhaps even to the whole island of Britain – that *two* demes have united:

> Stonehenge can be understood as a monument of unification, integrating the cosmological aspects of earth, sun and moon into a single entity which also united the ancestors of the people of Britain in the form of Welsh bluestones and English sarsens. (Parker Pearson 2012: 342)

It took strong stuff – the alignment of sun, moon, season and place, plus the communal effort required to quarry, shape, lug and erect 20-foot (6.7 m) megaliths, and the separation of landscapes into those that served the living and the dead, respectively – to carry a political narrative about *demic concentration* (unity of knowledge).

This symbolic expression of identity was certainly cultural but, equally clearly, what is meant by 'culture' cannot be confined to inherited custom or reduced to mere ornament, the leisure pursuit of the affluent. This was culture as cutting-edge innovation, uniting many branches of knowledge as well as people, and stretching the entire society's capabilities. In addition to artistic talent and communicative purpose, it required the most up-to-date knowledge of science, technology, and cosmology of the day. It tested the limits of the group's practical powers of coordination, logistics and labour, and their relations with other groups, from Wales to Wessex. We don't know what went on in and around the Stonehenge-Durrington Walls complex, but it's not a wild guess to suggest that it included storytelling by voice, music and dance as well as through stone and timber. The landscape's use for gathering, feasting and processing in the presence of ancestors, both recent and remote (for which there is evidence), suggests that 'culture' was the prime achievement of a powerful and wealthy polity. The story 'written' in the stones may be that of two demes uniting as one, a story of *scaling up culture*. We don't know the details, but the scale of Stonehenge itself tells us how important it was as a signal – Parker Pearson says its spectacular scale 'puts it in a league of its own, beyond anything else in Britain at that time' (2012: 340).

But it wasn't to last. Stonehenge was among the last of the megalithic monuments (only Silbury Hill is later), constructed in a time when the transformation from Neolithic to Copper/Bronze Age was already under way. It marked the end of a certain 'regime', not its beginning, such that – not for the last time – 'the greatest monumental spectacles preceded the regime's demise' (Parker Pearson 2012: 344–5). New technologies (copper; bronze) and new cultural practices (Beaker people) were diffused; new forms of land division were established (shifting from open grazing to field farming); and new sources of wealth were opened up (arable soils in eastern Britain). The 'Big Men' who presided over the local deme began to be buried in personal graves (round barrows). Culture and wealth were still displayed – Parker Pearson remarks on the 'sheer scale of Bronze Age bling' (p. 350), but it took the form of 'personal adornment and family burial monuments' (p. 352), a costly signalling practice that combined reverence for the dead with a very pointed message to the living:

> These people wanted to show off their wealth. Burying this amount of gold-work with a dead relative was an extraordinarily ostentatious thing to do; the people who arranged these funerals were able to show that they were so rich that they could easily spare large quantities of gold. (p. 350)

'Demic concentration' was valued still, but change occurred in how it was narrated in monuments and story. Polities were scaled up further into states and kingdoms, spurred by new weapons technologies and the ability of elite families to monopolize them (Gintis 2012). But now the political narrative was not about the group or what it knew as a whole. Individualistic personalization of political unity characterized Bronze and Iron Age *stories*. These have survived more or less unchanged in form and function over millennia, with successive political leaders using the same words for the same purposes.

Evolution creates the narrative – Gilgamesh, Ashurbanipal, Isaiah and George W. Bush

The oldest recorded story in the world is *The Epic of Gilgamesh*, originating in the Fertile Crescent not far from where Göbekli Tepe stands. King Gilgamesh may have existed, around 2,600 BCE, about 7,000 years after Göbekli Tepe, contemporaneously with Stonehenge's first stage. A celebrated version of this story is preserved at the British Museum on the so-called Flood Tablet, from the library of Assyrian king Ashurbanipal at Nineveh (Iraq), seventh century BCE (nearly 9,000 years after Göbekli Tepe). Its decipherment in the decade following Darwin's *Origin of Species* caused a sensation (MacGregor 2011), because on one of his adventures Gilgamesh is told the story of a flood in terms that bear an uncanny resemblance to the biblical (Noah's) flood story, thereby challenging the latter's divine provenance even as it confirmed its historical plausibility. It re-projected the story of human civilization back from the supernatural to the political: it wasn't divine intervention that caused the Flood; it was a traveller's tale.

As a political narrative the *Epic of Gilgamesh* still resonates, for its plot remains familiar, even in the news media. Christopher Booker (2004) has identified seven basic plots that are structural transformations of ancient tales, continuing in contemporary stories, in literature and on screen. They are: Overcoming the Monster; Rags to Riches; The Quest; Voyage and Return; Rebirth; Comedy; Tragedy. Booker includes *Gilgamesh* among stories with the most basic plot, 'overcoming the monster', along with the story of Perseus (the Gorgon), Theseus (the Minotaur), Beowulf (Grendel), Little Red Riding Hood (the wolf); and, more recently, Dracula, H. G. Wells' *War of the Worlds*, *The Seven Samurai/ Magnificent Seven*, *Jaws*, *Alien*, *Dr No* and *Star Wars – A New Hope*.

Applying this model to political communication, we can readily see the basic plots reiterated on the nightly news. A telling example was George W. Bush's 'Mission Accomplished' speech, delivered aboard USS *Abraham Lincoln* on 1 May 2003, immediately after the initial open combat phase of the Iraq invasion. Instantly controversial, as victory in the so-called War on Terror was far from 'accomplished', the speech was also notable for the biblical rhetoric that Bush invoked to celebrate how US forces had 'overcome the monster' unleashed at 9/11. The President concluded:

> All of you – all in this generation of our military – have taken up the highest calling of history. You are defending your country, and protecting the innocent

from harm. And wherever you go, you carry a message of hope – a message that is ancient, and ever new. In the words of the prophet Isaiah: 'To the captives, Come out! and to those in darkness, Be free!'.[43]

Using the full resources of the modern 'warfare state' (Edgerton 2006; Sparrow 2011), and in the face of monstrous unseen adversaries, Bush invoked an ancient story to *reconstitute* the post-9/11 polity.

Gotcha?[44] – The big guns of storytelling . . . Fall silent?

We should consider whether such continuity over the *longue durée* has something to do with the cultural-evolutionary adaptation of humans. It may explain one of the mechanisms by which '*Homo narans*' (Fisher 1984) maintains large, complex demes of non-kin in cooperative, albeit competitive, polities. Here again, Mark Pagel (2012, 2012b) is instructive.[45] Like the archaeologists Klaus Schmidt and Danielle Stordeur, he too sees culture as primary. Culture is the 'survival vehicle' for the survival of human groups or demes. As such, culture is characterized not so much by aesthetics as by allegiance of individuals to their deme. Pagel argues:

> The fact that cultural allegiance is most vividly expressed not in ethical behaviour but aggressive parochialism suggests it has been instrumental in protecting human beings throughout their evolution. (Pagel 2012b)

Culture is the group-making mechanism that humans evolved for survival *in groups*. Göbekli Tepe is one of the earliest surviving representations of that mechanism; 'polities' are culture's abstracted and formalized continuing form. When it comes to telling stories, Pagel's notion of 'aggressive parochialism' is all too familiar in media studies as the 'universal-adversarial' stance in journalism. The 'we'-group is taken to be *universal*: it includes everyone in the deme; and all

---

[43] Text at: www.cbsnews.com/stories/2003/05/01/iraq/main551946.shtml. Isaiah's Jewish 'captives' were held by the Assyrian king Sennacherib. The next king of Assyria but one was Ashurbanipal, so the link to Gilgamesh is not far-fetched: Gilgamesh's story and Ashurbanipal's deme were Isaiah's 'Bad Neighbours' (Chapter 4: Malvoisine).

[44] See *Wikipedia*: The Sun (Gotcha).

[45] See also a useful review of Pagel 2012a here: www.independent.co.uk/arts-entertainment/books/reviews/wired-for-culture-the-natural-history-of-human-cooperation-by-mark-pagel-7573966.html.

knowledge is available to it. 'They'-groups are taken to be *adversarial*: enemy, threat, deviant, dissident or deranged (see also Greene 2013).[46]

Hartley (1992a, 1992b) found that 'universal-adversarialism' is a chief characteristic of modern journalism. 'We' (say, Americans, following imperial habits), represent all humans; 'they' (others; the othered) are out to get us. There is, it follows, no better way to express who 'we' are than in what Charles Bean called 'the supreme test for fitness to exist': *warfare*. This structural characteristic of stories about cultural identity permeates many types of discourse across many domains of life. It is not confined to actual wars or international politics, but crops up wherever what Thorstein Veblen once called 'invidious comparison' is called for. In short, we're not just 'wired for culture', as Pagel puts it, but our stories are 'wired' for universal-adversarialism. Among others, news stories follow that formula.

Storytelling can be characterized as a carrier of information codes. Stories are designed for imitation, copying, sharing and emulation. They are a distribution mechanism for *how* to think (inductive reasoning; pattern recognition) and *what* to think. They store lessons, allowing social learning to cross generational, language and geospatial boundaries, reproducing the sequence of inductive logic that teaches a deme not only what to fear but what to do about it: how to outwit duplicitous adversaries, how to test unknown characters for truthfulness, how to signal prowess to enemies and lovers, how to behave courageously, and so on. Culture is the 'survival vehicle' for groups (demes); stories are the survival vehicle for culture. Stories like *The Epic of Gilgamesh* reflect archetypally on personal fear of death. The plot brings a realization of death's inevitability for the hero, but hope for reproduction through family, followers and 'our' strong city. Individuals may die, but their actions benefit the group, which thereby survives. So it was too with 'Mission Accomplished'. President Bush said: 'Those we lost were last seen on duty. Their final act on this earth was to fight a great evil, and bring liberty to others'. The dead made us free; so the story goes.

Culture and stories are mechanisms for transmitting cooperation and social learning (Thomas and Seely Brown 2011), and for developing externalized forms of shared knowledge (e.g. language, customs, institutions, technologies, tools etc.) that help to promote the survival of the group across time and place, even against the interests of individuals within the group, who die for unrelated genes, as it were. Cooperation overcomes 'selfish' genes (Dawkins 1976) by casting

---

[46] Note that the name given to many pre-modern nations, for example, Noongar (Western Australia) is simply their word for 'human being' (universal we). Conversely, many languages use pejorative terms for outsiders (adversarial they). Thus, all non-ancient Greeks were 'barbarians'. The Hebrew for 'opposite, adversary, accuser' is '*satan*'. The name 'Wales' is derived from the Norman-French word for 'foreigner' (they), whereas Welsh speakers name themselves the Cymry ('compatriots') (we).

members of the same tribe or deme as 'honorary relatives' (Pagel 2012), who look out for other members of the group, even though no genes are shared between them, and who, through acts of 'costly signalling', seek to impress strangers, even though they'll never meet them (Miller 2009; Gintis and Bowles 2011).

This is how cooperative trustworthiness is *tested*, allowing onlookers to judge what a given claim has cost the speaker; hard-won experience scoring higher than braggadocio, and it explains why *truth, trust, troth* and *truce* have the same etymological roots (Hartley 1992b: 48). In this sense, all storytelling is political, constituting the 'we'-community, seeking to create polities of trust, to expound the costs of cooperation for characters and deliver its symbolic rewards (Boyd 2009). Culture demands high levels of altruism towards the group and high levels of trust for insiders. Concomitantly, it instils distrust for outsiders or strangers. In contemporary news media, universal-adversarial journalism creates a 'they' identity, not only for direct enemies (monsters) but also for Tricksters (Hyde 2008), who may be masquerading as 'honorary relatives' to gain advantage of our deme's knowledge systems and information codes – to steal our semiotic cattle. On the other hand, we love stories where *our* Trickster steals *their* cattle! (Hartley 2012: ch. 9) Evolved mechanisms to counteract knowledge-theft may include *different languages* (the 'tower of Babel'), an early form of intellectual property protection, perhaps; and secret, arcane, cabbalistic or hermeneutic knowledge, including secret men's and women's business among indigenous demes. Modern nation-state genres of we/they exclusionary tactics include the differentiation of 'our' publicity from 'their' propaganda (Hartley 2006).

Scaling up

Storytelling seems to be universal among humans, but stories themselves have evolved only within specific 'we'-communities, often quite small or tribal demes. It is only in the past century or so that communications media, economic development and social network markets have expanded sufficiently to reach global scale. With global media networks comes the possibility that the differentiation of 'we' from 'they' – friends, family and lovers from strangers and enemies – may not be so easy any more, as stories themselves become literally universal across our far-flung species. Movies, music and publishing all aspire to global audiences and readerships; stories do well that appeal across previously impermeable demographic boundaries (e.g. J. K. Rowling). 'We' identities become much more abstract and distributed across complex networks.

How has storytelling kept pace with these changes? The most important change is that informal 'polities' can now be self-created, using the long-tail characteristics of large-scale social networks, where like-minded affinity or identity groups gather from among otherwise heterogeneous populations and communities of interest co-create their own political narrative, inaugurating an era of user-created citizenship.

When 'we' become 'they'

With the emergence of global communication networks with billions of users, the universal-adversarial formula now gets in the way. How can trust for 'we' but fear of 'they' identities be shared across the community when that group begins to approximate to humanity as a whole? In mainstream politics, narratives are emerging where humanity is both 'we' and 'they' at once – stories about climate change and environmental sustainability, for instance, or those about 'man's inhumanity to man' in war, displacement and refugee migration. Humanity at large is seen as the causal agent of those problems, and thus 'our' own adversary. We have literally become our own worst enemies. The monster our heroes must overcome is – ourselves. Human culture and technology seem to have evolved rather faster than human storytelling formats, so the universal-adversarial pattern no longer fits the facts. Demes are no longer 'tribal' or even nation-states. With contemporary digital media, we live in a semiosphere that is manifestly global and local at once. 'Our' deme may be organized around quite different rules of association among strangers than the ones that govern national citizenship.

Young Australasians camping out on the hills surrounding Anzac Cove are associating themselves with a political narrative of national origins, but they are also members of many other networks, complexly interconnected and of global extent, intensely meaningful for those involved but not necessarily shared by the people in the next tent, such that the distinction between 'we' and 'they' is as meaningless as a distinction between Australasian and Turkish graves on the peninsula, or between heroes and postmen.[47]

However, there seem to be no digital stories about this form of consciousness; only dutiful prayers to the ancestors, following a script written generations ago by war correspondents. So maybe digital storytelling isn't as radical and progressive as its commitment to self-expression for the ordinary person seems to suggest. Perhaps it needs to copy more forward-facing models; Tavi Gevinson, perhaps.

---

[47] See Atatürk's words about this when he visited Gallipoli in 1934 as President of Turkey: www.awm. gov.au/encyclopedia/ataturk.asp.

Digital storytelling activists need to be open to opportunities. Trying to avoid the pitfalls of mainstream and commercial media does not exempt any 'alternative' from the need to use scaled-up communicative systems. 'We' need new ways to organize, distribute and communicate new senses of virtual 'we' communities that are not founded on universal-adversarialism.

'The legacy of my father'

The 'big guns' are preparing, as we write, for the 2015 centenary of Gallipoli. Mainstream media are gearing up for World War I centenary. The BBC – largest public service broadcaster in the world – is also *deming up* with Rupert Murdoch, its most adversarial commercial competitor, in an alliance of opposites. That there is no love lost between these titans of storytelling is well known. However, the 'star' of 'one of the most important programmes' in the BBC's coverage of the centenary of World War I has been announced: Rupert Murdoch himself, who is being interviewed for a BBC film that will 'tell the tragedy of Gallipoli'. *The Independent* had the story:

> In an hour-long interview with the BBC, conducted at the New York headquarters of his global business News Corp, the media mogul has talked of his pride in his late father's actions and how they inspired him to begin a career in newspapers. . . . He said he was anxious to keep the memory of his father's achievements alive. 'I have always kept in mind very much the, if you like, legacy of my father and the influence he had on me and I have his picture prominently on the wall of my study at home. We do feel – I feel – that's a family obligation'. [48]

What was his father's legacy? According to this story, 'Keith Arthur Murdoch was a young Australian war correspondent who changed the direction of the war by exposing the 1915 Gallipoli campaign as a disaster'. The BBC's filmmaker, Denys Blakeway, told *The Independent* that 'the 60-minute film, due to be screened on BBC2 in 2015, "will hinge on Rupert Murdoch's father's action"'. Clearly, the narrative die is already cast. Rupert Murdoch's father 'changed the direction of the war', and *Gallipoli* (2015) will 'hinge' on his action. The BBC media release dutifully recycles this 'fact' as an axiom.

---

[48] This and related quotations from here: www.independent.co.uk/news/uk/home-news/bbc-unveils-the-star-of-its-first-world-war-anniversary-coverage--rupert-murdoch-8884028.html.

Murdoch himself already has form in this respect. He bankrolled Peter Weir's 1981 movie *Gallipoli* (starring Mel Gibson).[49] That film, to Weir's later 'regret', falsified the event for purposes of national (Australian) pride:

> The charge at The Nek on August 7, 1915, which provides the film's climax, did take place but an Australian, rather than a British officer, ordered the final charge. The film gives the opposite impression, something Peter Weir has said he regrets. 'The implication was that we were Pom bashing' he told David Stratton . . .[50]

Thus, through the heroics of Rupert Murdoch's father, Australians 'overcame the monster' – not the Turks but the 'Colonial Power' – and founded a nation based on white egalitarian mateship. The 'Minister for Veterans Affairs and Minister Assisting the Prime Minister on the Centenary of ANZAC', speaking on behalf of the Australian government and people at the Dawn Service at Gallipoli in 2013, gave official credence to the legend:

> Although it was so dreadful, it has become central to our nation's story. A hallmark in defining our nationhood and what we see as important in terms of mateship, service, sacrifice, courage and commitment'.[51]

Australian mateship being what it is, Anzac Day is now sponsored by VB beer. Their 'Raise a Glass' campaign is fronted by retired army general Peter Cosgrove (future Governor General of Australia), who says: 'Wherever you are, whatever you're drinking, raise a glass to those who serve'. VB will even arrange for General Cosgrove, AC, MC, to phone you with a wake-up call for the Dawn Service, over whose centenary he will preside as head of state in 2015.[52] This seems to be the political narrative that has already been marshalled to 'inspire a new generation to understand what happened', as the Director General of the BBC put it at the launch of the broadcaster's plans for the World War I centenary coverage.[53]

---

[49] See: wwwmcc.murdoch.edu.au/ReadingRoom/film/dbase/2002/gallipoli2.htm, with details of Murdoch's funding (through Associated R&R).

[50] Paul Byrnes, at: http://aso.gov.au/titles/features/gallipoli/notes/.

[51] Warren Snowdon speaking on 25 April 2013: www.theaustralian.com.au/in-depth/anzac-day/gallipoli-calamity-defined-a-nation-warren-snowdon-told-dawn-service-at-anzac-cove/story-e6frgdaf-1226629387147#sthash.fhqgofsJ.dpuf.

[52] https://www.raiseaglass.com.au/. And see: Pete Mitcham, aka Prof Pilsner (25 April 2013), 'Raise a glass – of scepticism', *Brewsnews*: www.brewsnews.com.au/2013/04/raise-a-glass-of-scepticism/. Wake-up call:www.victoriabitter.com.au/2013/04/this-anzac-day-theres-no-excuse/.

[53] www.radiotimes.com/news/2013-10-16/bbc-to-create-digital-cenotaph-for-ww1-anniversary-with-biggest-ever-broadcasting-season.

Digital stories to constitute a new polity

Finally we should return to digital storytelling. Can it do better than this? The *form* of digital storytelling has been well established, and its *purpose*, to open up the storytelling capabilities of digital media to everyone, remains laudable. But the *contents* of vernacular, unrehearsed stories unwittingly reproduce the political narrative that 'constitutes the polity' by mythologizing 'our' origins – unless conscious effort is made by digital storytelling activists and agencies to try something new. If a 'new generation' needs to be inspired to 'understand what happened', would it not be better to develop an alternative approach, based on the example of people from that generation, such as Tavi Gevinson, rather than relying on big-gun war correspondents and mythmakers like the Murdochs, Weir, Bean, Ashmead-Bartlett, Cosgrove and Carlton United Brewery – even the BBC. If we truly want to honour our granddads, and find new ways to constitute the globally networked polity, where foe-creation is self-destruction, we must find room for stories that do not go 'over the top', but, rather, we must understand how the very concept of 'we' is as much of a threat to ordinary people's understanding, well-being and peace as any monster. As a Greek user called '*eleni b*', on the photo-sharing site Pinterest, wisely noted (albeit, quoting literary evolutionist Jonathan Gottschall 2012):

> The metaphor behind the Trojan Horse: The audience accepts the story because, for a human, a good story always seems like a gift. But the story is actually just a delivery system for the teller's agenda. A story is a trick for sneaking a message into the fortified citadel of the human mind.[54]

As the citizens of another legendary city in Turkey discovered, it's always wise to beware of Greeks bearing gifts. Is there a Trojan Horse in the citadel of stories? The potential is there for digital media and social networks to democratize storytelling without universalizing adversarial 'aggressive parochialism'; and non-professional people may learn to tell a wider range of stories than the few that dominate national politics, the movies, journalism and education. The hope is that 'user-created citizenship' will *revise* not *reproduce* our understanding of 'who we are as a people' (as British PM David Cameron said about World War I commemorations).[55] But the indications are not altogether

---

[54] See: www.pinterest.com/pin/254383078925276152/ and: www.fastcocreate.com/1680581/why-storytelling-is-the-ultimate-weapon.

[55] Quoted here: www.independent.co.uk/news/uk/home-news/jeremy-paxman-blasts-david-cameron-over-wwi-centenary-comments-8866630.html.

positive. Digital storytelling in the context of Gallipoli seems to have been captured by institutional agencies that use it to disseminate existing meanings, while the generative journalistic story goes unchallenged, even when aspects are known to be not true. Digital storytelling faces powerful competition from the pros,[56] so it needs to develop sharper self-consciousness about the importance of storytelling as a whole, and a sophisticated understanding of the generative role that narrative plays in constituting who 'we' are. Given that digital media and social networks have already made what constitutes 'our' deme more risky, complex, open, uncertain and multivalent than ever before, it is urgent for progressive innovations like the digital storytelling movement – and cultural theory – to catch up. We need a model for universal (i.e. global in scale and digitally networked) but non-adversarial storytelling (i.e. stories that don't indulge in foe-creation for self-expression). Can it be done? Let's give it a try!

---

[56] As well as allowing Keith Murdoch pride of place in the Gallipoli story, the BBC planned to do exactly what digital storytelling is good at: 'we will tell well-known stories from fresh perspectives and original stories so far untold'. (Adrian Van Klaveren, controller for the BBC's World War One Centenary): www.mirror.co.uk/tv/tv-news/rupert-murdoch-joins-bbc-digital-2459368.

4

Malvoisine

Bad Neighbours

In the same year [June 1216], Louis [prince of France], with a powerful force of knights and soldiers laid siege to Dover castle, having first sent to his father [Philip II] for a petraria [stone-thrower or trebuchet] which was called in French 'Malvoisine;' and the French having disposed this and other engines before the castle, they began to batter the walls incessantly.

Roger of Wendover 1235[1]

Culture is knowledge that makes 'we'-groups: demes. A 'we'-group is a locus of identity and cooperation. It determines, in advance of individual choice, with whom we may cooperate, and which other groups we may oppose. It is built around a common inheritance in ways of seeing the world and interpreting its contents and meaning. Culture is a system of references – through symbols and artefacts, and all manner of practices and prospects – that forms a knowledge base for a 'we'-group. Culture is group-making knowledge.

The *'product'* of culture is not the work of art or way of life, but the *deme* that in turn makes *newness*, in an open-ended, adaptive mode of *productivity*, not according to a pre-existing definition of what each 'culture' is said to 'contain'; that is, facing the group's future, not the past. Thus, the 'product' of culture is a deme: a distinguishable subpopulation of semiospherically organized and socially networked non-kin (externalized brains), with common 'institutions of language' and rules for the production of meaningfulness within a contextualized

---

[1] Roger of Wendover's *Flowers of History, Comprising the History of England from the Descent of the Saxons to A.D. 1235* (ed. J. Giles, 1849), p. 374: (http://archive.org/stream/rogerofwendovers02rog eiala#page/374/mode/2up). Roger of Wendover's section of this MS covered the years 1216–35; the MS was first printed in 1567; this version was published in 1849; the relevant page (374) can be read at Archive.org. See also: *Wikipedia*: Flores Historiarum.

'niche' (actual, like a city, or virtual, as online). Demes are largely scale free, because they can range in size from a 'small-world' social network of six or seven persons (a 'hunting party') to the global 'community' of 7 billion individuals. But even when we imagine all humanity as one deme, as does the Australian multicultural broadcasting network SBS TV with its tagline: 'Seven Billion Stories and counting',[2] there are still many differences and sub-subpopulations to account for across that number.

We are looking for the 'productivity' of scale, of increasing complexity and proximity. But we are also looking for 'creative destruction' among demes, to ascertain whether actions that seem destructive according to one logic, for example, invasion, or besieging one's neighbour, may prove to be 'productive' according to another, for example, by consolidating knowledge and transmitting it to descendant demes.

The themes of this chapter are two interrelated aspects that unfold from this: namely what happens as culture grows to *global scale* – and thus as a 'we'-group extends to its global limit. Who or what takes the role of 'they'; or is it possible to maintain group cohesion without 'bad neighbours'? Demic growth is a process that sometimes appears to be gradual and incremental, but sometimes it is 'non-linear', achieving Romer's (1990) 'take-off' or 'whoosh' (McCloskey 2010), a 'tipping point' (complexity theory) or 'explosion' (Lotman 2009). In the latter case of rapid expansion, the question arises about what happens at each *boundary* of other 'we'-groups along the way – a clash we call 'Malviosine', literally 'Bad Neighbour', which marks adversarial competition between 'we'-groups, or demic (cultural) conflict, of increasingly global proportions.

Exponential 'take off' is not a cultural phenomenon per se; it is in large part caused by the economic and technological forces that drive globalization, such as the flows of factors of commodities, labour, capital and information, or advances in communication and transport. Local cultural phenomena can rise to global significance on the waves of this process, through a phenomenon we can dub 'innovation at the margins' (Tacchi 2004: 100), or what Leadbeater and Wong (2010) call 'learning from the extremes'. Rapid, large-scale expansion is also a cultural phenomenon, because with 'demic diffusion' the culture of one local place is pushed into others, potentially across the globe (Cowen 2004).

---

[2] 'Seven Billion Stories' spells out the acronym of SBS (officially, Special Broadcasting Service). SBS has linked this slogan to the UN's '7 Billion Actions' initiative: See www.sbs.com.au/7billion.

Evolutionary cultural dynamics become a site of group conflict. As knowledge grows, so does culture. Where the 'logic' of scientific discovery may be a Popperian (1963, 1972) evolutionary process of conjecture and refutation, culturally it can give rise to intergroup warfare.

H. sapiens is an extremely groupish animal; that is our evolutionary niche. We cooperate, voluntarily, more than any other life form (Nowak 2011). We are a language-using, high-trusting, instinctively cooperative animal and, to a first approximation, this is why we have culture. Culture is the evolutionary mechanism by which we achieve group-based cooperative pay-offs (Mesoudi 2011). 'High' culture – J. S. Bach or William Shakespeare – may well include the 'flower of human achievement'. However, it is 'ordinary culture' (Williams 1958) that holds everyone together in a deme, however large. Demes form tightly coordinated groups of trust and identity through shared meaning making. Our groupishness is also groupish: we make in-groups and out-groups (Tajfel 1970, 1974) or universal-adversarial 'we'-groups and 'they'-groups, (as examined in Chapter 3) – and thus cultural growth implies group growth, which implies that social and cultural *dynamics* work along the *boundaries* of groups and through the creation of *changed* groups and *new* groups. Importantly, this process also works through group *conflict*.

At the global scale, rapid expansion becomes a major problem for the theory of culture, especially since the *study* of culture has long been accepted as the means for forming judgement, taste, ethical comportment and appreciation of the inner life of others, especially among governors, administrators and statesmen, from Sir Thomas Elyot's (1531) *Boke named The Governour* to the 'imperial archive' (Richards 1993) and the foundations of modern literary and aesthetic criticism. Such a disciplinary history may be interested in how conflict is conducted – for instance in novels and artworks – but the next step, seeing culture *itself* as conflictual and aggressive to out-groups – is not generally taken, because if the question of violent conflict is addressed at all, the purpose is to consider how to minimize, regulate or overcome it, rather than to analyse it as a causal component of cultural identity and interaction. So the question remains: what happens when cultural growth interacts with groupishness? Can human cooperation (among fellow-deme members) and conflict (with outsiders) be integrated, such that even *conquest* (of one deme by another) actually results in greater *cooperation* at higher levels of integration, by consolidating and extended the distribution of otherwise local knowledge? Does expansion result in a multicultural global village, or in a cultural Cold

War? How do people navigate this space? Is this a global commons? Or is it a realm of contestation?

Big cooperation – Universal or adversarial?

The problem of large-scale cooperation has been approached in many different ways in the sciences. William Hamilton's theory of kin selection (Hamilton 1964) is the foundation stone in explaining altruism in biology (altruism = individually costly cooperation, making groups). Kin-selection theory offered a gene-centred explanation of how social insects (*Hymenoptera* such as bees, termites and ants) build large cooperative societies through the concept of 'inclusive fitness'. The key fact is that a colony is made of closely related individuals (e.g. the honeybees, *Apis cerana*, in a beehive are all sisters). E. O. Wilson (2012) has challenged this theory of the evolution of 'eusociality' by proposing *multilevel selection* rather than kin selection (Nowak 2011). The precise nature of the evolutionary mechanism by which large-scale cooperative groups emerge in nature is debated, but it is not our primary concern here. Our specific concern, instead, is with the role of culture in cooperation.

Theories of kin selection or multilevel selection do make demands on a range of informational and communication properties between individuals in a group. For a start, individual animals need to be able to recognize kin (genetic relatedness) and to discriminate behaviour based on recognition. A beehive or termite colony is also a complex information processing and communicative system that is achieved with various chemical messengers (pheromones, for instance), and it is well known that foraging bees communicate to others in the hive the direction and distance to nectar, pollen and water that they've discovered through the 'waggle dance'. This may be dancing, but it is not culture. Indeed, bee dancing is as much a part of bee genes as are bee wings. It is a closed communicative system – bees can transmit GPS coordinates to their sisters, but not awareness of their self, sociality or knowledge. But humans are different. Human dancing is cultural (Blacking 1984) and, while it may serve similar functions of communication (whether expressive, costly signalling, ritualistic or innovative),[3] it is a learned and acquired behaviour that has *meaning within a group*. Bees' dance repertoire is restricted, but human dance forms are open,

---

[3] For example, since 2008 the American Association for the Advancement of Science has supported a contest to 'dance your phd': http://gonzolabs.org/dance/.

such that the waltz, ballet or folk dances send a very different message from pogo, twerking or the Apache dance.[4]

Mark Pagel (2012) argues that open-ended human cooperation is special because it has been able to achieve a much larger scale than other organisms, including other eusocial organisms, by developing extended kin mechanisms, or ways of treating others as 'honorary kin'. Pagel explains that this is what language does. By extension, the work of identifying 'honorary relatives' is the role of all other cultural markers (or 'social text'), whatever subsidiary functions they may perform, and this in turn underlies the act of *interpretation*, which is also groupish, belonging to *demes* (as opposed to *description*, as in scientific method and mathematical logic). Pagel argues that this is why there are so many languages (or dances, or genres of artistic expression, and so on). Importantly, it is why we do not end up with a single language, even if that would be functionally efficient, were communication of messages the entire purpose of language. A single universal language – Esperanto, say – is not evolutionarily efficient because that does not solve the problem of knowing with whom to cooperate, or whom to oppose. It does not solve the 'we-group/they-group' problem. Indeed, this would only be evolutionarily viable if there were no groups (only individuals), or more specifically, no group boundaries. In short, the evolution of mutually untranslatable languages is an early solution to the problem of 'intellectual property' – individuals outside the speech community have no access to knowledge that may be freely shared among colinguals.

We argue that this is an ongoing and evolving problem that cultural science can pick up where evolutionary anthropology leaves off, with the notion that there are new group-creating mechanisms (new languages; new dances) that enable the kin-selection mechanism to extend far beyond immediate kin into a much larger world. We ask: what happens at *very* large, effectively infinite scale of massive numbers of people – global populations – with equally mind-boggling scale of 'big data', information and communication?

This is the problem of scale. On the one hand, there are utopian ideals of universalism that gave us the *Rights of Man* (Paine 1792), Esperanto and endeavours to create global government (Mazower 2012), the 'great big melting pot' of multiculturalism, or the so-called Global Village (McLuhan 1962).

---

[4] Apache dancing has nothing to do with the American Indian tribe of that name; it is the name of a spectacular 'fight-dance' craze that originated in Parisian youth/crime culture at the turn of the twentieth century. A notable example can be seen in the Crazy Gang movie of 1937, *O-kay for Sound* – a true expression of Malvoisine in dance! Accessible here: www.youtube.com/watch?v=8PDtdOTlYds. See also: www.streetswing.com/histmain/z3aposh.htm; www.jazzageclub.com/dancing/the-apache/

But then, on the other – the 'dark side' as it were – there is Malvoisine; intra-species or internecine and latterly global hostility, wars and terrorism, along with fractionations and balkanizations and the persistence of tribalisms and warring nation-states, and other xenophobic manifestations. There is a resistance to integration that seems deeply set in the human mind and consciousness, an atavistic instinct for *adversarialism* at least as strong as the enlightened progressive *universalism* of a global society.

The basic problem about scaling up, from an economics point of view, is that coordination and governance costs rise exponentially with the size of the group. Multiple factors feed into this, including the costs of information, transactions costs, the costs of monitoring and enforcement, along with the growing multiplicity of objectives and sources of conflict. This tends to put an upper boundary on the limits of hierarchic forms of organization that can only be overcome by breaking large organizations into modular units (Simon and March 1958). This same principle explains why large groups such as a nation are governed through smaller political units of states, province, cantons, city, borough, local council, and so on.

The exponential growth in complexity of coordination of increasing numbers of people yields a parallel problem in the growth of knowledge carried by each level. To the extent that growth in hierarchies can proceed through increasing scale, this invariably requires reduced complexity in knowledge carried by each element so that they are individually more predictable, manageable and governable. As the number of people in a group grows, and as the knowledge of that group grows, cooperation becomes increasingly expensive, and tends to break down at the point where the gains from it are no longer worth the costs of maintaining it. These costs are monotonic with size: as the number of agents rises, so does cost. Bigger is always more expensive, and at some point it becomes uneconomic – a group can be invaded at a cost that is not worth the fight. That determines how big a group can get.

We might expect to see groups – firms, for instance – get very large owing to the benefits gained from economies of scale and scope, and increasing returns from knowledge (Romer 1990). Yet economists have observed that it is the *market* that tends to get big, not firms, in which the price mechanism works as an institutional rule system for such large-scale coordination of economic activity (i.e. the economy is a spontaneous order, Hayek 1973; Potts 2013). The key insight therefore is that 'big cooperation' does not necessarily require big organizational groups (i.e. firms, most of which remain smallish). This is because the coordinating role is played by specific institutions, including the market mechanism, property rights, money and 'rules of the game' that do effectively scale to a global level. The price mechanism and market institutions are an evolved scalable solution to the coordination problem. Friedrich Hayek (1973: 37) explains that much of society and culture is a spontaneous order, as opposed to designed or planned:

> It would be no exaggeration to say that social theory begins with – and has an object only because of – the discovery that there exist orderly structures which are the product of the action of many men but are not the result of human design. In some fields this is now universally accepted. Although there was a time when men believed that even language and morals had been invented by some genius of the past, everybody recognizes now that they are the outcome of a process of evolution whose results nobody foresaw or designed.

For Hayek, culture evolved through group-selection mechanisms in which small groups developed modes of behaviour and acquired specific coordinating rules that enabled individuals within the group to cooperate effectively to gain knowledge and power over their environment in order to produce outcomes that ultimately outcompeted other groups. In Hayek's theory of cultural evolution the growth of 'cultural rules' is a consequence of groups outcompeting other groups, which then presumably are integrated into the now larger successful group. This underpins a theory of culture-as-institutions, but it does not yet furnish a theory of culture as group making. The problem remains: How does culture grow through ever larger groups? In evolutionary theory, the optimal size of a group adapts through selection working on a cost/benefit trade-off. A group should only ever get so big before the costs begin to outweigh the benefits, which is equivalently the problem of the limits to cooperation. The Hayekian solution elides this by arguing that institutions make groups, and that different institutions have different selection advantages that translate into differential group success. This explanation is elegant but incomplete. It lacks an account of the processes by which group formation occurs and of the processes by which the boundaries change and of what gets integrated and what is lost. For that, we need to consider the processes of cultural explosion or take-off to 'Big Culture'.

Big culture[5]

For Deirdre McCloskey (2010) the rise of modernity happened in a big 'whoosh' (her word), starting in the 1700s and continuing to this day. What is interesting about McCloskey – a Chicago-school economic historian – is that she attributes

---

[5] We don't like the term 'Big Culture'; but it is less barbarous than 'bigification'. Is there a better term?

this explosive emergent growth (the 'whoosh') not to coal or steel, or factory systems, or any of the other much favoured explanations for the industrial revolution, but instead to a revolution *inspired by rhetoric* (persuasive talk and values), which she calls the rise of 'bourgeois dignity':

> What made us modern, and rich, was a change in ideology, or 'rhetoric'. First in little Holland and then in Britain a new dignity and liberty for the middle class freed innovation. A unique wave of gadgets, and then a tsunami, raised incomes from \$3 a day to \$30 a day and beyond. . . . The most important secular event since the domestication of plants and animals depended on more than routine. It arose from liberties . . . and above all from a resulting revaluation of bourgeois life. (McCloskey 2010)

These days we speak of globalization in several registers. Most obviously economic, as an increasingly interconnected world system of economic production and consumption, but also in relation to a range of global public goods and global problems that reach beyond nation-states such as peace, security, disease, environmental pollution, migration and human rights. We also speak of globalized culture (Tomlinson 1996; Cowen 2004; Pieterse 2003), and 'world systems' of knowledge (Lee 2010). Cultural anthropologists and sociologists tend to view this through a lens of hegemonic cultural homogenization (McDonalds and Starbucks being two favourite bête noirs). Economists view it as an outworking of specialization and trade, bringing a larger consumption set and driving a flourishing of niche cultural production. The broader question, however, is not the process but the cultural dimensions of how scale arises. This is something that neither economists nor cultural critics have adequately addressed. We seek to understand not the cultural-ethical *effects* of globalization (boo or yay) but the cultural-evolutionary *causal* mechanisms and processes of group formation and dynamics that underpin any process of exponential growth or 'explosion'.

Such cultural 'explosions' are a theme of this book in such things as data ('big data', which is really about computational analytics), information storage (exobytes, yottabytes), digital cultural access and production (Google books, for instance), and cultural markets (e.g. Amazon). For McCloskey,[6] this is the great 'whoosh' of the twentieth century, when most economic output measures doubled, doubled, and then doubled again. Choice over consumer

---

[6] See McCloskey's site hosting research and writings on this topic – *Prudentia*: www.deirdremccloskey. com/.

goods is a thousand times greater than that a century ago (Beinhocker 2006). That is not just linear growth; it is exponential, power-law, or hyperbolic take-off. The semiotician Yuri Lotman (2009) describes this cultural process as 'explosion'.

Non-linear expansion is the difference between 'mass culture' (growth in which homogenizing forces dominate, potentially reducing variety) and 'Big Culture' (an explosion of variety and possibility, increasing uncertainty) – a concept related to 'big data' that we capitalize to indicate that it refers to culture at scale, as arrived at following the economic 'whoosh' or take-off of modernity. These present very different challenges. Big Culture, like big data but unlike mass culture, is mostly a story about the need for new tools and new mind-sets to navigate, explore and exploit the new possibilities that lie within. There are new consumption opportunities and new production possibilities, all of which require an entrepreneurial approach.

There are several dimensions to Big Culture. The human population gets bigger: 3 billion persons at the start of the twentieth century to over 7 billion, heading for a predicted peak of 9 billion by mid-twenty-first century. Cities get bigger with more people living in dense urban conglomerates than ever before; we have more close neighbours than ever before. Data and information get bigger through new digital technologies of computation, communication and storage, and more of the world is accessible at very low cost. Media get big through globe-spanning networks and near universal access (especially via mobile devices), and so we know more about the world in real time than ever before. Trade and markets get bigger and we have more opportunities to consume and contract and produce than ever before. Politics and society get bigger as representation grows and more issues become interlinked through recognition of the extent of global public goods and of the means to address them (poverty, health, pollution, climate, security, and so on). Supranational jurisdictions, from the United Nations and European Union to World Trade Organization, World Intellectual Property Organization and the rest, get bigger in number, importance and scale. Knowledge enlarges as a conjunction of all the above forces and mechanisms working through a vastly expanded educated population that operates globally (using English as the unifying 'lingua franca') and commitment of resources to innovation. What is striking is the extent to which we have largely normalized these explosive changes. It is not true to say that 'everyone' lives in Big Culture, but certainly a growing majority of the species does: it is population-wide in the biological as well as in the biopolitical sense.

An example of this is the modern phenomenon of celebrity, which in our model is an 'explosion' in the number of links that connect certain individual people to others (Barabási 2002; Hartley 2012: 188). There have always been important people (in mass culture they are controllers of distribution), but celebrity is a different concept. Celebrity is explosion of the individual in cultural connectedness: it is created at the conflux of big attention (big media) and big rewards (big markets). We see it in sports, religion, finance, management and any domain that is shaped by the social network market dynamics of attention and information feedback (Potts et al. 2008).

The point to note is that celebrity – a Big Culture phenomenon – is also *group making* (turning Big Culture into *our* culture) through a totemization of a personified representation of the meaning of a 'we'-group. The role of celebrity is to anchor a group (known in Twitterese as 'followers') into present-tense meaningfulness or future-facing conditions, which may be why newly minted celebrities are ever younger in the most prominent international popular-culture systems (Hollywood; music; social media). The phenomenon (not each individual celebrity) is created by the group, for the group. The presidential style of democratic leadership contests (e.g. US presidential elections) or the celebrity CEO (Jack Welch, Steve Jobs) are other instances of this kind of group making around a celebrity figure.

How big can Big Culture get? Sociologists employ the concept of 'imagined communities' (Anderson 1991), of which the ideal type is the nation-state. Imagined communities are constituted in mediated rhetoric (previously newspapers and broadcasting; now online), and in turn constitute the pathways through which cultural explosion ripples. New-media theorist Clay Shirky (2008) explains the growth of ad hoc communities (or organizations) through lowered transactions costs associated with 'social tools'. Group formation here is a mechanism by which explosion advances (note: explosion, not growth processes) by an expanded domain of a group, or through the rapid creation of new groups, rather than by a kind of institutional expansion, or imperialism, through which a set of rules is imposed upon or adopted by a larger population. This is perhaps a subtle distinction in abstract, but it goes to the heart of cultural science: culture evolves through a group process of meaning making, and not simply as differential information replication or social learning – it's not a species of 'efficient distribution' but of group making.

Explosion is a cultural mechanism of this complex evolutionary process of the growth of groups and the meaning they carry. Explosion invariably runs up against the reciprocal problem of group conflict, which is really 'contested meanings' but can be manifested in much worse behaviour.

Malvoisine

At the Siege of Acre in the Holy Land in 1191, so the storytellers say, King Philip II of France used siege engines, trebuchets or catapults for throwing rocks, flaming missiles, plague-ridden bodies or the heads of slain enemies, into enemy forts or citadels (Figure 4.1). One 'excellent' such machine he named Malvoisine or 'Bad Neighbour' (*Malam Vicinam*). It seems that the Turks returned these favours with their own engine, named '*Mal Cousine*' or 'Bad Cousin' (*Malam cognatam*):

> The king of France … concentrated on constructing siege machines and placing trebuchets [petrariae] in suitable places. He arranged for these to shoot continually day and night. He had one excellent one which he called 'Bad Neighbour' [Malvoisine]. The Turks in the city had another which they called 'Bad Relation' [Mal Cousine] and often used to smash 'Bad Neighbour' with its violent shots. The king kept rebuilding it until its continual bombardment partly destroyed the main city wall and shattered the Cursed Tower.[7]

Malvoisine eventually prevailed, shattering the city's 'Cursed Tower' (*Turrim Maledictam*). Later, in 1216, King Philip lent Malvoisine to his son, Prince Louis

Figure 4.1 A 'Bad Neighbour' in action. *Harper's New Monthly Magazine*, 22–29 June 1869.[8] *Monty Python and the Holy Grail* (1975) substituted a cow – and 'French taunting' – for the 'Greek fire' shown here.[9] Creative Commons license.

---

[7] Cited in Chevedden (2000): 97–8, from: *Itinerarium Peregrinorum et Gesta Regis Ricardi*, ed. Stubbs (1218–19), describing the Third Crusade (1189–92). See also *Wikipedia*: Itinerarium Regis Ricardi.
[8] Source: 'Engraving of thirteenth-century catapult for throwing Greek fire'. *Wikipedia*: Greek Fire Catapult (Harper's Engraving).png (Creative Commons license).
[9] *Monty Python and the Holy Grail* (1975): see: www.youtube.com/watch?v=9V7zbWNznbs.

of France, to batter Dover Castle, during the war between King John and the barons in England, after 'bad' King John had reneged on Magna Carta, signed under baronial duress at Runnymede in 1215. Like its many successors down to contemporary drones, robots and missiles, Malvoisine was a technological solution to a political problem. It didn't work, because Dover Castle was a 'new technology' itself, built to withstand such assaults.

Malvoisine – the doctrine of inter-demic contestation of meanings by assault – *names* a more general issue in cultural science. Considering that organized demes (tribes; states) can be armed with lethal weapons and use them to effect 'hostile takeovers' of competing groups, to the point where successful demes may enlarge, even to imperial scale, while defeated ones may disappear for ever, the question of violent destructiveness (or of cultural security, to put it another way) looms large.

If the adaptive function of culture is to ensure the survival of 'we'-groups in antagonistic competition with 'they'-groups, then two problems come into sharp focus when those groups confront one another, armed to the teeth, as they began to do 2 million years ago – before *H. sapiens* branched off from ancestral populations – with the emergence of projectile weapons among proto-human hominins (Gintis 2012: 6–7).

First, how can we explain group-on-group *violence*, destruction, and their institutionalized forms – warfare, oppression, coercion or even genocide of entire peoples by conquerors, rulers or neighbours – as part of *culture*, especially if we are reluctant to jettison the notion of culture as cooperation, creativity, and a civilizing influence? The second problem is more recent, resulting from Big Culture: when 'we' span the entire globe and the *entire species*, how can conflict be a fundamental component of 'demic' knowledge formation, where 'we'-groups grow their knowledge in competition with 'they'-groups, sometimes to the point of taking them over altogether (by demic diffusion, cultural transmission, accession, settlement, conquest, colonization)? In other words, how can demic knowledge remain adversarial when it becomes truly universal?

As to the first problem, Herbert Gintis (2012) has a definite view, as we described in Chapter 3: 'Demes': Projectile weapons, which could be used against large prey, were also good for killing rivals (2012: 6). Gintis conjectures therefore that coercive force had to give way to hegemonic persuasion. Counter-intuitively, in-group competitive violence produced the *communicative arts* of 'strong reciprocity' – persuasion, logic, analysis, politics, big brains, language – in short, culture. According to Gintis, technologically equipped culture, founded on lethal weapons, did not lead to destruction but to the growth of knowledge, and knowledge became the means by which simian-like troupes of hominins evolved to modern *H. sapiens*.

Applying the same logic to inter-demic conflict, Gintis concludes his 'behavioral synthesis' of human evolution with a narrative that associates the development of different forms of state (from monarchical-aristocratic to democratic) with the industrial evolution of new lethal technologies (from scarce and expensive to common and cheap), until 'The true hegemony of the foot soldier, and hence the origins of modern democracy, began with the perfection of the hand gun' (2012: 9). This certainly reads as a peculiarly US-centric model of democracy, and says nothing about weapons of mass destruction or the 'MAD' ('Mutually Assured Destruction') brinkmanship politics of the Cold War era, but it does argue strongly that wars *produce* knowledge, culture, technology and political arrangements – they co-create humanity.

This point has been widely discussed by economic historians of technology, particularly with respect to World War II, from which emerged radar, modern computing, operational logistics, rocketry, new alloys, jet engines and nuclear energy, among many other technological breakthroughs, which in turn had large-scale political and cultural effects. Taken at population-level, rather than at the level of individual winners and losers, this point of view suggests that Malvoisine has been a force for evolutionary adaptation from the get-go, even though its scale and effects have become more spectacular in the period since knowledge began to grow exponentially (or faster) after the invention of metallurgy, writing, cities and states.

This leads us to the second problem mentioned earlier: namely how you deal with more, and with ever more – the problem of scale – having reached the point along that exponential curve in the growth of knowledge, arms and population, when 'we' have no one left to fight, because Big Culture spans the globe and the species; and how can you trust 'universal' knowledge that has not been tested in inter-demic contest?

The 'bad neighbour' problem is perhaps the fundamental problem in the study of the evolution of sociality and the main barrier to large-scale cooperative emergent social orders. In evolutionary social theory, this problem is otherwise known as the problem of *altruism*, or the free-rider problem, as a limit to ever greater or ever higher levels of *cooperation*. But this is about the instability of cooperation in a static world of individual behaviour. What we are concerned with here is a variation on that, namely the greater incentive to *defection* with larger numbers (Olson 1965), organized as self-knowing groups. Game theory tells us that cooperation is only stable in small groups with complete information and monitoring. Beyond this scale, cooperation unravels as cooperative groups become increasingly valuable targets for invasion by uncooperative 'defectors'. Further, evolutionary game theory establishes that cooperation in repeated games can be sustained through reputational mechanisms (Fehr and Fischbacher 2003). Cooperation is not predicted to survive to global-scale context. As we go up through larger aggregations of social groups, the problem of bad neighbours – whether through defection or conflict – becomes a larger and more complex issue.

Bad neighbours have different knowledge. That is why they are different groups. Equivalently, good neighbours have similar or relatable knowledge: their group is self-knowing and its knowledge is shared. That is how cooperation is possible; knowledge among members is interoperable. But different knowledge ('out-knowledge' as it were) is also *valuable*, in that it is a source of innovation and spur to adaptation for in-groups. But when different knowledge exists in external groups, it is not available in a way that can be easily accessed or used. Indeed, it is something that tends to be repelled, in the language of immunology, as a 'foreign body'; and it may be strongly protected by the out-group who made it, who don't want you to filch it. A major potential source of novelty and innovation is new ideas from other groups, but cultural groupishness makes them difficult to acquire. This problem – of hostility to external knowledge, but a wish to benefit from what it knows – is not xenophobia; that is an explanation after the fact. Rather, the cultural science account follows the chain of causation – the evolution of meaningfulness in a group.

Nor is this simply a political or even a military problem. In cultures with advanced divisions of labour and knowledge systems, it applies just as much to expertise and indeed to knowledge itself. Groups have boundaries and the limits to the growth of knowledge are the dynamics of those boundaries. A Humean world (where all knowledge grows through inductive inference), or a Popperian world (where the growth of knowledge proceeds through conjecture and refutation), all to eventually become common knowledge, is a quasi-fiction first debunked in the sociology of science. Latour (2005) argued that science was also a human cultural endeavour and, just like other social-mediated processes, could be analysed as a kind of 'cultural text'. Science progresses as groups of scientists and their ideas are challenged and transformed. The so-called progress of science illustrates an externalized, demic principle that is consistent with the Kuhn/Lakatos model of scientific paradigms and research programmes. In *The Structure of Scientific Revolutions* Thomas Kuhn (1962) famously challenged the prevailing model of scientific 'progress by accumulation' (a growth model) with his model of paradigm shifts, which is a non-linear model of 'explosion'. Although he didn't use that terminology, this was in essence a model of scientists forming externalized demes, which rubbed up against competing groups but kept its internal knowledge insulated. In Imre Lakatos's (2001) model, 'hard core' propositions are protected by a belt of 'auxiliary hypotheses'. A scientific revolution occurs when these auxiliary hypotheses no longer hold and the hard-core axioms are exposed to challenge, in effect, changing the boundary of a group. So the standard model of scientific progress is actually based about 'we-group/they-group' dynamics and continuous threats from 'bad neighbours'. The Kuhnian 'paradigm shift' is explosive, with rapid expansion and transformation of a whole field, and the neglect of the existing paradigm.

The bad neighbour model of novelty and innovation is natural. Knowledge grows as it is tested, and testing knowledge involves placing it under tension and stress, running it up against very different perspectives. Contested knowledge is not untrue knowledge; it is knowledge that is subjected to strengthening through challenge. This is the logic of open economies: anyone can enter a market and seek to compete, and no position is protected. It is also the logic of open societies (Popper 1945), with their necessary constitutional guarantees of free speech and free assembly, and the tolerance of difference that this requires. Tolerance, rather than boundary-policing, becomes the highest form of civic behaviour, precisely because it exposes a 'we'-group to learning from 'they'-groups, against the evolutionary grain.

Systemic violence

Hard-won tolerance in the name of an open society, open knowledge and openness to dynamic change, all mean that the well-tempered inquiring mind is brought up short at the warlike, destructive implications of explosive and contested change. The notion of 'conquest as cooperation' (see Chapter 9: 'Extinction') is repellent, or seen as a contradiction in terms. Another name for it is imperialism, where Europe led the way.[10] Here, indeed, an important

---

[10] According to Laycock (2012), only 22 out of nearly 200 countries recognized by the United Nations 'were never invaded by the British'. *Daily Telegraph* (4 November 2012): 'British have invaded nine out of ten countries – so look out Luxembourg': www.telegraph.co.uk/history/9653497/British-have-invaded-nine-out-of-ten-countries-so-look-out-Luxembourg.html.

question about scaling up does need to be considered – the origin of violence. Competition, conflict, 'creative destruction' and conquest may result in the elimination of entire cities, peoples, and landscapes, and with them the loss of entire cultures, languages and knowledge. How can this be claimed as part of the process whereby cultures *grow* their knowledge?

Consider whether human violence is *natural*, or *cultural*; is it a product of behaviour or civilization? Do 'contested meanings' require that the 'winner takes all' and the loser loses everything? Does the cause of violence lie in human behaviour ('hard-wired in the Pleistocene', so to say); or is it better explained in the scaled-up complex systems that result from accelerated wealth, knowledge, technology and civilization? Some writers (Elias 1939; Pinker 2011) favour the first explanation; others (Benkler 2011; Gintis 2012) the latter. The answer has important implications for cultural science. If the former (natural behaviour of individuals), then scaling up makes little difference; there isn't much that we can do about it, beyond strong security and policing to keep these naturally violent propensities in check, or (which is the same thing) by handing violence over to the state to exercise as a monopoly (in the form of war and punishment) in order to regulate its use in face-to-face communication and across society. The 'civilising process' (Elias 1939 and elsewhere) is seen as the slow defeat of that state of nature in which the 'war of all against all' renders life 'solitary, poor, nasty, brutish, and short' (Hobbes 1651: XIII.9). As Mark Twain had put it in 1897 (ch. 47):

> The joy of killing! the joy of seeing killing done – these are traits of the human race at large. We white people are merely modified Thugs; Thugs fretting under the restraints of a not very thick skin of Civilization.

But if it is the latter ('nurture' or cultural systems), if violence is an *outcome* of scaling up the growth of knowledge and other assets, or (which is the same thing) if violence is *demic* and a property of adversarial cultural systems, not a behavioural property of individual humans, then it immediately becomes a specific problem for cultural science; with clear 'policy' implications – that invasive violence and 'creative destruction' need to be separated and demic boundaries maintained in dynamic contestation without recourse to violence. Such shifts, from 'Mars' to 'Venus',[11] war to trade, force to law, power to 'soft power', have been successfully effected in various domains, both geopolitical and social. It is states that need discipline, not competitive knowledge systems.

[11] See: www.presseurop.eu/en/content/article/1783481-mars-and-venus-10-years.

The trouble is that we persist in telling ourselves stories that naturalize person-to-person violence. So the origin of violence as a problem of knowledge needs to be understood across at least two dimensions: in the stories we tell ourselves as well as in fact. The *representation* of violence is important because it pervades our demic self-knowledge. We familiarize ourselves with stories that ascribe its cause to

- *Other groups* (adversarial 'they'-groups) – for instance our own 'bad neighbours', both external 'enemies' to the nation and internal 'threats' to order and safety, or the two combined ('the terrorist');
- *Other times* – projected from the 'here and now' to the medieval past, or earlier;
- *Other cultures* – especially those seen as 'barbarian', 'savage' or 'primitive';
- *Fantasy worlds* – science fiction, where we/they contestation or postmodern relativism may be projected into the future and thought-through to logical but unpalatable conclusions (e.g. *Star Trek*'s 'Omega Glory' and *The Hunger Games* or many another dystopian vision of totalitarian-consumerism).[12]

All these 'places' (places in rhetoric and discourse) are routinely represented as inherently Hobbesian for all, except 'our heroes', who are vindicated by winning, usually after acts of extreme, extra-legal violence. 'We' don't start it but, eventually provoked, 'our' hero fights it out, usually one-on-one (accompanied by explosions), until equilibrium is restored. Our stories require conflict and revel in violence, even child-on-child killing as in *The Hunger Games*, but it's not our fault.

The second dimension is that hard-to-reach zone that, given the amount of story in our heads, we might call 'not-story', that is, reality. It turns out that the *behavioural* truth may be close to the opposite of what our *demic* stories tell us. According to sociologists Siniša Malešević and Kevin Ryan (2013), 'recent research on the behaviour of individuals in violent situations shows that our species is neither good at nor comfortable with the use of violence'. They point out that Norbert Elias's influential model of 'the Civilizing Process'

---

[12] See *Wikipedia*: The Omega Glory. This 1968 Roddenberry episode of *Star Trek* places the 'Kohms' (communists) and 'Yangs' (Yankees) on a planet where their mutual hostility eventually returns them to *Lord of the Flies*-style primitivism; a common trope of modernist sci-fi anxious about Vietnam and the Cold War. *The Hunger Games* exemplifies an equally common trope in a world without external enemies, where 'we' pay the price of pleasure, abundance and choice by forcing impossible choices on the 16-year-old heroine: survival versus humanity; life versus love; compliance (government) versus rebellion (freedom). Her choices are vindicated by winning (rather than knowing).

(1939), where a *longue durée* directional trajectory is said to have led humans from a natural state of barbarism and bloodlust towards a civilized stage of self-restraint and control, is based on the prior existence of barbarism and an inherent belligerence among humans. It turns out, however, that there is little evidence for that presumption, and plenty of evidence against it.

Malešević and Ryan argue that a distinction must be made between (psychological) aggression and (social) violence, where – it transpires – violence of the kind that characterizes advanced, modern societies is not a recapitulation of an earlier or more primitive stage of evolution, but a product of civilization itself:

> In contrast to aggression . . . collective violence entails sophisticated coordi-
> nation, organization, control and at least some degree of planning. In this sense
> aggressive behaviour is almost the exact opposite of organized violent action, as
> instead of acting on impulse, successful collective violence presupposes restraint.
> The goal-oriented use of physical force requires cool headedness, instrumental
> rationality and self-control. Hence rather than being stifled by the Civilising
> Process, complex forms of organized violence, such as warfare, revolutions
> and terrorism, are only possible with the development of civilization. (Malešević
> and Ryan 2013)

Malešević and Ryan point out that soldiers are spurred to action not by bloodlust but by what Australians call 'mateship':

> . . . one's platoon starts to resemble one's close-knit family. . . . Hence it is not
> the joy of fighting that binds warriors together, it is an unprecedented and
> heightened sense of micro solidarity that stimulates this special feeling in
> individuals. The 'joy of war' is not the joy of killing and death but the joy of life
> and love. (Malešević and Ryan 2013)

'Micro-solidarity' (mateship) is a *demic* phenomenon, belonging to culture not behaviour, and it is this that motivates military *behaviour*, which is otherwise often characterized by an avoidance of killing. It follows that contemporary modernity and globalized civilization need to answer for violence, not humanity's state of nature via some evolutionary throwback. As Malešević and Ryan conclude, 'total war, the Holocaust, gas chambers, gulags, organized suicide bombings and the atomic annihilation of entire cities' are only possible and only show up at the latest stage of civilization; they are not its negation but its completion. Malvoisine is not a medieval joke because the joke is on 'us': Malešević and Ryan point out that the Nazis' genocidal killing squads were led by 'highly educated individuals: economists, solicitors, academics'; a third of their commanders had doctorates.

Violence produced modernity, and modernity uses violence, for the best imaginable reasons and purposes:

> It is modernity's legacy of Enlightenment that fosters the grand and often mutually incompatible ideological blueprints for creating an ideal society, and it is modernity alone that can provide the efficient bureaucratic apparatus, the science and technology capable of implementing these grand vistas of a brave new world. . . . It is civilization, not the lack of it, that is at the heart of the organized and protracted mass slaughter of millions of human beings. (Malešević and Ryan 2013)

There's a case to answer: recruiting whole populations to the 'common substantive purpose' of a state, however benignly that purpose is imagined, be it for profit, salvation, progress or racial domination (Oakeshott (1975: 114, 319), is to recruit humanity to violence on a scale never before realized, no matter how much we fill our heads with visions of 'naturally' violent berserk premoderns and fantasy monsters. We are indeed our own worst enemies.

Does this mean that demic knowledge – Big Culture – is inherently violent and destructive, even if individuals are not; and that our universal-adversarial mode of group identification is inevitably corroding and destroying the very global unity that Big Culture has produced? We don't know; but the evidence – especially from the realms of politics, journalism and fiction (including games), if not science – is that the *representation* of demic knowledge cannot operate without an adversary, so once demes have expanded to global scale the pattern is to turn inward – to look for the 'enemy within' (if not foreigners then Communists, terrorists, paedophiles, etc.), or to externalize the threat beyond humanity (climate change, pandemics, aliens, etc.). But the reality may well be different. Violence ensues not from natural aggressiveness but 'sophisticated coordination, organization, control . . . planning, cool headedness, instrumental rationality and self-control', as Malešević and Ryan point out. Self-organizing complex groups like demes and cultures need to be cajoled, marshalled and deployed using central planning and direct coercion (e.g. conscription). In other words, competitive adversarial competition is cultural, but violence is not natural – it is imposed by something more like mass culture than Big Culture. The problem of Malvoisine is that contestation has been taken over by central planners and states. Self-organizing competitive systems may well manage to get along without it (see Chapter 5: 'Citizens').

What happens when culture gets really big?

In much cultural studies and cultural economy literature (Tomlinson 1996; Pieterse 2003), the prospect of globalized culture is seen as a threat of the loss or devaluation of small local culture (which is often taken to be its idealized size), under an onslaught of homogenizing mass cultural markets or hegemonic mass cultural production. Anti-globalization movements largely treat it as axiomatic that globalized culture is 'a bad thing'. But globalized culture can mean many specific and complex things.

It is useful to frame this through the lens of globalized economic activity with respect to international trade. The economic case for the net welfare benefits of open trade is overwhelming and on solid footing: no serious economist disputes this (Clemens 2011: 85).[13] But that does not mean that these welfare gains are obvious, or even intuitive. It takes careful thinking and counterfactual observation to appreciate the arguments from comparative advantage, say. It also requires that one can appreciate that the welfare gains come from specialization, and hinge on falling costs of transport and communication (a truism for most of the past 300 years), along with maintained citizenship in a global community.

But can the same arguments be made about cultural globalization? The economist Tyler Cowen (1998, 2004) elaborates a gains-from-trade argument that shows not only why consumers benefit from increased variety and better preference matching, but also how small local or niche cultural producers gain from the ability to reach into a larger market. However, the cultural science perspective on globalization is not an extension of the gains-from-trade model. It does not predict specialization on the producer side and increased real income and variety on the consumer side. Culture can be an exchangeable commodity and or capitalized 'output'; the more salient point is that a globalized culture is less an argument about the quantity or quality of individual cultural consumption or production, but about its demic effect. Culture is productive of newness and knowledge and the globalization of culture can be immediately framed as a larger demic population and thus a broader social base for innovation.

A globalized culture has more demic frontiers of externalized knowledge populations: a greater number of 'we-group/they-group' boundaries. In a bigger, more globalized culture, Malvoisine will be a larger issue. Along with the standard-issue anti-globalization concerns that demand cultural protectionism

---

[13] People can of course be against globalization in defence of their private interests as producers; the economic logic applies to aggregate welfare gains for all producers and all consumers.

(which we discuss in Chapter 9: 'Extinction'), it is common to frame this as an issue of multiculturalism. A number of modern parliamentary democracies (including Australia and Canada) have explicit multicultural policies intended to enable a multiplicity of cultures to occupy the same national space without favouring one group over others, and through endeavours to minimize conflict, often by minimizing contact or through social engineering to promote tolerance and criminalize antagonism. This contrasts with assimilationist or 'melting pot' approaches (the United States pre–World War II, for instance, or Italy, France and Germany in the nineteenth century), which seek to prioritize values of national citizenship above culturally ethnic, racial or regional loyalties (see Chapter 5: 'Citizens'). It is not unreasonable to frame the question of globalized culture as this same debate (multiculturalism vs. assimilation) carried to world scale (Pultar 2014).

Globalized culture clearly presents greater opportunity for conflict along wider frontiers of potential miscommunication, or outright clash of value systems. A defensive extension of nation-state models of multicultural tolerance (whether learned or enforced) or priority-shifting assimilationist blending may be the only path to cultural harmony and peace at the global scale. But this is not the path of cultural science. The problem with that approach is that it trades off against innovation, newness and indeed cultural renewal, all of which actively require the tensions of clashing and conflicted systems at the margin of demic knowledge. Both multicultural tolerance (by isolating and protecting difference) and assimilationist higher values (by de-valuing and blending difference) have the same dynamic consequence, in minimizing sources of newness, regeneration and evolutionary drive.

Innovation can come from investment of resources (inputs) into research and development. Yet that is not the only source; just the most controlled. Innovation and the discovery and creation of newness, as the precursor to the ongoing updating and adaptationist project of regeneration, also come from the outworking of tensions at the margins of systems, which is to say at the boundaries of 'we'-groups and 'they'-groups. This is something that becomes more powerful at scale. Discovery and regeneration is a process of shifting boundaries as ideas from a 'they'-group are made meaningful to a 'we'-group. When the Rolling Stones made the 'ideas' of rhythm and blues and soul music ('they'-group) meaningful to an audience that could understand rock and roll ('we'-group), this was regenerative innovation. Igor Stravinsky did a similar thing for folk music in *The Rite of Spring*, and Pablo Picasso for African and Oceanic tribal mask art in *Les Demoiselles D'Avignon*.

Globalized culture presents powerful opportunities for cultural innovation and renewal. But at the same time it must be recognized that this will be largely unpredictable, mostly uncontrollable, full of surprise and waste, with many apparent near-field losses (that will invariably be noisily fought). Globalization is itself a mechanism of cultural renewal, although rarely through the central officially sanctioned and mainstream pathways. Instead, this unfolds as an emergent product of the messy margins and conflicted tensions of a self-organizing and evolving open global system.

Here is where the answer to the question of violence must be sought. It is state-sponsored enterprise that imposes a potentially lethal 'common substantive purpose' on citizens, not the self-organizing quest for 'newness under uncertainty' among citizens. Increasingly, the 'bad neighbour' turns out to be your own friendly authorities, whose mission to civilize, pacify and protect you results in tall stories backed up by 'security' forces armed to the teeth, not infrequently facing down their own citizens, who make up the majority of casualties in many contemporary wars. Thus, it is not civilization (if by that is meant self-organizing complex associations) that causes violence, but the appropriation of its technological and bureaucratic machinery by piratical states that has caused its exponential rise since the American Civil War (the first to experience machine guns).

The explosion of culture is perhaps the defining challenge of postmodernity. The problems of scale and growth are the real problems of cultural studies, and the central problems that cultural science seeks to address. These problems of rapid large-scale change (Lotman's 'explosion', McCloskey's 'whoosh') and their intersection with a context of globalization, which tends (rightly) to place them in the context of forces beyond individual or government control, also tends to lead many scholars, experts and leaders of thought and people to worry about these forces and outcomes. Cultural studies, in particular, tends to be pessimistic about the prospects of Big Culture. But cultural science isn't. Our point is that just because something is not easily managed and controlled does not necessarily make it bad and risky, or inherently violent. The nature of cultural production and renewal is perhaps much more like this than we have previously appreciated. By and large, we have been experiencing cultural globalization for a long time now (at least since the early modern 'age of exploration'), and it is a primary source of newness, innovation and cultural regeneration. It just doesn't look like that as it is happening, when it tends to feel more like conflict, tension and confusion. It is only after the event that its meaning becomes obvious, as changes in knowledge and group boundaries become apparent. Cultural science is the study of this process.

5

Citizens

Demic Concentration Creates Knowledge

To be attached to the subdivision, to love the little platoon we belong to in society, is the first principle (the germ as it were) of public affections. It is the first link in the series by which we proceed towards a love to our country, and to mankind.

Edmund Burke 1790: Vol. XXIV, Part 3, para 75

What is a citizen?

An implication of cultural science is that this whole citizenship malarkey may be about more than just voting, demanding rights and asserting group identity. Citizens might also be *creating knowledge* through the mechanism of externalized, meso-level innovation. Citizenship can shape group making, which is demic, and productive of knowledge. By establishing a more stable sense of what a given deme is and how it differs from others, the process of 'demic concentration' can lead to a knowledge-making citizenry. In this chapter, we outline this cultural science model of citizenry and explore some of its implications.

Standard models of citizenship mostly replicate the concerns of each analytic domain that seeks to explain it. Political philosophy views citizenship through a 'social contract' lens, seeing an historical and logical framework of rights and obligations connecting the citizen and the state. This is the constitutional and institutional expression of rational citizenship. It approaches citizenship through a local, bottom-up model of civic association based on Burke's 'little platoon' (see the quotation at the head of this chapter). Alexis de Tocqueville underscored this insight in *Democracy in America*, with his claim that it is *free* citizens, specifically, who cooperate in local associations to build civic communities.

For cultural sociologists and cultural-studies theorists, citizenship is foremost about the formation of groups within the body politic, and the construction of identity associated with those groups: progressive citizenship (or 'social justice') is when this works through political solidarity with weak or historically marginalized groups. But this same logic can work as an exclusionary mechanism, where citizenship identity works through rejecting claims to equal treatment by outsiders or new groups ('tyranny of the majority'). In both cases, citizenship is an expressive political performance associated with coalition formation variously to challenge existing power structures; form new power structures; or reinforce existing power structures.

Economists, game theorists and other students of collective action tend to view citizenship not as a bundle of rights, or as social identity, but more abstractly through the lens of a social dilemma (Dawes 1980) or 'public goods game'. By starting with the instability of large-scale cooperation, following Hobbes, this implies that collective action problems require coercion (Olson 1965). The state will have a legitimate monopoly on violence,[1] and a citizen is defined in effect as a subject who willingly submits to this arrangement in return for benefits that may include political franchise, rent transfers from other groups (e.g. copyright 'protection') or participation in some political enterprise (Oakeshott 1975). Citizenship is thus approached from the perspective of a 'calculus of consent' (Buchanan and Tullock 1962).[2] This approach analyses citizenship – and governmental authority arising from the consent of the governed – as an input into the production of a public good, focusing on the costs and benefits to individuals within a citizen group. A further angle is civil society, which is group formation arising from voluntary self-governance – Burke's 'little platoons'. This local citizenship, as voluntary association to get things done, connects to the concept of a commons (Ostrom 1990).

Cultural science builds on previous concepts to model citizenship as '*demic association that makes knowledge*'. Free citizens, in cooperating freely to build communities, will also make a deme; a 'we'-community. Such demes will be semiotically productive of knowledge, to the extent that they interact with 'they'-groups. We have long known that much knowledge exists in individual people (what economists call 'human capital') and in organizations, such as

---

[1] Note also Mancur Olson's (1982) 'stationary bandit' model of the origin of the state; and our discussion of Norbert Elias's essentially Hobbesian view of human nature, with civilization itself as the 'coercive' mechanism, in Chapter 4.

[2] This is exemplified in the 'Public Choice' school of economics, which is the rational choice approach to political action, or 'politics without romance' as James Buchanan puts it.

firms, who combine capital with people to do things. But the citizenry has never much been thought of as a site of knowledge, which is to say of productivity. Cultural science gives us reason to suspect that citizenship might be more than just politicized agency, but might also be creative and productive. What we have in mind here is a new audit of the particular ledgers of knowledge in a society.

Citizenship theory begins with the city-states of ancient Greece, denoting membership of a *polis* (although cities as such are much older – see Chapter 3: 'Demes'). The concept of citizenship is the link between a person and the state, initially coterminous with the city, specifically, Athens. People had initially been organized in family groups (*phratries*) and noble families (*genes* – plural of *genos*, 'kin') ruled the roost. In about 500BCE citizenship was reformed to link to *demes*, which were based on districts and population, counterbalancing to some extent the influence of the aristocratic families (genes). The people (*demos*) of Attica were organized into 139 demes and thence into 10 tribes or *phyles*, from among which public officials were elected, juries selected, and so on (Hornblower and Spawforth 2005). Revenue-raising and religious observances were organized at the local, demic level. Thus, ancient citizenship formalized the shift from kin to non-kin as the organizational mode of civic association.

In modernity the concept of citizenship was extended to nationality, at which scale it was first theorized in the Enlightenment (Diderot et al. 1753: 488–9, entry on 'Citoyen'; and see Paine 1792), which specifies a bundle of rights of the state towards the citizen and responsibilities of the citizen to the state. The relation between a person and a monarchy, by comparison, is that of subject, not a citizen.[3] Citizenship is usually acquired by having been born in a nation (although not conferred until the age of majority), or it can subsequently be acquired through several processes including naturalization, marriage and sponsorship. Significantly, a state can refuse citizenship on a range of grounds. With a few exceptions citizenship cannot be bought, sold or transferred. It can however be multiplied – a citizen can hold dual nationality in many jurisdictions, and 'European Citizens' (members of the EU) enjoy civic rights in 28 countries.

A citizen is entitled to a bundle of rights associated with the state, which usually include the right to live within the boundaries of the nation and to

---

[3] British 'subjects', for instance, became 'citizens' only after the British Nationality Act 1981 became law in 1983.

be afforded some protections and freedoms. In turn, citizenship will entail
obligations that may include compulsory participation in the justice system
(jury duty) or in national defence (military service), among others. Citizenship
may entail rights to social insurance and services, usually including health and
education. It may also extend to the franchise of participation in democracy,
obligations over taxation, and obligations over personal registration and
submission of private data for the purposes of statecraft, which has been a
state prerogative since the compilation of the *Domesday Book* for William the
Conqueror in 1086.[4]

In the academic literature, there are three established fundamental approaches
to the concept of citizenship:

(i) *The 'civil' or 'liberal' approach*, where the state exists to help citizens and to
protect rights, favouring a weak state and individual freedom;

(ii) *The active, or 'enterprise' approach*, where a state exists to universalize a
'common substantive purpose' (Oakeshott 1975) such as the 'rights of
man' (French Revolution) or universal rights (American Revolution),
sometimes by force (e.g. World War II and the Vietnam War), or the
modern social and corporate welfare state, where the citizen has no option
but to participate in the state's 'enterprise'.

(iii) *The 'critical' or 'ideological' approach*, which analyses modern citizenship
in the name of subjectivities that it fails to emancipate, especially those
based on class (Marxism), gender (feminism), the raced, colonial, ethnic,
migrant or multicultural subject (e.g. Mandela 1994: 35–6; Saada 2012),
and many 'others' who do not conform to a dominant identity.

As it is globalized, abstracted and conducted through shared semiosis (see
Chapter 6: 'Meaningfulness') and social networks, the concept of citizenship has
shifted from institutional arrangements towards action around meaningfulness.
A modernized version of the 'republic of letters' takes up this aspect, such that
we can add a fourth approach, that of 'media citizenship' or 'cultural citizenship'
(Hartley 2009a):

(iv) The *creative, cultural or DIY approach*, where citizens create their own
forms of 'association among strangers' using the affordances of digital and
interactive media, social networks, and their experiences and practices as

---

[4]   See: www.nationalarchives.gov.uk/domesday/.

audiences and consumers, within a market environment and what would previously have been understood as private life (e.g. Hartley 2012: ch. 6; Miller 2006; Papacharissi 2010; Baym 2010; Jenkins et al. 2013).

This creative-associative conceptualization of *media or cultural citizenship* is at the core of a cultural science approach. A citizen group is self-assembling and may be self-polarizing (Sunstein 2002). Rather than seeking to be politically acknowledged, as in the case of groups pursuing the goals of 'identity politics', or seeking to gain or rebalance power relations, this is a view of citizenship that seeks to be *productive* through the mechanism of voluntary association through social learning (Richey 2013), and the creation of demic knowledge.

Rational citizen theory

A different line of approach to citizenship arises out of economics and game theory, centred on what we might call 'rational citizenship'. 'Rational citizenship studies' therefore refers to analyses running from microeconomics, game theory, public choice theory, new institutional economics and the rational agent approach to political studies, that explain the choices and actions of citizens by the institutional incentives they face. This concept, or something like it, animates most critiques of the choice-theoretic approach to citizenship analysis (Taylor-Gooby 2008: ch. 5).

In rational citizen theory, a citizen is a member of a group, or 'club' (Buchanan 1965). A nation-state is a very large club (it produces many benefits that are excludable, so it is not a public good), which needs to solve 'collective action' problems. The basic problem in rational citizen theory is the *social dilemma* (Dawes 1980) – how to engender large-scale cooperation when each individual agent's rational move is not to cooperate, that is, not to contribute to the public good as a citizen ('to defect', in the language of the theory), but yet to seek the benefits of citizenship (to 'free-ride'). From this perspective the problem of citizenship is how to create 'good citizens', or people who will consistently play 'cooperatively' against other citizens.

Economics has already taken a hard look at itself, and asked whether studying economics tends to make people more likely to defect in social dilemmas, making them *bad citizens* (Frank et al. 1996). In contrast, part of the founding project of cultural studies (Hoggart 1957) was to produce the *right sort* of citizens by inculcating the enfranchised and recently literate majority in the project of progressive citizenship. A possible bridge between these domains is suggested by Frijters and Foster (2012), who specifically refer to love and power in groups, in which one may read citizenship as a species of *rational submission*. Another line of argument is to model citizenship as a form of *group decision-making* that relies on the superior information processing power of groups, such that joining a group is a contribution to improved decision-making and outcomes (Mendelberg 2002), although this does not address the free-rider problem.

Rational citizenship can also be modelled as a conspicuous and costly form of signalling of otherwise unobservable qualities that are important for social coordination, such as long-term commitment to a community (Spence 1973). The unintended consequence of this costly-signalling form of 'conspicuous citizenship' is the formation of groups as demes that have superior information processing (as shown earlier) and knowledge-producing properties compared with uncoordinated individuals. This is where active citizenship and networking among elites, including philanthropy and support for the arts, welfare and enjoyment of others, nevertheless attracts suspicion, because the groups engaged in such activities appear to be self-selecting with masonic tendencies – the 'Establishment', benefitting from the 'old school tie'.

The same concern about cooperation in public goods games (social dilemmas) sits at the core of the *commons* literature (Ostrom 1990), yet there is almost no connection made between this and citizenship studies. A possible explanation is that whereas citizenship concerns are inherently of the *polis*, the city-state, or the good burghers of the town (McCloskey 2010), discussion of the commons is based around natural resources, agriculture and matters of the country, concerned with forests, grazing pastures, fishing grounds and irrigation systems. Citizens live in towns; country and rural folk tend towards the commons. A new bridging literature may be developing, in respect of *knowledge commons* (Ostrom and Hess 2011) and the innovation commons.

The evolutionary puzzle of citizenship

Citizenship is a form of cooperation. But large-scale cooperation is evolutionarily unstable because it can usually be invaded by free-riders. A citizen is therefore an unexpected evolutionary object. Coordination costs rise exponentially with the size of a group. It is driven by the costs of information, transactions, monitoring and enforcement, and, in consequence, the cost of multiplying objectives and sources of conflict. Hence organizational growth is achieved often most effectively by breaking large organizations into modular units (Simon and March 1958). Large groups such as nations are governed through smaller political units of states, province, cantons, city, borough, local council, and so on. In turn citizenship thereby occurs at multiple scales and determines how big a group can get. This is the model pioneered in Classical Greece.

Large-scale systems of coordination (such as an economy) tend not to be groups, but rather *institutional rule systems* such as markets, which do effectively scale to a global level, as discussed in Chapter 4 (earlier), noting Hayek's (1978: 9) argument that culture evolved through mechanisms of *group selection*.

Hayek's theory of cultural evolution is an instance of what Cavalli-Sforza (2000) calls 'demic diffusion'. This works as a theory of culture-as-knowledge that diffuses with population dynamics, but not as a theory of culture as group making, or what we call *demic concentration*. The argument here is that citizenship produces knowledge through the demic process of externalized knowledge within 'we'-groups, made of meaningfulness and identity. These 'we'-groups, constituted by their interaction with 'they'-groups (foreigners, aliens, barbarians, and so on) create knowledge. 'We' do so through a Lotman-style clash of difference (Chapter 6: 'Meaningfulness'), the mutual untranslatability of incommensurable systems or semiospheres (we/they in this case) that produce communication and thus meaningfulness out of cross-border interaction. What does this knowledge do? In part it recursively builds and maintains the group. But it also maintains the larger group formations that extend citizenship to higher levels, including the city.

Creative citizenship produces organizations to deliver social and civic goods, including the product of trusts and charitable foundations. NGOs are often interest groups or lobbies, which is a different concept motivating collective action, as centred about creating or expropriating a rent (Krueger 1974), or in some way getting others to act in a way to benefit the rent-seeking group. Creative citizenship, however, is entrepreneurial in the sense of creating knowledge and value that did not exist before, and thus adds to the sum of civic capital. Political service can come down on either side of this distinction, depending upon whether it is to benefit a group of cronies, or the creation of a social good through citizenship. A sense of duty can in this way be a creative form of citizenship.

Creative citizenship

The copious social-science scholarship that monopolizes citizenship studies is marked by a notable *lack* of attention to the role of creativity in acts of civic association. Scholarship proceeds quickly to institutional analysis. *Creativity* has been a dominant trope in humanities-based approaches to communal life, but the concept of *citizenship* is much more weakly theorized in this domain. However, it underlies the criticism of John Ruskin, Matthew Arnold and Walter Pater,[5] all of whom worked to a 'civic' sense of creativity. A flavour of it may be gained from Ruskin's distinction between 'political' economy (pertaining to citizens) and 'mercantile economy' (pertaining to 'power over labour'), in *Unto This Last* (1862), where citizenship is understood to be closer to the representation of beauty than of rights:

> Political economy (the economy of a State, or of citizens) consists simply in the production, preservation, and distribution, at fittest time and place, of useful or pleasurable things. The farmer who cuts his hay at the right time; the shipwright who drives his bolts well home in sound wood; the builder who lays good bricks in well-tempered mortar; the housewife who takes care of her furniture in the parlour, and guards against all waste in her kitchen; and the singer who rightly disciplines, and never overstrains her voice, are all political economists in the true and final sense: adding continually to the riches and well-being of the nation to which they belong. But mercantile economy, the economy of 'merces' or of 'pay', signifies the accumulation, in the hands of individuals, of legal or moral claim upon, or power over, the labour of others; every such claim implying precisely as much poverty or debt on one side, as it implies riches or right on the other. (Essay II: 'The Veins of Wealth')

This preoccupation with the 'fittest' artisanship and 'disciplined' creative expression, that is, beauty in everyday making, as the foundation of the 'riches and well-being of the nation', has lasted well beyond Ruskin's own era, just as Matthew Arnold's prescriptions about culture as the pursuit of perfection have long outlived the debates that inspired them. Both writers were influential in literary culture, their ideas being taken up and modified among critics down

---

[5] Pater's influential *The Renaissance: Studies in Art and Poetry* (1873), lauded the Classical Greek aspiration to make *beauty itself a civic virtue*, imputing that quality to the Renaissance, thereby inspiring the 'aesthetic movement' or 'art for art's sake'. See: www.authorama.com/renaissance-1. html.

to contemporary cultural studies, for whom Ruskin's notion of a 'political economy' based on the *creative industriousness of the citizenry* turned into a demand for 'critical literacy'. F. R. Leavis famously distinguished between 'culture' and 'civilization', as Ruskin had between 'political' and 'mercantile' economy, concluding that in the face of burgeoning 'civilization' (i.e. industrial mass culture), 'the citizen . . . must be trained . . . to resist' (Leavis and Thompson 1933: 3–4). The instrument of that training was a literary education, which was duly enforced in schools, just as these expanded to a universal, compulsory experience for all citizens. Training in discrimination, critical literacy and 'resistance' to the blandishments of commercial mass culture implies – and acquired – a strong sense of moral purpose, such that a literary education was soon construed as a training in *criticism* rather than *creation*, the idea being to turn out good citizens not good poets, artists or singers, much less farmers, shipwrights or builders.

Communication and cultural studies also borrowed perspectives from the behavioural sciences that dominated American university education in and after the 1950s. Here, the relationship between the state and the citizen was seen in terms of the one between mass communication and the mass audience, or commercial culture and the consumer. Studies tended to focus on 'media effects', where media messages (produced by corporations) caused behavioural changes in individuals. Investigators looked for positive effects (citizen-consumers may be persuaded to vote or buy 'our' way; this being the whole point of marketing and PR studies), or – more commonly – they sought out negative effects ('subjects' may be influenced to behave antisocially; or persuaded to resist or riot; or they may tune out altogether, suffering *ennui* or alienation).

A reaction against overly critical and behaviourist approaches was inevitable. It surfaced in and after the 1960s, during which period a new generation experienced its own forms of political, cultural and personal emancipation *through* the commercial culture that the critical Victorians and their 'mass society' successors sought to resist. 'Practical criticism' declined in favour of 'creative writing' and other types of artistic training, starting with tertiary education, including preparing students *for* rather than arming them *against* the media in practice-based and production courses.

From the late nineteenth century onwards – with the increasing ubiquity of the popular press, publishing, cinema and broadcasting – citizenship and consumption, commercial marketing and political propaganda, information and ideology, were increasingly hard to tell apart, especially as states and political parties as well as news media and entertainment networks were all using the same persuasive techniques to reach the same population. As Scammell (2000: 351–2) put it: 'the act of consumption is becoming increasingly suffused with citizenship characteristics and considerations. . . . It is no longer possible to cut the deck neatly between citizenship and civic duty, on one side, and consumption and self interest, on the other'. It seemed that democracy and markets needed each other.

Those who had not experienced totalitarianism, world wars or the Cold War – that is, 'Gen X' and its successors – were 'media natives'. They could see no need to resist commercial media, but were drawn instead to seek employment and artistic fulfilment in a media-rich environment. Ordinary consumers experienced continuous improvements in technological affordances, and practical competence was extended socially and self-improved (e.g. by YouTube tutorials), such that previously professional or craft skills (e.g. in writing, graphics, audio-visual production and editing) were 'democratized' across whole populations (Bruns 2008; Cheshire 2013; Flowers 2008; Rose 2012). Pretty soon, astute observers like Stephen Coleman (2003, 2005) noted that general audiences, who 'studied' forms of association via entertainment formats, could teach 'political junkies', who insisted on political or critical purity, a thing or two about civic values. Similarly, 'pro-ams' (Leadbeater and Miller 2004) and 'makers' (Anderson 2012) were the heralded as 'new innovators', leading a 'new industrial revolution'.

Technological and economic trends were transforming the media landscape as a whole, with the emergence of digital technologies (Bollier 2008), the internet (Benkler 2006; Zittrain 2008), interactive and mobile media (Goggin 2008; Goggin and Clark 2009), and social network markets (Potts et al. 2008). At the same time, media and communication studies matured, absorbing 'critical' citizenship from literary studies, 'political' citizenship from social sciences, and 'creative production' from vocational training. Gradually new approaches to the concept of citizenship were clarified and established.

Although the 'critical' and 'media effects' traditions have proven resilient in educational settings, dissatisfaction with their presumption of a 'command-and-control' model of centralized mass communication manipulating individualized (behavioural) consumers has increased with the emergence of interactive, participatory, digital media, and the concomitant spread of the notion of the user (who is, among other things, an *information*-user: Gans 2012), the maker (Anderson 2012) or creative consumer (Jenkins et al. 2013).

It is from this humanistic tradition that the recent concept of the *creative citizen* has developed, not from citizenship studies directly, nor from political communication or the social sciences, which in general remain sceptical about user-agency (O'Connor 2010). Thence, attention readily shifts across to 'new media', where the *use* of mediated representations, including user-created content and socially networked association, leads to consideration of '*DIY citizenship*', and to what may be termed a 'play theory of citizenship' (Stephenson 1967; Gray et al. 2009; Hartley 2012: ch. 6),[6] where user-citizens make their own forms of association and civic meaningfulness *out of* the resources of entertainment media, private life and consumption, often while disengaging from formal civic participation (e.g. not registering to vote), and from consumption of erstwhile 'organs of enlightenment' (the press) that had constructed and instructed the 'informed' citizen. Thus, observers noted simultaneous *disengagement* with the industrial-era technologies of democracy, and *rapid uptake* of 'new' digital, mobile and social media, such that accusations of 'civic apathy' coincide with exponential growth of user-interactivity (see Harris et al. 2010).

Emergent concepts of creative citizenship for the globalized, digital era result from the clash of erstwhile conceptual opposites, especially those of 'the citizen' versus 'the consumer', producing new meaningfulness by novel combinations of consumption and making, private life and civic participation, 'the politics of the personal' and the use of digital social networks to agitate for change. Concepts of the public sphere have been reworked accordingly (Warner 2005; Baym 2010; Papacharissi 2010; Harris et al. 2010), and studies of collective action focus not on elections but on voluntarist or affect-based activism 'on the street' or in the 'dance-off' (Hartley 2012: ch. 6), on single-issue campaigns (e.g. Sea Shepherd, Greenpeace), on organized lobbying using social networks (Get-Up!), as well as direct – but informal – political intervention (Occupy, 99%, Arab and other 'Springs'), and various forms of crowdsourcing and crowdfunding for worthwhile civic initiatives. These are all part of a larger concept of *creative citizenship*, building out from demic knowledge. Creative citizenship as a field of research has by now also intersected with 'creative economy' research and policymaking.

---

[6] A 'play theory of citizenship' pays homage to William Stephenson's (1967) *Play Theory of Mass Communication*, where he seeks to counterbalance the focus on control and information with a focus on enjoyment and play.

Health care versus racketeering?

Where there are citizens, so there must be cities, both of them creative. Since 2009, according to UN figures,[7] living in cities is the majority human experience, as it has been since 1950 in developed countries, and soon will be everywhere. Cities are the focus of creative productivity, by citizens themselves, as well as by firms, industries and institutions. Not surprisingly, the idea of the creative industries or creative economy has become increasingly prominent in cultural policy and economic planning internationally (Bakhshi et al. 2013). Like other good ideas, it has not gone uncontested. For instance, introducing a collection of papers about creative cities, Phil Cooke and Luciana Lazzeretti (2008) produced an adversarial (we/they) account, making a very pointed distinction – amounting to a 'clash of systems' – between the 'cultural economy' and the 'creative industries'. They set these in opposition:

- *Cultural economy*: 'lengthily trained artists, singers, curators and musicians' with 'an aesthetic status comparable to that of many health-care systems'; its source is in the academy and public institutions.
- *Creative industries*: 'entrepreneurship bordering on racketeering' where: 'all make money, some criminally large amounts thereof'; their sources are the street, the market and private enterprise. (Cooke and Lazzeretti 2008: 1–2)

This illustrates a strand of thinking in economic and sociological thought, as well as in the arts and cultural critique, which prefers public culture to private enterprise, especially in relation to culture and creativity. That preference, for one side only of the public/private divide, produces these two different models of creative purpose. If we were to follow Cooke and Lazzeretti's terminology, arguments for subsidized arts and culture to ensure the well-being of the populace would be called the 'health-care' model; whereas favouring development for profit would be called the 'racketeering' model. The prejudicial nature of the distinction is obvious, but despite the invidious comparison and the ambiguities and mixtures associated with everyday experience, it describes well-known and institutionally embedded distinctions, summarized in Table 5.1:

---

[7] E.g. http://esa.un.org/unup/

Table 5.1 Differentiating the cultural and the creative (adapted from Hartley et al. 2012: 68)

	Cultural economy	**Creative industries**
	'Health care'	'Racketeering'
Mode	Art	Entertainment
Locus	Cultural institution (GLAM)	Scene, festival, mall, novelty
Value	National identity	Global diversity and difference
Attractant	Prestige	Social network (street, media, clubs, crowds)
Agency	Citizenship	Digital literacy
Temporality	Daytime	Night-time
Demographic	Adult	Youth
Research	*Journal of Cultural Economy*	*Journal of Cultural Economics*

Defenders of public culture ('health care') want to protect it from market forces ('racketeering'), but from the point of view of a creative city, it is important that both of the columns in Table 5.1 are co-present, at a jostling semiospheric boundary. Rather than choose between the oppositions, then, we should see them in structured and productive conflict; and by combining them, we can propose a different purpose for creativity – neither health care nor racketeering but *innovation*. This model is posited on a systems view of the creative process, where value lies in the 'clash of systems' that result in the 'emergence' and elaboration of new ideas, which in turn result in change and renewal in complex environments. Yuri Lotman's approach would predict that such innovation occurs where systems collide; where there is friction, buzz and complexity in the 'the hottest spots for the semioticising process', along the boundaries of the semiosphere (Lotman 1990: 136; see also Leadbeater and Wong 2010).

Historically, such tensions are worked through in cities – not in warfare – where asymmetrical, incommensurable and mutually untranslatable systems meet and mix on the street. A creative city is one where ideas thrive, driving both economic and cultural growth (see Chapter 9: 'Extinction'). But ideas only thrive where they are competitive, contested, can be implemented in practice, and where difference and variety stimulate originality and novelty, to allow for the emergence of newness (Hutter et al. 2010). Historically, this process is most intense in urban locations, especially regional or national capitals, with a diversity of arts and crafts, as well as mechanisms for the exchange of ideas, including markets. Creativity and cities were made for each other, but the process is 'non-linear'. It relies on complex systems interacting and clashing, producing what Vedres and Stark (2010) call 'structural folds' or inter-cohesion within networks, arguing that 'entrepreneurship in the business-group context is driven by the intersection of cohesive groups where actors have familiar access to diverse resources available for recombination' (2010: 1151).

The city as a human invention is highly evolved for dealing with proximate variety, change and difference in the growth and coordination of knowledge and ideas. Clash and difference drive change and innovation, which produce increasing elaboration. The creative city is one where inter-cohesive 'clusters of clusters' emerge, to enable the self-management of increasing complexity and the growth and elaboration of knowledge.

'Racketeering' and 'health care' need to remain in close enough proximity to interact and cross-fertilize. In great cities, this productive opposition is literally built in: high-end cultural institutions including galleries, museums and universities are clustered in one district; street markets, shopping malls and the headquarters of global media companies in others. This is the basis for Michael Porter's urban cluster theory. Clustering is the historic, initially unplanned solution to problems of complexity; cities are the cumulative result. Complexity itself springs from myriad individual and organizational actions, stimulated by competitive difference among creative artists, 'the characteristic dialectic of disagreement, dissatisfaction, even alienation' (Cooke and Lazzeretti 2008: 4) that triggers new work, which is by definition novel, original and innovative. This rationale for the arts is the same as that for the market-based creative industries, despite the differences that divide them (Beinhocker 2006). And both are needed for a creative city – all thrive on complexity, competition, clash, creativity and coordination.

Artists, consumers and the clash of systems

When applied to the person of the artist, it is easy to see how 'the clash of systems' adds value to individual talent and energy, in China for instance:

In China, the artist might be an impresario, an amateur, an iconoclast or a state-employed 'cultural worker'. She might be a film director, performer, singer, poet, painter or video artist. The role of the artist has changed over time: from agent of change to state functionary, from iconoclast to craftsperson, and more recently to economic agent. (Keane 2013: 127)

It would be hard to maintain these activities, functions and personae if (as *Little Britain*'s Daffyd might have said) you're the only artist in the village. Cross-fertilization among systems is bound to be slower or less rich in choices in regional, rural and remote areas. Artists are part of the productivity of the city; their most innovative activities are best understood as products of *urban semiosis*.

Of course artists have always been economic agents. Indeed, according to Swedberg (2006), the young Joseph Schumpeter used them to model his heroic concept of the entrepreneur, upon which figure evolutionary economics is founded, as shown in Table 5.2:

Table 5.2 Schumpeter's 'curious parallels' between entrepreneur and artist (from Hartley et al. 2013: 'Agency'; see: Swedberg 2006: 250)

The static majority	The entrepreneur/the artist
– Seeks equilibrium	– Breaks out of an equilibrium
– Repeats what has already been done	– Does what is new
– Passive, low energy	– Active, energetic
– Followers	– Leader
– Accepts existing ways of doing things	– Puts together new combinations
– Feels strong inner resistance to change	– Feels no inner resistance to change
– Feels hostility to new actions of others	– Battles resistance to his actions
– Makes a rational choice among existing alternates	– Makes an intuitive choice among a multitude of new alternates
– Motivated exclusively by needs and stops when these are satisfied	– Motivated by power and joy in creation
– Commands no resources and has no use for new resources	– Command no resources but borrow what they need

This formula for the creative city focuses on businesses (enterprise), makers (artists, craft-workers and artisans) and the production process (especially in creative media, where it is fully industrialized). There is one element missing: the audience and consumer. The creative industries are unlike other sections of the economy, because *supply precedes demand* – people don't know whether they will like a new creative production till it comes out (Caves 2000). For artists and creative enterprises to succeed, they need to be inter-cohesive with a 'structurally folded', well-informed and attentive audience, with whom they can maintain a dialogic relationship, using various mechanisms for generating and 'bundling' novelty for their attention (Potts 2011).

Further, since the emergence of digital and participatory media, audiences have become productive in their own right. The historic difference between producers and consumers – experts and amateurs – is under challenge. With the growth of social media and user-created content, the productivity of the system as a whole is increased. Digital technologies link and mix user-created content seamlessly with enterprise-touched content (as in YouTube), and the ease of uploading 'content' means that creative activities by non-professionals – musicians, bloggers, pranksters – can command global attention or create new niche markets. Consumers and producers are linked in mutually participatory networks. Hence, creative cities require a creative population – one that's connected by high-speed broadband as well as by open streets – as part of its complement of artists and enterprises.

One of the most prominent signs of this new sensibility is street art deriving from anonymous graffiti. This is 'user-created content' with the added spice of attracting official disapproval. It was quickly canonized – shifting from 'anomalous' to 'law-affirming' textuality – in 'cool' cities, via artists like Keith Haring (1980s New York), Banksy in Bristol (UK) and others (Banet-Weiser 2011), with examples preserved in situ as tourist attractions, for example, the 5Pointz 'Aerosol Art Center' in Long Island, the Berlin Wall, or Melbourne's lanes. It is now so mainstream that city councils encourage and license it, creating a new distinction between 'street art' (allowed) and 'graffiti tagging' (erased).[8] Graffiti is a visible marker of bottom-up creativity in urban life. Sometimes it's an expression of anonymous nocturnal youthful presence, sometimes of darker moods brought on by contemporary events, for example: on official buildings in former East Germany

---

[8] The city of Melbourne has adopted lane art as a selling point in its tourism profile. It has developed rules for deciding between art and graffiti, and a license for artists and property owners who want to keep their street art: www.melbourne.vic.gov.au/ForResidents/StreetCleaningandGraffiti/GraffitiStreetArt/Pages/Whatisstreetart.aspx.

after unification, where Hartley saw the line '*First they bring us culture; then they take our flats*' sprayed (in German) on a wall in Weimar; around Beijing and Hong Kong in support of artist Ai Weiwei in 2011; or across many cities from Istanbul through the Middle East and North Africa during the Arab Spring, for instance following the incident of the 'woman in the blue bra' in Egypt, December 2011. This is urban semiosis at its most direct, and it requires a productive, dynamic 'clash' between the previously distinct categories of artist and consumer-citizen.

Given the importance of users as producers, learning and experimentation are vital elements of creativity, but they are missing from standard creative industries models. New ideas may come from outside the industrial context of expert specialization, to include learning among myriad users, and learning from networks-as-agents. This kind of networked and creative learning is informal, distributed, peer-to-peer, just-in-time and imitative. For the ordinary citizen, it is often associated with entertainment formats rather than the formal education system. But that population is now a productive resource in its own right. Thus a prerequisite for further economic growth is education – formal and informal – for the growth of creative productivity and interaction among users. However, as for creative industries, so for education: it isn't the 'provider' that matters so much as the 'user'.

Cities with concentrated student populations lead global creativity tables, and those students lead diversification. According to Malcolm Gillies (2013), 100,000 of London's half-million students are international students, and a 'majority of undergraduates studying in London declare themselves to be other than "white British"'. Students are global mixers, early adopters, have relatively high disposable income (spare cash for novelties), are mobile, experimental, flock to special events, festivals, and colonize neglected quarters with low rents, frequently reviving them in the process. Thus, they perform a *social learning* function for cities. This is not an instrumental *training* job for higher education and schools; it is a cultural function of 'natural pedagogy' (Csibra and Gergely 2011), conducted informally in the 'clash of systems' that people experience as part of urban life. In fact, people need to cluster, both physically and online, just as much as producers do.

In such a lively environment, creative innovation accelerates both formally (education and the arts) and informally (participation and the media). Innovation itself can now be seen as both 'elaborate' production by expert organizations, and 'emergent' meanings arising from distributed, self-organizing social networks. What links them all is ideas. As John Howkins (2009) puts it, 'ideas are the new currency'. This kind of currency is not always monetized. Some ideas circulate entirely outside of the market, operating in social networks and in economies of attention. For others, many creative artists and start-up businesses illustrate the truism that 'emergent ideas' and making money, especially Cooke and Lazzeretti's 'criminally large amounts thereof', may be separated not by sector or ideology but merely by time – today's YouTube video from the margins may launch tomorrow's HNWI (high net worth individual) in the tax haven (e.g. Psy).

Civic associations need not only be for political purposes, or for addressing social problems or creating public goods. These all have collective action and free-rider problems because they require an individual cost to produce a public benefit. But there are other classes of civic association that are often enjoyable to participate in, and which also produce social benefit. These are directly creative acts of citizenship such as public festivals (such as eisteddfod competitions, comedy festivals, jazz or world music festivals, the various 'fringe' festivals, or any manner of subject, product, or regionally themed festival (books, food, cars, local produce, and so on).

This manner of knowledge can be cumulatively, recursively and combinatorially expressive of the deme as well as producing abstract (de-demed) knowledge. Dance, music, art, literature, food that is produced for the consumption by that same group works to concentrate a deme. It builds civic community through the creation of meaningfulness. These are produced and consumed within the deme.

The productivity of festivals is not only in demic construction and maintenance, but also in creative re-constitution. Potts (2011) argues that festivals are a prime instance of an institutional form called a 'novelty bundling markets', which is a species of market that has developed to address the problem of lowering the costs of the production and consumption of novelty by combining expert bundling of novelty with lowered costs of experimental sampling of new goods. Novelty bundling markets are central to media markets and cities: they facilitate economic and sociocultural innovation by improving the productivity of novelty uptake.

Standard models in theory of citizenship focus on the relation between individual and state, and on collective action problems among strangers. In all cases, a citizen is treated as a problem of groups with respect to cooperation, ethics, identity, duty and power; but it is not much treated as a problem of creativity and knowledge. Cultural science examines how citizenship can indeed be creative and productive of knowledge because it follows the same logic of an externalized deme.

Part Two

Groups Make Knowledge

Meaningfulness

The Growth of Knowledge

My Oxford philosophy tutor, who had a curious habit of crawling under the table while giving his tutorials, commented in a high British voice coming from under the table, 'It's all very well to talk about evolution, Mr. Boulding, but what evolves, what evolves, what evolves?' After 40 years I have at least a glimmering of the answer. What evolves is something very much like knowledge.

Kenneth Boulding, *Ecodynamics*, 1978: 33

What evolves?

In cultural evolution, what is it that evolves? The standard answer is some self-replicating information unit translated into analytic-cultural space. Richard Dawkins' concept of the 'meme', for example, offers the abstraction that culture is made of replicating units of information, enabling us to model cultural evolution as a process of differentially selective information-updating on stochastic priors and discrete choices (Boyd and Richerson 2005; Mesoudi 2011). But does this approach, centred around replicating units of information (as cultural particles), actually make sense as a theory of the growth of knowledge and the dynamics of culture?

We think the answer is no, and for a simple reason: namely the unit of cultural dynamics and of knowledge dynamics is, at least outside of stylized and abstracted analytic set-ups, rarely given and obvious. Instead, it is the very thing that is revealed, or that emerges from the dynamic processes. Our contention is that this unit is what seems to be evolving, or is what is contested in cultural evolutionary processes. We think of it not as a discrete packet of replicating information, or indeed as any gene analogue, but rather as some locus of connections in a broader complex system (Kauffman 1995; Potts 2000). This unit, in other words, is not a unit of knowledge, or even of discrete information, but rather something different; namely *a unit of meaning* or of *meaningfulness*. This is a statement about a space of complex evolving connections that is closer in analytic form to semiotics than to genetics. In this chapter, we develop this notion of meaningfulness as the basic analytic unit in a theory of the evolutionary dynamics of culture and knowledge.

It is not contentious to define cultural studies as an inquiry into (or a deep reading of) contextualized meaning in the 'social text'. Cultural science has the same objective, but comes at it with an account of the forces that generate and construct meaning. Such forces are often politicized, in a radicalized perspective that is an atavistic feature of cultural studies, as Scott Lash (2007) explains:

> Cultural studies has been perhaps primarily concerned from its outset with the question of power, and it is through hegemony – or its equivalent – that its analysts have understood power to be effective.... Hegemony means domination through consent as much as coercion. It has meant domination through ideology or discourse.

Cultural science however, is not built around a theory of power as prime mover in the construction of meaning, as 'hegemonic domination through ideology or discourse'. Rather, it sees meaning as the emergent product of evolutionary forces, not revolutionary ones (in the Marxist sense), which operate at the level of the storytelling deme, and about which knowledge forms. Cultural science does make room for a theory of rapid transformation but, following Lotman (2009), we call it 'explosion' and explain it via systems thinking rather than historical 'laws' (see Chapter 9 : 'Exinction').

Knowledge, culture and meaningfulness are distinct domains of evolution – each can be conceptualized and studied separately by holding the other two constant. Thus there are theories of how *knowledge evolves* (in evolutionary epistemology, Popper 2002; Campbell 1960). There are theories of how *culture evolves* (in evolutionary anthropology, Boyd and Richerson 1985; Mesoudi 2011). And there are theories of how linguistic *meaning evolves* (in topological semiosis, Lemke 1999). Cultural science is the endeavour to join these three into a unified theory of how culture evolves through the evolution of meaningfulness, shaping the evolution of knowledge, within and between groups (demes) that are themselves dynamic, scale free and ephemeral.

Something very much like knowledge

David George Ritchie was a late-nineteenth-century Scottish philosopher. He advanced some of the opening arguments of what we now call 'universal Darwinism' and was an early proponent of the idea of cultural evolution. He was well ahead of his time, for what came to be known as *consilience* did not seriously develop until a century or so later under the more pointed rubric of E. O. Wilson's sociobiology (Wilson 1975, 1998). Ritchie recognized early the importance of evolutionary thinking in the ongoing development of the theory of culture and philosophy, and wanted to carve out an analytic space for it. Look at what he wrote:

> But in asserting that human society presents many phenomena that cannot be accounted for by natural selection in its purely biological sense, I am not denying the truth of the theory, but rather extending its range. There is going on a 'natural selection' of ideas, customs, institutions, irrespective of the natural selection of individuals and of races. (Ritchie 1896: 170–1)

This is an unmistakable agenda to integrate the sciences and humanities through a unified evolutionary way of thinking. A hundred years later, Daniel Dennett, another arch-Aristotelian philosopher, published a classic exposition and defence of Universal Darwinism in *Darwin's Dangerous Idea* (1995). Dennett opens with a riff on a speculative substance called a 'universal acid'. Now, because it is an acid, and because it is universal, universal acid burns through everything: nothing can contain it. In a wonderfully vivid metaphor, he proposes that the theory of evolution is indeed such a universal acid: it's uncontainable, and transforms everything it touches. Dennett's point was that despite many attempts to resist and contain it, evolutionary theory has been a universal acid that burnt through one hardened dogma after another, inexorably transforming human knowledge of life, the universe and everything. Dennett's observation about Darwin's theory extends across the natural and life sciences through engineering, mathematics, computer science, social sciences, the sciences of the mind and more, revolutionizing fields of knowledge, one after the other. The universal acid metaphor indeed seems apt.

Yet, worryingly for Dennett's thesis – with a few notable exceptions such as Dutton (2009) or Boyd (2009) – evolutionary theory has been widely resisted in the humanities. It has seemingly been contained, or even repelled. With the exceptions of the Foucauldian concept of biopower (Rabinow and Rose 2006;

Flew 2012: 49), biosocial approaches to feminism (Rossi 1977; Ellis 1991) and various approaches to posthumanism (Wolfe 2009), biosocial theorizing is rare in the typical humanities faculty, which is more interested in here-and-now power than in the nature/culture evolutionary nexus. To the extent that evolutionary thinking appears, it is likely to be portrayed as a target of attack, namely 'survival of the fittest' eugenics, for supposed anti-progressive thinking (compare our discussion in Chapter 1). Hence, despite the 'curiously parallel' nature of biological and cultural evolution, it seems that Richie and Dennett, to say nothing of Veblen and Wilson, Dutton or Boyd, among many others, have been empirically wrong in their optimistic sentiment about the universality of evolutionary theory in the domain of human knowledge.

So what gives? Does Dennett's universal acid burn through everything *except* for arts, culture and the humanities? Or is Dennett's conjecture still unrefuted because even universal acid takes some time to seep through (like the lurking Alien's acid blood in *Alien*)? Is culture now, belatedly, an evolutionary science too; or is it not, and never will be, because culture is about values (ethics) rather than facts (causation)? The study of culture and the knowledge domains of the humanities are among the last to be visited by evolutionary theory. We can think of three distinct accounts for this late arrival – that it was: (a) the most successfully defended; (b) furthest removed; or (c) trivial or metaphorical.

In (a) – 'best defended' – evolutionary theory is inappropriate in humanities and culture because alternative better theories have been proposed; specifically various strands of Marxism, Foucauldianism and postmodernism. In (b) – 'furthest removed' – it is because of human exceptionalism in nature, in that our higher consciousness and imagination places us so far beyond the effects of 'natural selection' that we ultimately make our own reality; these ideas travel under various guises of what is called 'constructivism'. In (c) – 'trivial application' – Dennett is wrong because the applications of evolutionary humanities touch but a tiny sliver of the true concerns of humanities interest and scholarship. Human culture is so deep and complex that theories derived from naturalistic explanations will be underdetermined in the realm of human culture.

Best defended

Proponents of 'best defended' point to the deep adoption and vigorous pushback of alternative accounts and narratives, and specifically the defence against the more laissez-faire implications of so-called social Darwinism. Here evolutionary theory was defeated early in the game by the anti-social-Darwinism rampart against the supposed liberal political readings of evolutionary theory that was prophylactic against its alleged political toxicity.

Furthest removed

Proponents of 'furthest removed' allow that evolutionary theory might be relevant in some proto-historical accounts, but it is now an exceptionally weak force because we humans have developed to such an extent that such base forces no longer apply with any strength, or at least not at the upper ends of the spectrum where the best and brightest of human achievements are cast. Explaining how is another matter, although Norbert Elias's (1939) theory of the 'civilizing process' is one influential attempt (see Chapter 4: 'Malvoisine'). Defeating base instincts in thought and expression, so as to achieve 'perfection', is at the core of the Arnoldian high-culture argument. It argues that evolutionary theory may well be true of 'them', as we were, but not of 'us', as we now are.

Trivial or metaphorical

Proponents of 'trivial or metaphorical' argue that evolutionary theory can't compete with, say, Continental Theory, or to put it another way, their conceptual frameworks are generated by the traditions of German-French philosophy, rather than the 'Anglo-Saxon' natural and empirical sciences. They do not deny its potential relevance, but emphasize that it simply does not deliver when confronted by head-to-head competition with the rich, compelling and intellectually exciting arguments from power, politics and social justice that come with the theorized critical readings of postmodernism. Such arguments will perhaps point to Richard Dawkins' (1976) self-replicating 'meme', or to the arguments over various forms of unnaturalness in evolutionary psychology, as prima facie evidence of the shallow and crude offerings of a scientific approach as compared to the variegated richness and nuance of even low-brow instantiations of Critical Theory.

These are not unreasonable arguments and it is not our intention to disassemble them. In all three it is an article of faith in modern humanities research that evolution has been variously repelled, inoculated or rebuffed, where it has not simply been ignored (Boyd et al. 2010; Tallis 2011; for a counter-position see Carroll 2011).

The problem of cultural evolution

Yet we maintain that no such thing has actually happened: the evolutionary debate in the humanities *is still yet to occur*. This is not because of effective defence or superseding logic but, rather, because an evolutionary application to the study of culture is simply *a much harder problem than has previously been appreciated*.

The problem has been stylized along two axes as: (1) the search for the 'genes of culture' (i.e. basic micro-units of replication) about which to fix an evolutionary theory of culture; or (2) as the evolutionary foundations of culture arising from an evolved human nature, which constrains the set of behaviours that generate culture and explains culture as a kind of 'extended phenotype' (Dawkins 1982) or social technology. Often, approaches will proceed as a combination of (1) cultural genetics, and (2) the genes for culture (Boyd and Richerson 2005).

'Cultural genetics' is the argument that cultural evolution is emergent from biological evolution. That is a standard and uncontentious line of reasoning; indeed, it is a point argued by Darwin himself and by his later synthesizer Julian Huxley:

> . . . the hitherto unexploited capacity whose fuller utilization not only made possible the rise of man to evolutionary dominance but initiated a new phase of evolution, was the cumulative communication of experience. The resultant sharable, transmissible, and progressively transformable tradition gave rise to a new type of entity or organization technically called cultural, and evolution in the psycho-social phase has been essentially cultural, not biological or genetic. (Huxley 1955: 7)

The upshot is the dedicated pursuit of the cultural equivalent of the gene, or the unit of cultural selection and cultural replication, which supposes the existence of some manner of 'cultural particle' (Findlay 1992; Laland et al. 1995; Pocklington and Best 1997; Mesoudi 2011). The study of cultural evolution will then concentrate on finding appropriate 'cultural replicators' in respect to which the human mind is a 'carrier' or 'vehicle' for such replicating cultural particles. Cultural genetics is then the search for the particles.

The 'genes for culture' argument is different; based not on the search for cultural particles per se, but rather for the units responsible for the ability to create and replicate them in the first place. Specifically, it is inquiry into the evolution of the neurological and cognitive capabilities to create, produce and socially reproduce culture through social learning. These cognitive capabilities are the elements of cultural evolution. This is the province of literary Darwinism that builds on evolutionary psychology and evolutionary neuroscience. This line tends to pass from evolutionary theory of the mind (shaped by the 'environment of evolutionary adaptedness') directly through to human high culture (art, literature, text, film) without the intervening stage of concern with the broader domain of cultural anthropology or evolution of technology, knowledge, and other 'artifacts, mentifacts and socifacts' (Huxley 1955: 9). The search for the units of cultural evolution is to be found expressed in the human mind, carried by the human genome, and shaped in the human ancestral environment by powerful forces, supposedly 'hard-wired' in the Pleistocene.

Yet, there is little agreement about the appropriate unit of cultural variation, selection and replication. Evolutionary theorists have always proceeded to assume some manner of information-like 'cultural unit', come what may, and at the same time cultural theorists have avoided any such analytic notion, tending towards self-referential definitions (a round-up of these questions can be found in Harold Fromm's two essays in *The Hudson Review*, 2003). The problem surely lies with the difficulty of the question – as per Kenneth Boulding's tutor's query, quoted at the head of this chapter – in respect of 'what actually evolves' in the process of cultural evolution. It took evolutionary biology more than 50 years to get a clear handle on the locus of evolution – from Mendel's pea cross-breeding experiments to Erwin Schrödinger's notion of an 'aperiodic crystal' to the base-chemical and then information-theoretic idea of the gene. This was a long hard struggle to get at the idea of a self-replicating unit of *information* as the basic analytic unit of evolutionary theory, a breakthrough that combined population genetics with natural selection, and which came to be known as 'neo-Darwinism' or 'the modern synthesis' (Huxley 1942).

Yet, as difficult as that challenge was, the locus of *cultural* evolution was and remains an even harder problem (Huxley 1955). It even defeated Michel Foucault, whose lectures on biopolitics were, according to his own account, intended to 'show how the central core of all these problems that I am presently trying to identify is what is called *population*. Consequently, this is the basis on which something like biopolitics could be formed' (2008: 21). But before he could get to population, Foucault felt that he had to understand the 'regime' of 'governmental reason' and 'economic truth' first, and so the entire lecture series (and subsequent book) was preoccupied with neoliberalism and did not return to the genealogy of biopolitics (Flew 2012). Hence, 'population' remained a socio-governmental construct, not a bio-cultural one (i.e. demes). And that is where it has stayed, even in the rigorous field of social theory, where Foucauldian biopower has drifted more towards *ethics* than to 'causal sequence'. Here's Nikolas Rose (2006), for instance, on the turn to 'bioethics':

> On the one hand, our vitality has been opened up as never before for economic exploitation and the extraction of biovalue, in a new bioeconomics that alters our very conception of ourselves in the same moment that it enables us to intervene upon ourselves in new ways. On the other hand, our somatic, corporeal neurochemical individuality has become opened up to choice, prudence, and responsibility, to experimentation, to contestation, and so to a politics of life itself. (Rose 2006: 'Introduction')

This simple observation – that identifying and theorizing the units of evolution was a very hard problem in biology and is an even harder problem in culture – underpins our motivation to develop this work in cultural science, and inspires us to seek a new approach in order to furnish an answer.

For the past century or so, most of those who have sought to generalize the Darwinian approach into the realm of human society and culture have arrived, like Kenneth Boulding, at an answer that makes the cultural unit of variation, selection and replication 'something very much like knowledge'. The most abstracted version is the 'meme', but other proposed cultural replicators include habits, routines and rules. Yet these identifications are not quite right; what evolves in respect of cultural evolution, instead, is not so much gene-like information, or generic knowledge, but something closer to *meaningfulness*: a propensity to peel off new meanings out of existing semiosis, and the diffusion of these through cultural 'units' or demes. In other words, the 'replicator' is an action not a thing; and (like sexual reproduction), meaningfulness is the 'newness' that arises from collisions at the intersection of two or more systems.

Meaningfulness evolves

In cultural science it is meaningfulness that evolves, 'demically'. However, it is misleading to represent this as referring to 'units of meaningfulness', as if merely seeking to re-label 'basic cultural unit' with 'basic unit of meaningfulness'. Instead, our claim is ontological and seeks to develop the idea that cultural evolution is the *emergence* of meaningfulness from *webs of associations* and relations and also by negotiation and *use within a deme* and between demes. Importantly, this is not a thing, or even information per se, but a structure of associations in action. It is these dynamic demic associations that evolve.

Moreover, this occurs semiotically, with reference to what it is not (it's a structure of difference), requiring a 'they' against which the demic meaning of a 'we'-group can be produced. Structures of association are produced when *different* semiotic spheres interact; the web of meaning develops not by internal growth but by productive encounters (not always friendly) between different systems. Cultural evolution is neither endogenous (self-generated within each 'species' of demic knowledge), nor exogenous (supplied from the outside); it results from the continuous and scale free (or fractal) dynamism of myriad systems colliding, clashing and connecting in constant proximity. The model is Lotman's semiosphere, not Shannon's linear communication (which the 'meme' requires). Among the 'systems' that clash are those that we are considering here: *knowledge; culture; sociality; meaning*, which are co-constituted and co-evolved, interinaimated (Richards 1936: 47–66) or folded (Vedres and Stark 2010); but also distinct, self-organizing and autopoietic, such that new information is generated by the encounter of each with an environment that includes the others, and the identity of each is determined by its bounded relations with others in the system. Thus, meaningfulness evolves and gains identity in a structure of associations with culture, knowledge and sociality.

Meaning and language; meaningfulness and culture

It is difficult to pin down what cultural studies 'is'. For example, in a recent comment to one of us, a senior social scientist suggested that it is more an 'attitude of mind' than a discipline.[1] Thus it is also hard to circumscribe domains of scope or exhaustive accounts of method. But it is nevertheless relatively straightforward to describe broadly what cultural studies is about; what it *does* (Storey 1996; Hartley 2003): namely an inquiry, itself generated as an irritant, provoked by unsatisfactory disciplinary arrangements inherited from the nineteenth century (Lee 2003), into the way in which *cultural meaning*, or even more broadly just *meaning*, is generated or produced through various social groupings, cultural practices or through the agency of broader institutions. Jeff Lewis (2002: 13) defines culture via a 'rather inclusive' approach as 'an assemblage of imaginings and meanings' that may overlap or clash, which operate through 'human groupings and social practices': that is, culture is meaningfulness *in use*; and that usage can be cooperative or contentious.

[1] Michael Hutter, informal conversation, WZB (2013).

Historically considered, cultural studies has also proceeded as an ideologically laden programme that has formulated its analysis with respect to the watchwords of subjectivity, gender, class, identity, nation, power and ideology, in order to develop this as a basis for social critique as a precursor to – or species of – political activism and political practice in the realm of discourse.[2] Cultural studies is unambiguously 'out and proud' as a product and discourse of the left (Dworkin 1997; Lee 2003; Hartley 2003). The programme is to study how meaning is produced in conditions of asymmetrical power relations, for example, through media representation, by and through various culturally impacting institutions (of class, gender, economic organization, etc.). Critique is conducted with a view to resistance to or reform of those same institutions.

The latter process extends to scepticism about the very process of producing meaning itself, leading to philosophical doubts about whether true meaningfulness can be achieved in language at all. Here, Continental philosophy in the German-French tradition signifies the extension of doubt not just to truth claims but to the very conceptualization of truth. Here is where a 'Nietzsche' deme (thought-group) parts company from a 'Darwin' one: philosophy diverges from science, even though both retain a rationalist method; the one applied to discourse, the other to phenomena outside of discourse. Continental philosophy pursued a rationalist disquiet about what language can claim about non-language, as well as what reason can claim through language (Lucy 2004). It was widely interpreted as 'irrealism' or unbelief in reality, otherwise labelled postmodernism, because of its axiom that 'there is no outside-the-text' (Derrida 1976: 158–9), but equally widely influential as part of a larger scale effort to democratize and politicize the production of knowledge itself. Thus, cultural science and Continental philosophy share the characteristic of trying to understand how meaning is possible in conditions of uncertainty, using language to analyse meaning; and it shares with science the characteristic of seeking the reduction of error in testable observations about causal sequence in phenomena.

Precursors to a science of meaning

Is there then a science of meaning? *Meaning* generally refers to the sense or significance of a word, phrase or utterance, or in general, of a sign. Charles Sanders Peirce (1868/1977) developed a taxonomy of signs, dividing them into icons,

---

[2] Cultural studies remains controversial in wider journalistic debate because of its political agenda: for instance here: www.spiked-online.com/newsite/article/cultural-studies-a-cancer-on-the-academy/#.UxA-Dl40_La.

indexes and symbols. Ferdinand de Saussure (1974) imagined semiotics as a science, although he did not live to develop it from synchronic (structural) to diachronic (evolutionary) status. He divided the sign into signifier and signified. Both these approaches focus on what 'units' there might be in the structure of language itself to support the extraction of meaningfulness from organized sequences or arrays of signs. But neither took the further step of seeking scientific explanation for the *uses* of such systems, from which meaningfulness arises.

For that, perhaps Valentin Vološinov (1929/73) was the first to produce a general 'philosophy of language' based on usage. His approach to language is dialogic, not based on the 'smallest signifying unit' of an abstract structure. It is from this tradition that we should be seeking explanations of meaningfulness; the same Russian Formalist tradition that included serial innovators in the study of meaningfulness such as Viktor Shklovsky ('defamiliarization'), Mikhail Bakhtin ('carnivalesque') and, later, Roman Jakobson ('functions of language'), Victor Erlich (*Russian Formalism*) and Yuri Lotman. For political reasons (inter-demic Soviet/Western conflict) this promising line of research was slow to influence international scholarship. Much of it was not translated till the 1970s, and by then it had become an arcane branch of literary criticism, caught up in the eddies of structuralism, deconstruction, and so on, rather than driving on from dynamics, sociality and use to a full evolutionary position on meaningfulness, which, however, as we've tried to indicate, is nascent, if not named, in Lotman's work (Ibrus and Torop 2014).

We are left, instead, with the analytic tradition. From the perspective of the utterer, meaning is the intention or purpose underlying such a sign-using communication ('what I really mean is . . .'); from the perspective of the hearer, meaning is whatever sense is made of the incoming signal ('I hear you . . .'). Thus, it follows that meaning is not inherent in a sign, but is the product of the negotiated social relationship among sign-users, and dependent on context: meaning requires sociality. Semantics, or the theory of meaning in analytic philosophy, concerns the relation between words (text) or abstract ideas and reality. Plato conceived of ontological ideal types in which we conceive of the meaning of a word, say 'circle' as corresponding to this ideal type of circle. John Locke extended this notion of *ideational semantics* to ideal communication in which linguistic meaning is communicated when an idea is encoded, communicated and decoded, such that the same idea is re-presented from one mind to another. Later, Bertrand Russell, following J. S. Mill, developed semantics into a theory of referential semantics or signs. The key insight of referential semantics was to *detach meaning from minds*, as was central to John Locke's empiricist programme, locating it instead in the world with the objects of its referents. Shifting meaningfulness from agents to objects was a general *modernist* manoeuvre, fulfilling one sense of the idea of 'objectivity' (Hartley 2009a: 28). The meaning of a word or an expression is simply whatever that expression applies to, thus rendering the word or expression arbitrary but conventional, unlike Plato's essentialist conception.

Yet there was a basic problem with referential semantics, which was revealed by mathematical logic. Gottlob Frege and later Donald Davidson recognized that meaning required more than just ideational connection or referential mapping, but also a sense of *truth*. Frege pointed out multiple expressions could have the same referent without having the same meaning. By adopting Alfred Tarski's theory of truth, Davidson pointed out simply that a referent can *lie*: a logically, grammatically meaningful phrase can pretend to refer to something, but may be a deliberate deception: for example, 'The King is dead' is a logically formed and grammatical sentence, but it is not necessarily true; indeed, it may be a deliberate deception and its meaning may hinge precisely on its truth value. The idea that meaning could be completely understood in terms of reference is only true when all communication is true (Roberts 2008). Worse, it leaves the entire world of imagination, storytelling, drama and dreams – the universe of semiosis – out of account (Eco 1976), and leaves open the unsettling (postmodern) option that all communication is false.

Beyond ideational semantics, referential semantics and truth-conditional semantics is the domain of *meaning in use*. In the approaches outlined above, it was implicit that meaning referred to units of linguistic expression – or words in a language – wherein the relation of natural language to an ideal language (in the Platonic sense) was discussed in terms of a purely logical language. From this perspective, the meaning of meaning was in essence a question for analytic philosophers (such as Frege, Russell, Quine, Davidson).

Meaning in use

But the concept of meaning that pervades cultural studies is of *meaning in use*, not in respect of a natural language compared to a purely logical language, but rather of a natural language compared to all other language-like domains constituted by the construction of expressive 'texts', such as other media – films, songs, art, architecture, and so on, and indeed extending to all social behaviours, actions, interactions that can be variously encoded and decoded, hence 'social text'. In this model, meaning is contextual and intertextual. The meaning of a word, phrase or utterance is not simply what it refers to but its relation to others in the system, and to its 'correspondence'. 'Words mean things that they make us think of' (Roberts 2008: 7) – the meaning is in the thinking, not the word only. It is the broader notion of meaning-in-use (rediscovered from Russian Formalism) that we take as our referent concept for cultural science.

We also need to demarcate meaning and meaningfulness. *Meaning* is the noun referring to the specific quality of having meaning, or the process of gaining a *recognized* value, salience, seriousness, importance or significance. Meaningfulness is the quality of making meaning *in a sociocultural context*. These do not quite amount to the same thing, as akin to the difference between *truth* and *truthfulness*. An agent can purposefully and honestly pursue truthfulness without necessarily producing truth (thus, news media can be truthful even when in error). Similarly, meaningfulness is a condition of communicative agency, not of the world beyond communication: it is the condition of seeking meaning in the context of sociality and identity (as per Recommendment 2 in Chapter 2: 'Externalism') in the process of interacting with the internal and external worlds of imagination, information and perception, but it is no guarantee of a particular meaning or any meaning at all. Thus, meaning belongs to language and discourse, but meaningfulness belongs to culture, demes and sociality.

It follows that not everything perceived will be *recognized* as meaningful, but will be filtered and restructured according to the sense-making system (e.g. language) in use (i.e. within a cultural context). Hence the structuralist axiom, borrowed from Heidegger, that 'language speaks us'. Meaningfulness is not really an analytic concept, but it is a central human and cultural notion, and closely related to the concept of *value* or *worth* (i.e. that which is meaningful is often also of value or has worth), and thereby of the motives for human action and interaction. We focus on meaningfulness (culture) rather than on meaning (language) because we ultimately seek to connect our analysis with a theory of actual human behaviour and choice in a social context (rather than analytic philosophy or deontic linguistics) and it is meaningfulness that shapes individual choice and social interactions by its connection to value within a deme.

A philosophy of plenty

We pursue a theory of the evolution of meaningfulness, as the evolution of the *quality of meaning across an interacting ('demic') population*. Mark Roberts (2008) proposes an evolutionary theory of meaning that is based on Donald Davidson's (1973) 'radical interpretation' theory of communication meaning. Roberts claims that radical interpretation works as an evolutionary correspondence theory of language in which mental representations of the world become more accurate through time through the mechanisms of evolutionary variation and selection. Yet Roberts (2008: 29) also recognizes the central analytic problem, namely that although 'a convenient unit, with a definite information content, the traditional gene, exists in biology, no such unit can be found in a theory of meaning'.

There is no 'unit of meaning' in an evolutionary theory of culture. But yet culture evolves as meaning evolves. How is this reconciled? Meaning is about the way we *reduce* the world to make choices in a world of plenty. This is closer to an economic interpretation of meaning, but one that describes a world of abundance rather than one of scarcity. Hartley (2003: ch. 1) dubs cultural studies a 'philosophy of plenty'. The difference is significant: with scarcity, choice is about trade-off and opportunity cost; a choice is defined with respect to what you give up. But with the abundance of ideas and information, and in a world of 'productive waste' (see Chapter 8), choice remains, but its logic is different. In a world of scarcity, a rational agent ranks all options to compute the lowest opportunity cost outcome. But with abundance, or plenitude, this is individually impossible, but feasible when externalized. Instead, choice centres about what to pay attention to, which engages deme-created knowledge. Choice follows the line of meaningfulness, and the role of culture is to construct this meaningfulness as an externalized reference system within which individual meaningful choices can be made. Meaningfulness enables individuals to use the knowledge of a deme.

Knowledge evolves

Evolution means the growth of knowledge. A particularly stark way to think about this, despite modern squeamishness about 'narratives of progress', is to conceive of evolution as giving rise to higher-order, more complex or *emergent* levels of organization that continue 'upwards' to greater complexity. The futurist Ray Kurzweil (2005) speculates about the possibility of an emergent 'singularity' in which knowledge becomes a property of the universe. He reasons how 'chemical knowledge' (self-replicating macro-molecules) and 'biological knowledge' (genes, organisms) are the lower levels of what might be six epochs of technological evolution[3]:

1. Physics and chemistry (geosphere);
2. Biology (biosphere);

---

[3] We show successive spheres of the Vernadsky/Lotman approach in brackets; suggesting that there are more 'spheres' to come.

3. Brains (semiosphere);
4. Technology (noösphere);
5. A merger of technology with human intelligence;
6. The universe *wakes up*.

Kurzweil's point is that knowledge builds on knowledge. It's a recursive production process in which the output of one cycle is an input into the next. This notion of a technological singularity, in which the growth of knowledge builds upon itself, giving rise to emergent levels of complexity, has been around for some time. It is a standard trope in science fiction; but science is catching up. Reality is about halfway along Kurzweil's runway. Such models paint a picture of human socio-technical progress as an evolutionary feedback process driving a series of emergent 'explosions' or 'take-off' events.

But this is not just speculation or science fiction: it is the mainstream working model in the philosophy of science. Karl Popper (1972) conceives of knowledge itself as growing through an evolutionary process of 'conjecture and refutation', which he saw as similar to the mechanisms of variation and selection. In *Conjectures and Refutations* (1963) he explains:

> Science must begin with myths, and with the criticism of myths; neither with the collection of observations, nor with the invention of experiments, but with the critical discussion of myths, and of magical techniques and practices. The scientific tradition is distinguished from the pre-scientific tradition in having two layers. Like the latter, it passes on its theories; but it also passes on a critical attitude towards them. The theories are passed on, not as dogmas, but rather with the challenge to discuss them and improve upon them.

The idea of the growth of knowledge as an evolutionary process – whereby one generation's truths are the next generation's 'myths' – extended to the study of other domains of distributed knowledge. Friedrich Hayek had made a similar point about the market and price system, in which entrepreneurs were agents (like scientists),[4] who proposed conjectures of what might produce value or profit, with the market system then acting as the selection mechanism. This idea is central to Austrian and evolutionary economics. For Hayek (1945) 'the economic order is a distributed and coordinated complex structure of knowledge'. Hayek's (1952) *The Sensory Order* made a similar claim proposing

---

[4] This same argument was made by the psychologist George Kelly (1955) in *Personal Construct Theory*, which modelled ordinary human behaviour in any complex environment as if the person were acting 'like a Popperian scientist', proposing hypotheses about what is going on within a frame of explanation, and seeking verification or refutation of these conjectures.

a theory of the mind as a complex structure of patterns and conjectural pattern matching.

An evolutionary approach to the study of culture as a growth-of-knowledge process inevitably invites comparison with other models and frameworks of socio-technical, economic and cultural evolution. The contention of cultural science is that they are all of a 'Darwinian' family, each making more or less the same claims and following the same logic of variation-selection-replication, differing only in instances relating to how the evolutionary mechanisms work and assumptions about what specifically is evolving.

The fact of the matter is that evolutionary theories in social sciences have a long history that plainly predates Darwin's 1859 *Origin of Species* and traces most directly back to the work of the eighteenth-century Scottish Enlightenment of David Hume, Adam Smith, Adam Ferguson and others. They recognized that the existence of order in society did not necessarily require a grand planner but could spontaneously emerge by self-organizing processes. Evolution theory first developed, in fact, in the human and social sciences, as a way of explaining emergent sociocultural and economic order, and then later transplanted into the natural sciences. Cultural science repatriates a native concept.

Consider a few examples. In the 1960s and 1970s several interdisciplinary scholars developed theories of 'societal evolution'. These were endeavours to integrate open system-dynamic theories of societal, technological and ecological systems that integrated proto-theories of complex systems and co-evolutionary dynamics. The work of Nicolas Georgescu-Roegen (1971) is a singular contribution that introduced the entropy law (the second law of thermodynamics) to establish an 'arrow of time' in economic dynamics, setting up the logic that only the growth of knowledge can offset this otherwise inexorable collapse (entropy) of economic systems.

Another pioneer was Kenneth Boulding (1978, 1981). Boulding's central idea was that social and economic systems are ultimately made of knowledge, and 'what evolves' in the process of societal and economic evolution is knowledge. He drew on French philosopher Teilhard de Chardin's 'noösphere' (sphere of thought or knowledge) to refer to this domain, as a parallel of the biosphere. In 'Economic development as an evolutionary system', Boulding explains that:

> What the economist calls 'capital' is nothing more than human knowledge imposed on the material world. Knowledge and the growth of knowledge, therefore, is the essential key to economic development. (Boulding 1977)

Joseph Schumpeter developed the theory of entrepreneur and innovation driven economic growth and development through the evolutionary mechanism of 'creative destruction'. In a famous passage Schumpeter (1942: 82) wrote:

> Capitalism, then, is by nature a form or method of economic change and not only never is but never can be stationary. And this evolutionary character of the capitalist process is not merely due to the fact that economic life goes on in a social and natural environment which changes and by its change alters the data of economic action. . . . It must be seen in its role in the perennial gale of creative destruction. (1942: 82)

Modern evolutionary economics builds from Richard Nelson and Sidney Winter (1982), who integrated Veblen's evolutionary theory of culture (institutions as habits and routines; technologies as knowledge) with Schumpeter's evolutionary theory of firms, markets and technology, to create a model in which what evolves are the *habits and routines of firms*.

Technology evolves

Brian Arthur (2009) explains, from a complex systems perspective, what technology is and how it evolves. He builds this around three core principles:

- All technologies harness and exploit some phenomenon (technologies put ideas to work for human purposes).
- All technologies are combinations (that's why technological advance accelerates).
- Components of technologies are also technologies (i.e. technology is recursive). This explains why as technology advances, markets increasingly resemble complex ecosystems.

For Arthur, the unit of a technology is the exploitation of some natural phenomenon that is then modularized, so as to be combined and recombined. Kevin Kelly (2010) represents technology as an ongoing supra-critical system that generates solutions to problems, wherein those solutions create new problems, which it then solves, creating new problems, ad infinitum (an obviously Popperian formulation).

Attention to modular components and the decomposability of complex systems (Simon 1962) inverts the standard question of 'What is it made of?' or 'What is the unit of selection/variation/replication?' Instead, in open systems, the central question becomes how these basic units or stable modules are revealed or discovered by the system itself. We think that the cultural science problem of the evolution of meaningfulness in culture is more like this, in seeking to discover a stable locus of cultural connections that emerges to define a deme.

Social learning

In evolutionary theory of culture, it is also units of knowledge that are said to evolve. Edwin Tylor (1871), a pioneer of anthropology, defined culture as 'that complex whole which includes knowledge, belief, art, law, morals, custom, and any other capabilities and habits acquired by man as a member of society'. This argues that these elements are the units of culture; the mechanism by which they evolve is *social learning*. Luca Cavalli-Sforza and Marcus Feldman (1981) and Boyd and Richerson (1985) established the mathematical models and quantitative approach that defines modern work on cultural microevolution in terms of social learning. Richard Dawkins (1982) similarly argued that the realm of ideas and human culture did not require a separate explanation, but could be naturalized as an extension of biological evolution. For modern Darwinian anthropologists, such as Alex Mesoudi (2008, 2011), cultural dynamics is an evolutionary social learning process with variation and differential replication operating over the space of possible units. Mesoudi and others argue that this approach can provide a general framework for social science (Hodgson and Knudsen 2010).

A different tack is taken by a handful of Renaissance scholars, who have sought to introduce Darwinism into the humanities with a particular focus on 'high culture' of art rather than on broader notions of material culture in anthropology. Specifically, Dennis Dutton, Joseph Carroll and Brian Boyd build out from an evolutionary theory of the human mind in which evolved human universals ('instincts') shaped by natural and sexual selection form patterns that can be observed in literature, stories and aesthetic choices. The Dutton/ Carroll/Boyd strategy does not seek to explain human culture per se from an evolutionary perspective, but rather seeks to develop the proposition that the elements of human culture (art, stories, literature; 'mentifacts') are the product of evolved human minds, and can therefore be explained using evolutionary theory. What they are arguing in effect is for the evolutionary explanation of the particular salience of aspects or patterns within human culture. We agree with this, but think rather that what they are really alighting upon is an account of meaningfulness (not minds).

Meaningful knowledge evolves

We don't disagree with the significance of social learning of units of knowledge. But our problem with these accounts of sociocultural and techno-economic evolution is that they do not explain how these cultural units – that subsequently replicate through social learning – get established in the first place. The cultural science approach is to argue that it is not knowledge that evolves per se (in an information theoretic sense), but rather meaningful knowledge (in a semiotic sense).

The cultural evolution of gentlemen
(a short but instructive digression)

A key breakthrough that underpinned the British Industrial Revolution (1760–1830) was the invention and then large-scale production of the gentleman. The gentleman was a cultural innovation. It was made from recombined elements of the idealized British aristocrat – such as a sense of fair play and decency, *noblesse oblige*, and a disinterested pursuit of truth (. . . and pheasants) – mixed with models of integrity drawn from other chivalrous romantic cultures and from artistic tradition. But the concept of the new gentleman, post-Cervantes' *Don Quixote*, also combined more applied components that spoke to a secular and material focus with 'making and doing' (i.e. Francis Bacon's *fabricants* as well as *savants*) or what we now call an engineer. The result was the *gentleman scholar*, concerned with science and literature; the *gentleman adventurer*, concerned with romance, leadership and discovery; and the *gentleman entrepreneur*, concerned with business and innovation.

These gentlemen and gentlewomen were entrepreneurial drivers of culture and society and economy. How so? They created new demes from extant cultural combinations. Indeed, in many cases there were not individuals, but societies – the most seminal being the *Royal Society of London for Improving Natural Knowledge* (1660) and the *Lunar Society of Birmingham* (1775). Crucially, their status arose not from aristocratic 'blood' but from the fruits of entrepreneurial success – money. Charles Dickens caught the unsettling implications of that transformation in *Great Expectations*. The main character, Pip, is the very model of a modern invented gentleman.

This observation about gentlemanly cultural 'dememanship' (so to speak) is not novel to us. It was made by Deirdre McCloskey (2006), who put the point in terms of the more general concept of 'bourgeois virtues'. The emergence of gentlemanly social norms amenable to a civil society also benefited a growing commercial society. As economic historian Joel Mokyr (2009: 387) explains, 'A new concept of gentleman arose, someone who did not behave opportunistically and could be trusted'. This was a broader cultural moment, as the winningly named Samuel Smiles (1859) writes in the first book of the future publishing mega-genre, called *Self-Help* that:

> The true gentleman has a keen sense of honour, scrupulously avoiding mean actions. His standard of probity in word and action is high. He does not shuffle or prevaricate, dodge or sulk; but is honest, upright, and straightforward. . . . Above all, the gentleman is truthful. He feels that truth is 'the summit of being', and the soul of rectitude in human affairs.

The gentleman was a product of a new cultural form emerging from a hybridized recombination of extant forms that then spreading through a population by a process of social imitation, entrained signalling and sign mechanisms, with a renewed or reconstructed focus of meaning. This new cultural form became a platform upon which many of the commercial and technological and industrial features of the British Industrial Revolution subsequently depended (Clark 2007). The cultural innovation of the gentleman was a deme of externalized knowledge within which new knowledge was created.

The nature of culture and beyond biosemiotics

Paul Willis captures a central presumption of the cultural studies canon: that much of what we take to be natural is actually cultural, which is to say socially constructed.

> It is one of the fundamental paradoxes of our social life that when we are at our most natural, our most everyday, we are also at our most cultural; that when we are in roles that look the most obvious and given, we are actually in roles that are constructed, learned and far from inevitable. (Willis 1979: 185)

The evolutionary canon reverses this, arguing that much of what we take to be cultural is actually natural, which is to say evolutionarily constructed. Cultural science seeks to intermediate this inquiry into the nature of culture.

The appearance of naturalness may be due to familiarity or mutual tacit consent. The work of politically oriented cultural studies since Barthes (1972), argues that culture is an ideological construction, for example, in the media, popular culture and commercial-political activities that strategically deploy signs and symbols to 'naturalize' socially constructed meanings, subject-positions and social relationships of subordination and hegemony. A significant task of cultural studies is to identify, reveal, 'demystify' and critique such reified constructs – that is, to deconstruct them.

But an equally significant task is to connect 'our' frameworks of explanation with broader understandings of the world. Practically, this means engaging with evolutionary theory as the framework with the best claim to offering an account of human nature to underpin a science of human culture. At the analytic core of evolutionary biology is the notion of self-replicating information. It is widely held that to extend the genetic model of evolution to the study of cultural change it is necessary that cultural units are identified and analytically represented in such a way that they are analogous to biological units of selection. A foundation of cultural science is to explain why this is wrong from an evolutionary semiotic perspective.

Terrence Deacon (1999) has explained the concept of a meme as a degenerate concept of a sign, that is, without the full triadic structure proposed by C. S. Peirce, but instead, only with the ability to be copied and thus to replicate (Pocklington and Best 1997; Wimsatt 1999). Memetics is thus semiology with the most analytically and empirically interesting bits discarded. But a better angle on this is to reverse the argument and instead of using it as a critique of memetics – which was Deacon's point – using it instead to develop the idea that semiotics can provide a general framework for the study of biology and life through the observation that the domains of life and the domain of sign systems are coextensive.

The approach that does this is called *biosemiotics* (Kull 2000; Kull et al. 2010). Kalevi Kull (1999: 386) indicates its scope and ambition:

> Biosemiotics can be defined as the science of signs in living systems. A principal and distinctive characteristic of semiotic biology lays in the understanding that living entities do not interact like mechanical bodies, but rather as messages, the pieces of the text. This means that the whole determinism is of another type. ... The phenomena of recognition, memory, categorization, mimicry, learning, communication are thus among those of interest for biosemiotic research, together with the application of the tools and notions of semiotics (text, translation, interpretation, semiosis, types of sign, meaning) in the biological realm. However, what makes biosemiotics important and interesting for science in general, is its attempt to research the origins of semiotic phenomena and together with it to pave a way of conjoining humanities with natural sciences,

culture with nature, through the proper understanding of the relationships between external and internal nature.

As evolutionary theory has come to focus on information replication and processing, with greater attention to sexual selection (which is largely about signalling and communication) compared to natural selection, and with the rise of epigenetics (Jablonka and Lamb 2005), generative grammars in complexity theory (Kauffman 2000), neural Darwinism (Edelman 1987), it is unsurprising that there has been a revival of interest in a richer communication-based and sign-based approaches to evolution. The rise of biosemiotics is not simply a further wrinkle in the neo-Darwinian model. It offers an entirely new view of evolutionary phenomena by emphasizing meaning, as Jesper Hoffmeyer (1996: 61) explains:

> In the biosemiotic conception, the life sphere is permeated by sign processes (semiosis) and signification. Whatever an organism senses also means something to it – food, escape, sexual reproduction etc., and all organisms are born into a semiosphere, which is to say a world of meaning and communication. . . . The semiosphere poses constraints or boundary conditions upon species populations since these are forced to occupy specific semiotic niches i.e. they will have to master a set of signs of visual, acoustic, olfactory, tactile and chemical origin in order to survive in the semiosphere. And it is entirely possible that these semiotic demands to populations are often a decisive challenge to success. For perhaps more than anything else, organic evolution testifies to the development of ever more sophisticated semiotic means for surviving in the semiosphere.

He concludes (1995: 369) with a bid for 'semiotic freedom':

> The most pronounced feature of organic evolution is not the creation of a multiplicity of amazing morphological structures, but the general expansion of 'semiotic freedom', that is to say the increase in richness or 'depth' of meaning that can be communicated.

Yuri Lotman's (2005) concept of the semiosphere thus provides a foundational analytic concept to bridge us from cultural studies and evolutionary cultural theory to a more fully fledged cultural science. At the heart of what we take from the semiosphere is the concept of an *umwelt*. It is often taken to mean 'environment', but is better translated as 'self-centred world', which is a building block for a demic conception of knowledge. In the context of an early biosemiotics, Jakob Uexkull defined an *umwelt* as 'constituted by a more or less broad set of elements called "causes of significance" or "marks" which are the only things that interest the animal' (Uexkull 1973). For Uexkull, these marks were the significant things in the environment that the animal paid attention to, and which thus constituted the animal's environment as perceived and communicated with, in the sense of the signs that it perceived and reacted to; in cultural science this is the signified and storied boundary of the deme. Knowledge is created and stabilized (generated and contained) within an *umwelt*.

The idea that Lotman picked up and developed, building on the work of Vernadsky (1938, 1943), is that when two or more *umwelts* interact this creates a *semiosphere*. Hence Lotman's contribution to this conception of animal-in-symbolic-environment is to recognize that animals, including human animals, also make signs of causes of significance, as well as perceiving and reacting to them, and that these productions then constitute the environment of other such animals.[5] The concept of the semiosphere is that of a mutually constructed sign-space based on natural signs (animal behaviours and environmental cues) but which extends to artificial (produced or made) signs.

The space of the 'evolution of meaning' that we seek to investigate ranges across this domain. Our purpose here is not to set out biosemiotics as a lodestar in itself, but to turn it around again and suggest how this approach is an instance of what we mean by the reformed notion of the evolution of meaning within a deme. Meaning is not just something that we critically read into things, 'through a text deeply' as it were. Meaning is not just a referential signifier that can be 'interpreted' post hoc. Meaningfulness is constructed and communicated in a semiosphere. Meaning evolves in the semiosphere, and the semiosphere is made of interacting *umwelts*. The semiosphere is a competitive environment in which signs are engaged in a competitive 'struggle for attention' (Lanham 2006) in a world that is superabundant in such information and signs.

Two key factors distinguish evolution (of meaning) in the semiosphere from evolution (of genes) in the biosphere:

1. Signs can co-opt other signs;
2. New signs can be identified or created in situ.

Signs can co-opt other signs because the production of signs is made with signs, recursively. The process of creation may literally be combining signs into another sign, or in more roundabout ways by referencing other signs, by building upon them, negating them, parsing them, entraining them, and so on. This is a lot more like a group selection or multi-level selection process

---

[5] An environment of mutually constituted produced signs is also central to 'costly signalling' in the evolutionary theory of sexual selection, for example, the 'handicap principle' of Zahavi (1977).

than an individual selection model (Sober and Wilson 1998; Runciman 2009). The meaning in a sign system is constrained by recombination, so a larger sign system space has more possible meanings than a smaller space (Yuri Lotman bells this particular cat with the concept of 'explosion'). This same process may also give rise to further *emergent* units as particular systems of sign referents become self-generating or autopoietic (Maturana and Varela 1980; Potts 2000). New signs can be created, identified, discovered or revealed as additionalities to the system of signs, not necessarily displacing existing signs, but changing the relations among them. 'The evolution of knowledge builds on the emergence and evolution of signs' says Carsten Herrmann-Pillath (2009: 18). This is what makes an evolutionary semiotic culture productive; first of meaning, and then of things.

Meaningfulness and marriageability

Yuri Lotman's concept of the semiosphere offers a systems model to analyse 'the clash of systems' as a condition for the existence, interaction, and sustainability of meaningfulness and creativity. Individuals on the ground may experience competitive and adversarial relations, even extending to life-or-death conflicts, as between predator and prey in an ecosystem. But these clashes may, at a higher level of integration, be seen as part of a structure for maintaining sustainability among different users of a given environment. Conflicts of this type may be 'creatively destructive' in the Schumpeterian sense, leading to greater diversity across the system as a whole.

A traditional structural-semiotic explanation of the 'play of difference' is confined to the operations of textual signs (Derrida 1976: 278–94). But Lotman's system-semiotics is social. It derives thought (new ideas) not from mind or even from *langue* but from interlocution; text is always dialogue. Here, where system-differences between the textual and the social intersect, is where meaningfulness is most productive. Thus, the attempt must be made to link semiotic systems like language with social systems like cities, and both with knowledge systems like cultural theory, to ascertain how the interactions (clashes) within and among them can be seen as related and mutually causal. Apparently different phenomena – creativity, cities, complexity and 'the clash of systems' – may be seen as components of larger interacting spheres (Page 2011). Difference, dialogue, turn-taking, conflict, and so on, are not evidence of mutual incompatibility or antagonism, as critical theory has tended to assume since Marxism, but rather are part of a global process of cultural productivity.

A good practical example of how the 'clash of systems' generates productivity out of difference is *marriageability*. Marriage is easily understood a near-universal cultural practice with wide local variations, that is both personal and economic. It requires the bringing together of different families, with the risk of incompatibility and conflict as well as the hope for cooperation and reproductive success, on which individuals, social systems and biological species equally depend. It is always caught up in other systems – religious, legal, economic – and in some places is more formal and rule-bound as a result.

However, marriage also requires an open system for optimum choice of partners. Indeed, for George Bernard Shaw, 'complete marriageability between all sections of the community' was the only test for 'practical as opposed to arithmetical equality' in society (Shaw 1937, v: 66–9). In the 1920s and 1930s when he wrote that, there were still highly marked class differences that separated 'high society' from their live-in servants, so this remark must have seemed provocatively socialistic – and was presumably so intended, written as it was in *The Intelligent Woman's Guide to Socialism and Capitalism*, which was addressed to Shaw's sister-in-law Mary (who was married to a peer, Brigadier General Cholmondeley).

Its egalitarian challenge remains a very good test for sociocultural equality and the open society, as current international campaigns against forced marriage and for gay marriage amply demonstrate. But any such equality is produced out of difference. The incest taboo requires marriageability to be looked for among non-kin, the very neighbours from among whom enemies are also selected (Leach 1964). The same overall 'universe of the mind' generates positive links (love; marriage; offspring), and negative ones (Malvoisine, warfare, death) from the same structure of relationships. It is this type of risk-laden 'clash of systems' that characterizes not only marriage and enmity but also the ground and the terms on which they are staged (cities and culture). In other words, at the level of populations, rather than individuals, difference generates productivity and sustainability.

Contesting cultural order

A major source of today's theoretical drifting is postmodernism's aggressive vocabulary of subversion, demystification, transgression, violence, fissures,

> decentered subjects, fragmentation, dismantling master narratives, and so
> on. . . . (Patai and Corral 2005: 12)

For some, cultural studies is a political front line in the history of ideas and
a bleeding edge of progressive academic social practice, as Patai and Corral
(2005) intone. This line is often then aggressively naturalized, as for example by
E. O. Wilson (1975: 4), who held that:

> It may not be too much to say that sociology and the other social sciences, as
> well as the humanities, are the last branches of biology waiting to be included in
> the Modern Synthesis.

This is the contested and defended frontier of modern cultural theory, the
'Maginot Line' of C. P. Snow's 'two cultures'. In this world, cultural science is
the endeavour to broker a constructive peace in this ongoing cold war over the
analytical ownership of culture. The basic terms of settlement are that:

- Culture is not the issue, meaningfulness is;
- Meaningfulness evolves;
- Meaningfulness is complex and semiotic.

Evolutionary theories of information-based replicators only begin to get at the
deep complexity of cultural evolution: there is a lot that they can learn from
cultural studies. By the same token, the standard dynamic models of cultural
studies are seriously flawed: they should be replaced by evolutionary and
complex system models. Cultural science is the analytic mechanism by which
we make this mutual accommodation.

7

Newness

Innovation

The process of innovation is paradoxical, for it involves a curious cognitive function of recognizing what is not yet formulated as a category. . . . It is only in the process of attempting to make a transformation in the world that new problems can even be formulated. Generating novel recombinations is itself a kind of production requiring coordination and cooperation across different communities.

Vedres and Stark 2010: 1157

The Janus face of culture

Janus was a Roman god; the Greeks had no such deity. Janus was the god of beginnings and transitions, of change and time. He was depicted with two faces, looking simultaneously forward and backward, to the past and to the future. The theme of past and present is perennial and philosophic, to be found in every religion. But it carries with it the grittier theme of the old and the new; renewal, certainly, but also death or destruction.

Culture too is Janus-faced. It looks forward to new possibilities and to the future, and also backward to the past at what is old, some of which will be canonized as classic. A filter is at work here, where most of the past is discarded through critical assessment: it is wasted (as in the next chapter) by passage of time. Forward-looking culture is found in avant-garde performance, in experimental music, in the small tents at festivals and in some pop culture. Past-looking culture is found in museums, in the big tents in festivals, and on school curricula. Forward- and backward-looking cultures together make a cultural present. But the balance of these two is what matters.

Like Janus's conjoined faces, forward- and backward-looking cultures coexist in close proximity, separated by watersheds, subtle or vertiginous, whether in time or space. Back in the 1990s, the discombobulating jump from the end of TV music show *Rage* at 9 a.m. on Sunday mornings (i.e. extra-late Saturday night), to *Songs of Praise*, used to leave one of us with temporal whiplash. Similar experiences on the spatial plane can be had in walking about certain parts of London, Berlin or Beijing – the old and new clash noisily. At other times these boundaries are ruthlessly policed, seeking to expel all traces of the old from their midst (think of Left Bank Parisian artists in the *belle époque*, for instance), or in the pristine traditionalism that is classic when done by the elite (e.g. authentic-instrument music), but kitsch when adopted by the masses ('the good old days').

Our issue here is not with a valuation of the past – that is, with a cultural critique of the classics – but with the forces that construct a sociocultural system through time. The problem arises not because of the reproduction of culture – for that is essential – but in the way that the same cultural 'operating system', which is 'installed without our consent' (Pagel 2012), treats novelty and newness or its ability to generate novelty and newness. The value of newness is in the pathways it offers to the future. But this same novelty is what threatens the values of the past. An effective cultural reproductive system will therefore be well inoculated against newness. It will reject it, in the first instance, because such changes will threaten what is currently valued and known to be good. But an evolutionarily effective cultural system that seeks to live in a changing world, whether that change comes from the environment or from competition with 'they'-groups, will also be able to adapt to changes. That adaptation capability will depend on the cultural system's capability to develop new ideas. Novelty and newness will be the mechanism by which such adaption occurs. Cultures 'know' this at the level of stories, and have done so for thousands of years. They work through the conundrum with myths about how knowledge has to be stolen from the gods by a Trickster (Hermes; Prometheus), a necessary act of renewal that changes the relationship between gods and humanity forever (Hyde 2008); and about how the capacity of humanity to attain new knowledge eventually (after about 15 hours in Wagner's case) spells the twilight of the gods (*Götterdämmerung*).

The production of novelty and newness is not important because it is aesthetically sublime or Romantically agonistic, or because it reflects human perfection, as Kant said and others have since implied (Arnold, Ruskin, Keynes, Bloom 1998, et al.). It is important simply because it is needed for survival. We need new ideas to live in a changing environment. That is an evolutionary social imperative, not an aesthetic cultural one. Cultural novelty is of value because it provides us with new ways of thinking, which in turn enable us to think in new ways.

Not all cultures (demes) can generate or sustain novelty. They are threatened by it, for new ideas are untested and potentially destructive of the existing order. In an unchanging world, novelty is pure uncertainty and risk. But in a changing world, whether it is the environment or 'they' who are doing new things, new responses are required. They come from either a trust in the powers of visionary leaders to see what needs to be done, or they come from what complexity theory calls 'bottom-up' solutions that percolate from the variety and novelty generated within the system. The premise of cultural science is that these bottom-up solutions – this variety generated from within the system – are the only solution concepts that matter. This is novelty, or variety in the evolutionary scheme, and it is the grist upon which selection mechanisms then operate. This is rightly and insightfully how evolutionary cultural theorists in anthropology and sociology see this world (Mesoudi 2011). Cultural science seeks to build on these insights of the origin of newness.

The dynamic scale of cultural change

There is a scale to novelty and newness. Novelty doesn't matter at any particular moment in the present. Creativity, novelty, newness and innovation are not really essential or even important in people's lives on a day-to-day basis. Most of what we think and do is copied, conventional and routine, which is as it must be if we are to function at all. A random sampling of human history at any point from the Pleistocene age to the present, anywhere in the world, over any particular grouping of people, would statistically yield the result that 'nothing much happened'. Any real-time randomly sampled history will be tedious precisely because it is the play of existing ideas. New ideas are rare in actual history. They are the reason that historiography is constructed about new ideas, or the people that propose them.

Yet, here's the thing: in the long run, across human history and prehistory, creativity, novelty, newness and innovation are really the only things that matter. They're like genetic mutations in evolution, in that while you mostly don't notice them, they're all that count in the long term. In 2009, scientists at the Wellcome

Sanger Trust estimated that you've probably got 100–200 mutations that your parents didn't have. That's not so many across the billions of alleles in your genome, and unless you are extremely unlucky, you'll have no idea that they are there. Yet over eons, these mutations (interacting with selection, of course) are the reason that you're not a slime mould, or a ring-tailed lemur. Analytically, cultural 'mutations' should be viewed similarly.

Creativity, novelty, origination, newness and innovation in culture are like this. Up close, day-to-day, novelty doesn't really matter because most culture as it is practiced and experienced – high culture and ordinary culture alike – runs through well-rehearsed scripts and routines. We are already familiar with most of the music we listen to, in timbre or genre if not in exact lyrical form. Most of the foods we eat we have eaten before. Most of the ideas we think with are domesticated workhorses within our deme. Robert Hughes' (1991) 'shock of the new' is a rare event, which is why it matters.

The thing about the rare mutation – the new idea – is that it will affect not just you, but all who follow in your deme. For example, you might digest lactose slightly better than your parents; or you might calculate the area under a quadratic equation with greater accuracy than your teachers; or see a connection between African death masks and European portraiture. The point is that so too might all of your demic descendants who adopt your idea. It is the implication that this change can be copied or replicated through potentially vast scale to become a basis upon which further changes can then be made that makes newness (as opposed to mere novelty) seemingly mundane up close, but so profound at a distance.

In cultural science, the cultural significance of newness is not an inquiry into the causes of artistic genius or aesthetic vision (Boden 1990; Simonton 1999; Galenson 2008). It is, rather, an inquiry into the process by which a new idea is recognized and then adopted and diffused through a population, and the process by which that demic (or meso) population then retains that idea (Dopfer and Potts 2008). Joseph Schumpeter (1942) called this process 'creative destruction'. We call it 'demic newness'.

There is no singular science of novelty. Rather, from biochemistry through the evolutionary, behavioural and social sciences and the humanities there are different approaches to the theoretical conception of novelty and newness. These can be seen in the different concepts used to describe or reference novelty through mutation, variation, variety-generation, origination, creativity, imagination, newness, discovery and innovation, among others. We will trace these out in order to highlight an overarching pattern of three distinct approaches, the third of which we associate with the cultural science approach to novelty in the form of demic newness. Our goal here is to show how we get from: (1) a biological science conception of novelty – from determinism to *randomness*; (2) through a behavioural and social-science conception of novelty – from systems to individual minds, or *consciousness*; to (3) a cultural science conception of novelty – from individuals to *demes*. Each level supervenes on the previous.

Randomness makes variety

The Laplacian/Newtonian world-view of classical physics is exemplified in the field-theoretic formulations of rational mechanics. In this world, all particles exist in a space-time continuum of universal force fields. In principle, if you know the position and momentum of every particle you can calculate the entire future history of the universe. This type of extreme determinism shows up in social-science models based on rational mechanics, such as both neoclassical economics and Marxism (Potts 2000). What is missing is randomness (Herrmann-Pillath 2013).

Randomness entered physics through thermodynamics – the entropy law – which posited an arrow of time with the tendency of all closed systems to run down the entropy gradient from order to disorder. Here randomness is entirely destructive. Modern physics emerged through quantization, which had at its core quantum indeterminacy, or the fundamentally unknowable state of nature at the level of a quantum particle. Here randomness is ontological. Modern information theory (developed by John von Neumann and Claude Shannon) emerged with the recognition that communication requires randomness embedded in a message. Here randomness is constructive.

Darwinian evolutionary theory is also built on randomness, in the form of the first of the three constitutive mechanisms of variation, selection and replication. The fuel of evolutionary selection is the variation in a population, and thus for the evolutionary mechanism to continue to function there must exist a variety-generation mechanism. There are several, including random mutation in an allele, sexual recombination, which involves the random mixing of two chromosomes. The idea that randomness generates variety, and that variety is discovered or revealed by random or quasi-random movements within a space (a field, a population or a system) is the first of our theories of novelty.

A subsequent evaluative mechanism (e.g. natural selection) then values that new point in space, leading to differential replication. This class of model is very abstract and can be applied over a very wide domain, from genetics to machine learning algorithms.

Once we can see this as 'random movement within a space' we can further identify this as 'search' and then appreciate how a further mechanism can be added, in the form of investment. A system or population will devote some fraction of its resources (time, energy, workers) to investment in search. This is expressed in its most abstract form in modern economic growth models of research and development (R&D) investment (Romer 1990). For any given system-environment ensemble, there will be an optimal investment in the generation of variety.

Machine learning and artificial intelligence have an analogous need for variety-generation that is then subject to selection and replication. The model is lifted directly from biological analogy mixed with random number generators to arrive at a complex mix of computational iteration using stochastic variation. These models are algorithmic, grinding away to produce continuous streams of novelty that become grist for the mill of a selection mechanism. In these situations, creativity and novelty are essentially reduced to random variation about known solutions and the use of adapted heuristics to create variation from existing solutions. This model is also widespread in the social sciences, especially in economics, where the Schumpeterian entrepreneur is the variety-generation mechanism, searching or experimenting in the space of value-creating propositions, and the market mechanism is the selection process. It is in this sense that biological evolution (Campbell 1960), economic evolution (Schumpeter 1942; Nelson and Winter 1982), technological evolution (Arthur 2009), and the sociological version of cultural evolution (Mesoudi 2011) are all homologous in the equivalent form of a mechanism of variety-generation coupled to a mechanism of selection.

It is important to appreciate that these models of variety-generation as random motion (in a space), coupled with post hoc selection for high value movements (in that space), are actually models of search, not of creativity. To call variation a 'creative process' is a metaphor. Specifically, these models do not account for the higher order conjectural processes at work in human creativity that rely on the creation of 'models of the world' as the space in which creativity operates before being translated into real world contexts. As Kant pointed out long ago, we do not interact directly with pure sense data but through interpretations that attach meaning and significance. Creativity operates through these constructions. This is why an evolutionary cultural science approach to creative novelty cannot proceed from a variation-based model of creativity.

Consciousness makes creativity

In the modern scientific conception, randomness is a foundation of the universe and of life. In the modern Romantic conception, creative agency is the foundation of the individual. This is a different formulation, centred on the free will of agency (compared to the deterministic will of God, say, or fate) in which the human being is capable of making choices, requiring of them some conscious mechanism of imagination, or creativity. This conscious class of model is essentially (and methodologically) individualistic, supposing an intelligence, perception and imagination centred about an agent in the world. It is humanistic and Romantic, and well removed from the deterministic particle of classical physics or medieval theology, because it builds about the study of creativity in the individual human being, whether as *H. sapiens*, or as a more abstracted social agent. This can be observed in the many special treatments of creativity in neuroscience, cognitive science, behavioural and social psychology, design studies, organizational and management theory, education theory, arts and literature, history and philosophy (Boden 1994; Csikszentmihalyi 1996; Simonton 1999).

These models link novelty and newness in the world to creativity in the individual human agent. Creativity is not random variation in a space, as in the previous definition of variety, but is closer to a process of making new connections between things, and thus a filling in of the field space of the world, rather than a motion in the world's space. The creative agent adds to the content of the world by re-forming it, or imagining it, in new ways. Creativity is a subset of adaptive intelligence proceeding from imagination through to the realization of novel objective forms, solutions or products. It is subjective cognition and experimental action that results in objective difference. Creativity is an individual act (of insight, of genius) that makes the world different.

In neuropsychology and behavioural psychology creativity and novelty-generation separate into two distinct modalities: that internal to the agent (mental properties) and those relating to agent–environment interactions. Internal models emphasize experience and time devoted to problems, and the ability to recombine aspects of one problem space to another through framing and analogical reasoning, which involves creativity as a kind of imaginative leveraging of knowledge (Boden 1990). These explanations load on general cognitive capacity, whether fast and intuitive or cumulative and experiential. Csikszentmihalyi (1996) proposes a theory of creativity based about what he calls 'flow', which is in effect a type of all-absorbing concentration in which the person becomes absorbed into their intense effort in an ultimately satisfying way. Creativity is a result of skilled behavioural abstraction and concentration.

In the consciousness model of novelty, creativity comes from the intelligence and imagination of individual human minds. Creativity is promoted by conditioning these individual minds, directly through training or indirectly through attention to the environment in which they operate. This model is so widely adopted, both formally and in the implicit framing of questions and problems, that we might as well call this the 'standard social-science model of novelty'. It argues that novelty is generated by individual minds (as creativity) and that this is affected by the conditions of the individual (intelligence, knowledge, experience, genius), and by the organizational and institutional environment in which that individual acts. Education and organizational theory favour the environmental side of creativity, supposing that all people (including children) are inherently creative and that the expression of creativity is a consequence of environmental, organizational or institutional enablers. Both of these are 'control' parameters, in that creativity can therefore be dialled up or down by investment in individual 'creative human capital' or by manipulation of the individual's organizational and institutional environment. The work of Edward de Bono (1985) on individual creativity and Richard Florida (2002) on institutional creativity are two poles that exemplify this model.

The standard social-science model of novelty is widely entrenched, with good reason. It makes sense of individual creative actions and propensities, and it defines institutional (and therefore political) control mechanisms. It fits well with the standard social-science model of methodological individualism and with the standard policy model of institutional incentive design. Yet there are problems. In following the imperative of methodological individualism in assuming that novelty comes from individuals (because individuals are the locus of choice), it also assumes that knowledge resides in individuals. Cultural science departs from this with the principle of externalism (Chapter 2), and the knowledge unit of a deme (Chapter 3), which returns here as the unit of creativity.

Furthermore, both the random model and the Romantic model are agnostic and doctrinaire about the identity of any novelty. They make it axiomatically obvious. This is a point about which cultural studies is highly sceptical – as framed through such concepts as 'social construction of' and 'contested meanings', but the real import is that novelty does not arrive with labels. What counts as a new idea is the result of a process of collective evaluation or emergence. Obviously there are individuals who propose and champion any particular novelty (an entrepreneur, for instance), but the process by which a novelty is identified and constructed remains unexplained in the standard social-science model.

For example, consider the value of copying. High modernist theories of novelty and creativity see the value of creativity in the creative production itself, not in the subsequent adoption or copying processes. But simple economic logic implies that value is created in adoption and copying (discussion of rights and property is really about the distribution of the surplus value created by that joint process). The value of a creative act is revealed by the extent of adoption and copying processes that follow. It is the deme of an idea that determines its value, not the originator.

The cultural science model of novelty does not discount or reject the random model of novelty as variation (subject to selection) or the Romantic model of novelty as individual creativity. It seeks to incorporate both these perspectives. They are both parsimonious explanations (the principle of Occam's Razor is satisfied) and well supported by empirical evidence. What the cultural science approach seeks to do is to develop them to the next level, as it were, by recognizing what they constitutionally fail to account for: namely externalism, meaningfulness, demic knowledge ('we'-groups), conflict, scale, waste and extinction (as further developed in Chapters 8 and 9). The upshot is an account of the creative source of novelty lying not in the tidy abstractions of individual or in society, but in the messy new cultural science concept of a deme (or 'we'-group), which is an externalized unit of knowledge, and what we think of as the main cultural carrier and progenitor.

Demes make newness

Cultural newness arises from within a deme. This is an externalized process of discovery and negotiation of new meaningfulness through the tensions of 'we'-group interactions with 'they'-group boundary conditions. Randomness (or generative waste) and Romantic individual imagination and creativity are obviously involved in this process. But the central cultural science proposition is that the creation of newness occurs at the level of the deme; it is *demic*.

After the classical theory of randomness as search in a space, and the modern theory of novelty as individual creativity in an institutional environment, comes the postmodern conception of novelty as demic newness. Culture produces newness and innovation through externalist, demic and wasteful mechanisms (Chapters 2, 3 and 8) that result in explosions and extinctions (Chapters 6 and 9). The classical and modernist view is that creative individuals (as a kind of random particle) produce novelty and that institutional mechanisms select over this. Culture is the result of this process. But the postmodern cultural science approach is that culture itself produces knowledge and meaning because of its generative capacities in producing complex spaces that bring freedom and tension into balance.

Cities, for example, can produce novelty through their assemblage of ideas and tensions. Democracy can produce novelty through its 'we-group/they-group' intermediation. Journalism can produce novelty through positing and mediating knowledge clashes ('both sides of the story'). The canonized artists of the Renaissance (Michelangelo, et al.) were not artists at the time: they were artisans and entrepreneurs who created new sources of meaningfulness. They had artistic talent to be sure, but that is not why we know them. Mostly, we don't care about the extent to which their works were done by apprentices; and we don't know the work of their talented contemporaries. Shakespeare was a brilliant entrepreneur, as well as a writer. His Globe Theatre project was the original model for venture capital in cultural production, in that his company was one of the earliest joint stock ventures, creating new audiences for popular entertainment (Hartley 2013). The origin of the cultural juggernaut of Australian Indigenous art is in significant part thanks to a New Yorker called Fred Myers (2002), who intermediated and constructed the meaning of these works for other demes, and thus established their value in the international art market. The genius of Damien Hirst, Jeffery Koons and Andy Warhol is as much in marketing as making. This takes nothing away from their artistic talent but does go towards explaining their significance (Lanham 2006). Culture produces newness by intermediating in a world of cultural abundance that as a mass experience really is a new and epochal phenomenon (Hoggart 2004).

The properties of a deme that contribute to the discovery of newness and the production of innovation emerge from how it sets up freedoms and deals with conflict. It is with how it puts people together and manages the chaos that may ensue in a way that enables good ideas to circulate (McNair 2006). The more the folkways and institutions of a culture function like a common pool resource, the more effective they will be in generating novelty and in driving innovation. In this respect, a good model of culture-driven demic innovation comes from the study of creative commons and knowledge commons, which builds on the work of Elinor Ostrom (1990) in relation to the governance of natural resource commons. A commons is a space where a group of people interested in an idea (i.e. a deme) can create or manage a resource of value. The overarching finding from research on successful commons is that it attributes good outcomes to good rules, not to good people. Good rules (along with good stories: Chapter 3) make viable demes. This is a template for cultural science.

The economic sociology of newness: 'Irritating impact'

Michael Hutter and his colleagues (2010) explain that:

> We understand newness as a concept denoting events, products, ideas, technologies, works of art, and processes of collaboration or coordination that have an irritating impact when they occur.

This view of novelty and innovation as *newness* is a different concept from novelty in the previous models (as variety or creativity). Newness here is hard and unloved. Newness comes from an outworking of tensions, frictions, dissonance, ambiguity and problems that eventually reveal new possibilities or opportunities to be seized and exploited to create or extract value.

The model of newness has been developed in economic sociology by David Stark at Columbia University and by Michael Hutter and his team at WZB Berlin.[1] At the heart of their approach is the idea of multiple value propositions, or what French sociologists Luc Boltanski and Laurent Thévenot (2006) call 'orders of worth'. They elaborate a sociological theory of value framework of six orders of worth – civic, market, inspired, fame, industrial and domestic – that applies in all calculative economic situations. David Stark builds on this, using the concept of 'structural folds' proposing a new model of novelty-generation and entrepreneurship based on the *dissonance* or frictions that occur between multiple evaluative criteria of worth, specifically emphasizing the notion that these dissonances can be and often are deliberately set up (Vedres and Stark 2010).[2]

Stark (2009: 15) explains that, 'Entrepreneurship is the ability to keep multiple evaluative principles in play and to exploit the resulting friction of their

---

[1] WZB: Wissenschaftszentrum Berlin für Sozialforschung. Social Science Research Centre Berlin.
[2] Stark (2009) *The Sense of Dissonance*, conducts ethnographic analysis of organizational contexts in three situations of organizational 'heterarchy' (a socialist factory, a new media start-up and an arbitrage trading room) in each case finding that the key driver of entrepreneurial discovery is the tensions and frictions or the dissonance created by the interplay of different evaluative criteria of worth.

interplay'. He argues that this type of innovation is not 'search' in the planning and engineering sense above, but is closer to a process of 'search when you don't know what you're looking for, but will recognize it when you find it'. Spatially and structurally organized dissonance can contribute to the discovery and realization of entrepreneurial opportunities. This is modelled with the concept of 'structural folds' (Vedres and Stark 2010), contrasted with Ronald Burt's entrepreneurial brokerage concept of 'structural holes'. In Stark's model, organizational dissonance is the mechanism that underpins how creative friction yields organizational reflexivity to create an 'ecology of knowledge' in which multiple and potentially conflicting evaluative principles and criteria of worth are in play and are entrepreneurially resolved into singular assessments of value (Stark 2009: 142). Newness emerges from the resolution of conflict of multiple overlapping evaluative criteria to arrive at a singular value judgement.

Michael Hutter's research group (Hutter 2008, 2010, 2012) have been working along a similar line with a raft of projects organized about the theme of 'cultural sources of newness', in which:

> Newness lies at the core of innovations and emerges in cultural sources, which are analyzed as cultural configurations [or] cultural constellations. (Hutter et al. 2010)

Referencing the work of Boltanski, Thévenot and Stark, but building on this in the direction of ethnography and cultural geography as well as evolutionary economics, the WZB group argue that three kinds of processes are decisive for innovations:

- The continuous variation of cultural forms and practices;
- The evaluation of newness;
- The states of tension that arise within and between cultures.

Their approach thus emphasizes that innovations are neither obvious nor attributable to individual creativity, both statements that are near axiomatic in the standard random or Romantic approaches; but instead that newness is a cultural valuation process that is associated with particular constellations of cultural configurations in respect of proximity, collaboration, communication and meaning; an externalized meaningful deme, in other words. Furthermore, this is not a causal process in which culture is the input and novelty is the output. Rather, these cultural configurations – dissonant tensions and frictions in Stark's sense – create opportunities that may then be entrepreneurially recognized and acted upon. This is not unlike the economist Israel Kirzner's (1973) conception of entrepreneurship as 'alertness to opportunity'. Novelty and innovation *supervenes* on culture through the simultaneous creation of newness and opportunities.

Cultures do not generate newness as a property of a given culture as a whole, such that we may speak of that culture X being innovative and culture Y being less so. This is a fallacy of aggregation, where we suppose that because we may speak of individuals being creative or intelligent, we may speak likewise of cultures. Cultural sources of newness refers to cultural processes and constellations of cultural interactions that generate the necessary frictions, tensions and dissonance, usually across overlapping value propositions, or *meanings*, such that a deme identifies newness in the opportunity created and worth in the value that can be resolved.

This process may not even look or feel creative and innovative. As a site of tension, complexity and bricolage, it will likely be discordant, uncomfortable, problematic, challenging and unresolved – recognizably *wrong*. It is a cultural space in which alertness to opportunities to resolve such tensions can be a source of advance and a place where surprise is expected (Shackle 1972). This is an environment in which experimentation works as a discovery method, and where the act of play – of trying things out in a somewhat unstructured way – may be effective.

It is also an environment with benefits to heterogeneity, proximity, mixing and scale – cosmopolitan urban environments of the city, in other words, where ideas can run into each other, where accidental connections can take place, where opportunities are created and recognized. Social networks and novelty bundling markets (Potts 2011) are culture constellations that put ideas together in ways that create tensions and stresses that need to be resolved and in so doing create spaces and environments in which opportunities are revealed. This is how a deme produces innovation. It suggests a reinterpretation of the work on the economics of cities as sites of creativity and innovation. Richard Florida (2002, 2005) has been at the vanguard of the human capital model of creative cities, in which creative cities are the result of attractors for creative people. Currid (2007) focuses this argument on the cultural and creative scene, as a competitive advantage for some cities, which is closer to the meaning we are advancing here, in that she is emphasizing the edginess and the social and fashion scene as a key part of the mechanism (Aspers 2010).

Yet, the cultural science line of argument is perhaps closest to Jane Jacobs (1961, 1984) or Ed Glaeser (2011). Jacobs argued that cities work worst when they are extensively planned, rationalized and driven to exploit economic scale in single sectors, and work best, in the sense of being the most robust, the most capable of growth, when they evolve organically by ever increasing the complexity of their economic base. Nassim Taleb (2012) would call this property 'anti-fragile' rather than robust, in the sense that Jacob's cities actually gain from stressors and disorder rather than just being robust against them. In policy terms, Jacobs was against the developmental model and top-down planning and favoured mixed-use development and bottom-up planning: in essence the abolition of zoning laws. We also favour these ideas and see them as sources of value and growth (Hartley et al. 2012), because they organically generate the types of dense urban cultural ecologies that are conducive to the generation and realization of opportunities via demic concentration.

What do these cultural constellations need to make an 'irritating impact', whether at the scale of cities, or in the form of smaller clusters, local scenes, associations, or any other social form? We argue two basic properties are necessary: social networks and freedom. Social networks create the space and flows of information between people to enable these tensions and conflicts and dissonances to form (i.e. be communicable) in the first place. Freedom works towards ensuring that they don't then cause the system to overheat, blow up or destroy itself.

By *social networks* we mean any technology that enables coordination to be achieved by the sharing of information across a network. Clay Shirky (2008) and Charles Leadbeater (2008) have argued that the very nature of innovation and creativity is changing because of changing opportunities bought by opportunities that operate across social networks. For Shirky, what has changed is the lower Coasian 'transactions costs' of coordination and organization that make it possible to do things collectively on social networks that previously were far too costly or difficult to coordinate (Potts 2010). A dramatic fall in the costs of coordination impacts on the social network by driving the explosion of mass collaborative creativity. Leadbeater (2010) emphasizes the revolution in the opportunity space to share and collaborate in innovation and production using social media technology (Quiggin 2006). As for *freedom*, McCloskey (2006, 2010) explains that these are the core freedom principles underpinning capitalism.

It is not that newness per se is socially constructed, or that a particular novelty or innovation is a social construction, at least, not in the critical sense argued by Ian Hacking (2000). Rather, the very possibility of newness, novelty and innovation is constructed by particular cultural contexts and situations that enable ideas and meanings to interact in ways that create potential new opportunities that are brought into existence in a cultural context.

8

Waste

Reproductive Success

And consummation comes, and jars two hemispheres.

Thomas Hardy 1915

On the efficiency of cultural production

In this chapter, we examine a function to which evolution as a process is indifferent, but for which it supplies the mechanism: successful reproduction. Contemporary evolutionary theory relies on three types of selection to explain reproductive success: natural selection, sexual selection and kin selection. We will come to these shortly – and plan to add *cultural* or *demic selection* (akin to *group selection*) to the list – but first, we want to bring a little-discussed feature of reproduction into the discussion, which is waste. Reproduction is usually measured, and so it should be, by its success – the individual reproduces; the species survives. In the process, however, we find a *scale of productivity* that reaches well beyond the human power of imagination. But most of that productivity is wasted. Whether you're looking at life or artifice, most attempts at reproduction fail. The most valuable product of any species or system, the very vehicle of its future – children and brainchildren alike – wind up as nutrient for competitor species, or as lifeless sediment. They never come to fruition. They're lost, rejected, eaten, stolen, infertile, unused, forgotten . . . dissolved into other life-forms or dumped in landfill. Success is valued, but its *efficiency* goes unremarked.

In this chapter, we want to put these two facts alongside each other: exorbitant creative productivity on the one hand, wastefulness beyond imagination on the other, to ask: What is this apparent inefficiency *for*? Evolution is an indifferent process. Does its indifference extend to efficiency? Or does that combination – productivity and waste at scale – perform a fitness-enhancing function in the successful reproduction of complex adaptive systems? In short, what is the *use* of waste?

Understanding the evolution of complexity (artistic, biological or otherwise) requires attention to *systems* rather than to *individuals*. In conditions of change, uncertainty and dynamism, not to mention competitive and predatory neighbours, something other than individuals is required because, like most of their offspring, individual creators are wasted too. Whether we're discussing biological creatures or human creativity, the *creator* does not survive in the *creation* – offspring and artwork alike owe nothing to the process or agents that made them. It's not the parent or artisan that survives, only their handiwork. The real question is the one posed by Yuri Lotman: '*How can a system develop and yet remain true to itself?*' (Lotman 2009: 1; Hartley 2012: 212–13). Perhaps the answer is simply wastefulness. It is the price of successful reproduction of complex adaptive systems – not of individuals.

The answer matters because we are interested in economic as well as in cultural analysis; in productivity and efficiency as well as in culture and language. Paying attention to wastefulness in the productivity of large-scale self-reproducing systems leads to a consideration of how it occurs, in culture (for instance, in language) and nature (for instance, in sexual reproduction). Thus, our investigation into successful reproduction in nature and culture may offer insights for economic analysis and policy too: at the very least, prompting a reconsideration of the concept of 'waste' as inefficient or unproductive. As to what it is for – the function of 'creative wastefulness' – we conclude that it is an *innovation mechanism*. It allows *newness to emerge*. And the mechanism isn't efficiency; it's *proximity*.

Inevitably, a chapter about successful reproduction is a chapter about children, both biological offspring and metaphorical brainchildren, that is, ideas and artworks. What connects *children* and waste? Certainly the process of *natural selection* is profligate. The offspring of many creatures and other life-forms (e.g. plants) are destroyed or devoured by the million; perhaps most of the children of most organisms. This apparent wastefulness is what it takes for those species to survive predation. *Sexual selection* is also notoriously wasteful, biologically and semiotically, exhibiting 'energetically wasteful displays' (Fitch 2005) with both 'costly signaling' (Gintis et al. 2001) and 'conspicuous consumption' (Veblen 1899).

In this chapter, we also consider *kin selection* (Bergstrom 2003), which brings *communication* into the picture (Fitch 2005), not least between parent and child, before proposing a further mode of selection, which we call *cultural, or demic selection*, which is comparable with *group selection* (Bowles and

Gintis 2011; Gintis 2012; Runciman 2009). Two new issues for cultural science arise out of all this: first, *communication* and waste; and second, *children* and waste. Given the high value routinely placed on both communication and children, it may be necessary to revaluate wastefulness, from being a negative to being a positive component of culture, which has implications for economics.

Along the selective continuum, from natural and sexual selection to kin selection and cultural or demic selection, the same mechanisms are at work, whether reproduction takes place in biological systems (natural and sexual selection) or communication/cultural systems (kin and cultural selection). The long-standing habit of seeing language, culture, knowledge and meaningfulness as somehow different (or even exempt) from evolution and complexity cannot be sustained. This has implications for evolutionary science and cultural studies alike: it is no longer possible for either to leave the other out of account. Consilience is the only reasonable method to adopt in order to investigate 'reproductive success', including what it costs in bodies and brains, organisms and information, individuals and ideas, or orgasms and offspring.

Trillions and trillions

Particles, distances, stars, exoplanets . . . and thus, possibly, also astrobiological life-forms are all measured in units of 10 to the power of 12 or greater; all the way up to the so-called googol (10 to the power of 100 or 10 with 100 noughts). Despite the evidence of our human consciousness, which doesn't deal in trillions, trillions abound at the level of 'me' as well as at that of 'the universe'. It's not just that we're *made of* trillions of cells and host trillions of microorganisms, but also that we routinely *process* trillions of bits of information, incoming via our sensory organs and then filtered down to perceptible levels by our central nervous system. We're immersed in trillions; we make our unique selves up as we go along by filtering trillions. Thus, as the cyberneticist Heinz von Foerster put it: 'The world, as we perceive it, is our own invention'.[1] It's an invention that we create by radically reducing to something that *can* be perceived – something *meaningful* – the otherwise unimaginable scale of possibilities and probabilities in the world beyond the uncertain boundaries of 'me' and 'we'.

---

[1] See: www.univie.ac.at/constructivism/HvF.htm. The direct translation from the original German ('Was wir als Wirklichkeit wahrnehmen, ist unsere Erfindung') is: 'That which we assume as reality, is our invention'.

Where these trillions intersect with individual choices and actions is most readily recognized in the matter of sexual reproduction. Success relies not only on *producing* those billions of spermatozoa, but also on systems for *eliminating* most of them from the race. That being so, what should we make of all the billions of eggs and trillions of spermatozoa that don't fertilize? Are they simply wasted? It certainly looks as though this is the case (bearing in mind that one organism's 'waste' is another's dinner), and in this, humans are very far from unique. Wastefulness at the scale of 10 to the power of 12 or more is typical across many different classes of life. It can colour the planet, as when pine pollen floats down rivers and gilds entire lake surfaces in the boreal forests. Needless to say, rather few new pine trees eventuate from the many miles and tons of pollen dust produced each year. The same applies when coral spawns. So many eggs and sperm are broadcast that slicks form on the surface, and onlookers in nearby coastal resorts can mistake the result for algae blooms, or pollution. If broadcast coral eggs are successfully fertilized, they produce larvae called planulae. These may eventually settle and grow into new coral, but most don't make it: 'The time between planula formation and settlement is a period of exceptionally high mortality for coral larvae.'[2] They are devoured by the billion.

Large, long-lived animals and plants play the same game. They inundate predators with tasty morsels. Flowering plants beg insects and birds to eat their fruit. Turtles feed most of their hatchlings, say all but two or three in every thousand, to predators and other lethal hazards (Frazer 1992). Many of them are perfectly viable individuals, just as 'fit' to survive as those that do, but they are willingly sacrificed to the laws of chance. This system of reproduction is not about individuals but about probabilities (the probability being that individuals won't survive but the species will).

In the evolutionary arms race between predator and prey, the secret weapon for parents seeking reproductive success, to be fired indiscriminately into the mouths of waiting monsters, *are the children*. Such wastefulness may be thought to be inefficiency, if not worse. Shouldn't every child be a wanted child? But this is not a matter of species failing to evolve efficient or moral means to transmit their genes into the future. We know this because species that are among the most wasteful in this respect are also among the longest lasting. Corals go back

---

[2] US National Oceanic and Atmospheric Administration: http://coralreef.noaa.gov/aboutcorals/coral101/reproduction/.

to the Silurian period; trees such as the ginkgo to the Permian; and pines such as the Wollemi pine to the Jurassic.

Apparently more 'efficient' species with few live offspring, such as humans, also make a probability lottery out of reproduction, but they do it at the point of conception rather than at birth (and we should not forget the billions of cohabiting organisms from bacteria to house-mites that make a living out of our 'wasted' cells). Thus, we should not be fooled into thinking that linear transmission – in the manner of Claude Shannon's wire-based model of communication – would be more efficient than one based on scale and proximity. The spectacular wastefulness of reproduction turns out to have a function, but one that can only be discerned at the system level, not that of the individual, whose motivations, choices, desires and so on are neither here nor there as they disappear down the nearest gullet. It is this: *waste allows newness to emerge.*

Cultural efficiency

Waste is so normal in *language use* that it has never become a problem requiring a solution through scholarly research or policy solution in communication sciences. The idea of language *efficiency* never arises; we know of no branch of cultural or economic inquiry that is dedicated to the production of a 'language efficiency quotient' or of a 'coefficient of cultural performance'. Talk, as they persistently say, is cheap.

There are, as everyone knows, semiotic systems where communicative efficiency would be valued if only it could be achieved; that is, in marketing, publicity, advertising, public relations, and so on, where someone (some organization) wants the message to 'cut through', for commercial, political or advocacy reasons. But here the 'problem' is not directly linguistic or cultural. The object of the exercise is not so much to make language more efficient; its naturally wasteful tendencies are taken for granted. Strategies are directed towards *defeating* those tendencies, by sheer semiotic force. Indeed, both commercial and political communications are called 'campaigns'. The military metaphor implies that what is wanted is the *conquest* of people's attention (see Chapters 4: 'Malvoisine'; and 9: 'Extinction'). To achieve victory, that is, to create a linear causal chain between the intentions of the paying advertiser and desired alterations in the behaviour of consumer-citizens (via semiotic/linguistic mediation), requires an army. The scale of that army can be gauged by what it spends. The US communications industry alone spent over a trillion US dollars in 2012, expected to rise to nearly US$1.5 trillion by 2016.[3] Troops of professionals are employed, marshalled and deployed by the captains general of commerce and community, augmented by political campaigners, lobbyists and myriad firms, industry sectors, reformists, associations, activists and advocates, plus entire fields of scholarly research, all dedicated to raising the low efficiency of *sending messages* (improving the efficiency of *language systems* as a whole is too hard), in whatever medium, for whatever purpose.

The best that anyone can hope for is that such high-investment messages will attract the attention of some people sometimes (without guaranteed consequent behavioural actions). Advertising really *wants* to do something to you and to make you to do something, but mostly you don't do it. So despite military strength investment, cultural and linguistic efficiency is not achieved in marketing communication, and the return on investment (improving one's share of sales, votes, attitudes) is always uncertain. Inevitably, even where investment, purpose and creative expertise are most intense (e.g. in retail sales and at elections), much of the linguistic product is simply wasted. As John Wanamaker, the so-called father of advertising, is reputed to have put it, 'Half the money I spend on advertising is wasted; the trouble is, I don't know which half'.[4] The best the campaign industry can manage is *proximity* – they sell 'eyeballs' to their clients, because they can indeed gather populations (Hartley 1999) and amass their attention through the media. On the grounds that people like to copy high-status behaviour (Earls 2009; Bentley et al. 2011), some of that attention may convert to sales.

But even such 'reproductive success' is indirect: what happens after a signal hits an eyeball remains radically uncertain. In short, *if advertising worked, we wouldn't need it*. If it were in fact possible to get the message across *efficiently*, there'd be no call for an industry (and an academic field) continuously devoted to renewing the attempt, 24/7, across all media. If you want higher efficiency of utterance, where what is said *performs* the desired action (Austin 1962), that is, where communicative cause and effect are conjoined in the utterance, you had better train as a judge: only in such formal institutional settings do utterances successfully enact what the speaker intends (and only then because these are ritualized expressions of monopolistic state force): 'I sentence you to two years.'

---

[3] 'New VSS Forecast 2012–2016'. *Veronis Suhler Stevenson* (www.vssforecast.com): www.vss.com/imgs/VSSForecast20122016PressRelease.pdf.

[4] John Wanamaker (1838–1922), merchant; religious, civic, political leader; and sometime US Postmaster General: http://pabook.libraries.psu.edu/palitmap/bios/Wanamaker__John.html.

The reality, however, is that most sentences float by unheeded, no matter how forcefully expressed or how much is spent on them, even if they appear to be directly addressed to 'me' by a high-value representative of the 'we'-group, for example, a winsome child, pop culture celebrity, prominent public figure or suchlike secular stand-in for the otherwise indifferent gods. We ignore them all, in droves, even when the information they seek to impart is 'for our own good' – our health, well-being or pecuniary advantage. Ruthless viewer scepticism is often warranted, of course; it's a protective membrane around our very sensitive demic connectivity receptors. Even where advertising *does* work, among the proportion of the population who do take notice and subsequently act on a message, the unforeseen consequences (obesity; alcoholism; smoking-related illness) can be dramatic and not necessarily positive.

Beyond the special case of the communications and campaign industry, semiotic waste abounds. All of publishing and the creative and entertainment industries in general face the same 'problem' of not being able to achieve communicative efficiency – even when communication is their stock-in-trade. This results in the peculiar structure of those industries, which reduce risk by producing a repertoire of potential choices for consumers (Garnham 1987), because nobody knows in advance what will prove popular (Caves 2000).

Uncertainty can be reduced, for instance in Hollywood, where competition for a declining movie-audience with plenty of options elsewhere has produced a counter-intuitive strategy for risk reduction, which is to spend even more money: the $200m blockbuster about superheroes, aliens or catastrophes is more likely to succeed at the box office (in the all-important first-weekend of release) than the $5m to $35m handcrafted film based on the cultural realities and human scale that made Hollywood so successful in the past (these types of movies are now called 'Oscar-bait'). Common sense might suggest that a $35m investment in a good story that touches the audience's lives and experience would constitute a lower risk than $200m spent on pure adolescent fantasy; but that's not the way things work in the world of semiotic productivity.

Communication doesn't work as a linear conveyance of information from A to B. Instead, most of it is neglected, rejected, resisted or consigned to the bargain bin. Talent or genius is no predictor of success. It takes luck, wiliness and time – as well as entrepreneurial energy and intensive investment – to 'win' the top spot in the rather brutal 'winner takes all' logic of the power law distribution curve that separates the blockbuster from the damp squib. There will always be one Shakespeare, J. K. Rowling, *Citizen Kane* or Beyoncé at the top; concomitantly there is a very long tail of best endeavours that miss that mark. That logic – the famous 'long tail' (Anderson 2008) of 'social network markets' (Potts et al. 2008) – requires that most who aim for the top will be 'wasting' their time; but nobody knows in advance who is the time-waster or who will win. Sometimes the $35m independent low-budget film can trump the $200m blockbuster, so the 'sure thing' can stumble, but that doesn't change boardroom calculations. As blockbusters like *The Lone Ranger* bombed in the 2013 'summer of doom', more were being announced: *Pirates of the Caribbean 5, Thor 2, Fantastic Four 3* and a reboot of *Godzilla* among others.[5] Waste is the *chief characteristic* of the entire creative production system, answering uncertainty with overproduction. This goes especially for its *most* creative productivity, because innovative, experimental or avant-garde entertainments (art) typically underrate – their risk is high; take up low. The best is often simply ignored.

Meanwhile, creative insiders have pointed to a potential new source of renewal for creative innovation: not film, but television. In a 'revolutionary' reversal of the historically entrenched taste-hierarchy that sees movies as an art form and TV as trash, respected actor/director/producer Kevin Spacey devoted his lecture at the 2013 Edinburgh International Television Festival to praising TV's new 'golden age'. He named *The Sopranos, The Wire, Game of Thrones, Breaking Bad* and *House of Cards* among 17 shows that comprise the 'most powerful and inescapable evidence that the king of television is the creatives'. Here, the principle of corporate wastefulness still triumphs over innovative creativity. Most of the creatives' ideas never make it to the screen. Thousands of scripts are presented or commissioned for US networks to be whittled down in an annual cull. Only 100-odd pilot shows are produced; of these, only tens are aired; of these, only two or three make it to season two (Gitlin 1983). This is just in Hollywood. For the purposes of Spacey's argument, the rest of the world may as well not exist. He named only 17 shows – all American – to demonstrate a 'golden age' for creative success. In short, Spacey's argument for more creativity actually amounts to a call for *more waste*. He wants industry leadership that, 'rather than playing it safe', is 'emboldened and empowered to support our mission; to have an environment . . . that is willing to take risks, experiment, be prepared to fail by aiming higher'.[6] The action he advocates – 'If you wanna compete, you've got to get into the original content game' – is modelled on

---

[5]   See: www.theguardian.com/film/2013/jul/26/blockbuster-film-industry-fan-base-box-office.
[6]   See: www.smh.com.au/entertainment/box-seat/in-tv-risk-is-everything-kevin-spacey-lists-tvs-best-17-shows-and-calls-for-more-20130823-2sfvq.html#ixzz2cwEvbcY2; and see: www.theguardian.com/media/2013/aug/22/kevin-spacey-tv-golden-age.

biological reproduction. This tactic entails the inevitable mass destruction of most high-investment stories to ensure success for the fortunate few. Spacey's much-vaunted creative 'kings' behave like turtles: they produce many eggs to ensure a few adults.

If the 'best that has been thought and said' is doomed to predation, consider how much less 'efficient' must be the low-stakes day-to-day communication of ordinary mortals. Indeed, most of what everyone says has no 'effect' beyond the fact of its utterance. If that is waste, then language is not only the most complex human invention but also its most wasteful. Consider this: each person speaks about 10,000 words a day. Annually, that's 3.65 million words per person. For 7 billion people, that's about 25 quadrillion (25,000,000,000,000,000) words uttered by humans each year. About 100 billion humans have ever lived; so that's about 1 octillion utterances, or 10 to the power of 27, or about the number of atoms in a human body. Conservatively estimated, each individual person utters more than 100 million words over a lifetime; and every sentence is unique. It's hard even to imagine what might constitute a 'language efficiency quotient' or 'coefficient of cultural performance', much less 'reproductive success' in this context. The scale of 'wastefulness' suggests that utterance has an entirely different value in and for a speech community; one based on keeping in touch or signalling, mostly among kin or deme, rather than offering more competition for the 'original content game'.

Children and waste

Clearly, language is not produced for *functional* purposes; efficiency doesn't come into it. But productivity does. To explore this aspect of cultural reproduction, we must turn to the role of children – the 'product' of any successful reproduction system. In this book, we see children and young people as especially important, playing a key role in the reproduction of meaningfulness within 'we'-groups. They take a lead in projecting the 'cultural survival vehicle' of their demes into the future. But here, once again, instead of finding recognition of that role and its value, we find mind-boggling waste. Indeed, at the analytical level, waste turns out to be *categorical*. The entire category of children's utterance is discounted, in life and social theory alike. It 'doesn't count' because it is mere game, play, or inconsequential make-believe, a rehearsal at best with no effect on society, politics, culture, economics or any other system beyond dubious 'learning outcomes' for the juvenile concerned.

But we think that children's utterance and play are productive of something of the highest importance for cultural survival; namely the renewal of the deme's 'we'-identity, through imitation, copying, sharing, tweaking and converting inconsequential utterance and ideas (play, day-dreaming, mischief) into new creative content and connectivity. Through such activities, the culture is reinvented every day anew by and among the peer group that faces their own uncertain future as makers of 'our' future. In short, we argue that human children are not wasteful, but productive, through their future-facing practices of integration into language, communication and culture; 'practice' here meaning experiment and rehearsal as well as action.

The idea that children are not only the *outcome* but also the *agents* of cultural reproduction (survival of the 'we'-group) is certainly counter-intuitive. But 'children' or 'offspring' are habitually regarded as an 'on-off' category (all-child or all-adult, without gradient). If the fact of humanity's long maturation process is taken into account, it can more easily be recognized that children are long-term interlocutors within family, neighbourhood and mediated communication. Completion of the parental function does not occur until a generation has been successfully reared; conventionally 25 years, which is also the age, again conventionally, at which 'youth' clicks over into 'adulthood'. The generations overlap, producing a continuous stream of children whose care, management and induction into the language and knowledge of the 'we'-community is institutionalized both within and beyond their immediate family, and whose social learning proceeds continuously as they pick up capabilities, and their language, knowledge and social networks expand. Thus a continuous slow-wave of new children – on a gradient from infant to toddler to tween; teen to 'yoof' – plays a significant and directive role in family organization, and thence in political, cultural, economic and social life more generally: but they do it, at least to begin with, largely through kin connectivity and through communication or *semiotic productivity*, not through industrial productivity as traditionally reckoned, even though children are also workers in many situations. It is in the communicative, semiotic, cultural and linguistic spheres of life that children may turn out to be productive in their own right – even as they also copy, imitate, rehearse, play and generally waste their time.

Nevertheless, children are discounted altogether in most accounts of culture, not to mention in the economy, in favour of an ideal abstract, the *rational-choice individual*, an assumed adult. Part of the reason for this assumption is that most evolutionary thinking about humans focuses on natural selection and sexual selection, where successful mating is the object of study. Children play no role in that process, and so they are almost entirely neglected in evolutionary theory. This biological fact colours social and semiotic facts that are rather different. Anthropologically, young people are 'impotent' (Leach 1965) until their adult powers are recognized by some ritual (puberty rites, exams, departure from home/village, employment, marriage). In economics and cultural studies too, children are not granted agency. Their semiotic and social productivity is rarely considered except in terms of risk (they are construed as victims rather than actors).

But recent work on reciprocal altruism and cooperation finds that '*kin selection*', or 'inclusive fitness' theory (Foster et al. 2006), needs to be added to *natural* and *sexual* selection, as what Tecumseh Fitch (2005: 212) calls 'the most significant recent addition to evolutionary theory'. Fitch's approach is important for our purposes, because he is concerned with the evolution of *language*, and sees kin selection as an 'elegant solution' to problems encountered in previous explanations. He writes: 'communicating kin often share each others' genetic best interests, so kin selection will favor an individual (especially a parent) who can increase a relative's (particularly, offspring) survival' (2005: 213). He comments: 'it is surprising that kin communication has been almost entirely neglected as an important force in language evolution' (2005: 214).

We would add that *kin communication* is not simply a matter of top-down or one-way 'parental care' (as it is almost always construed in the literature). It involves *both parent and offspring*: two communicative 'systems' whose capabilities, interests and languages differ (Lotman 1990).[7] Further, the 'offspring' of slow-maturation animals like humans hang around as 'children' (dependants) for a long time; they are not simply gaping beaks demanding food (stimuli to parental care), but – from the very start – they are autonomous interlocutors with a rapidly developing repertoire of communicative capabilities that they bring to encounters, and not just with parents. They may be 'impotent' (i.e. powerless) in relation to the business of the external world, but they are very active in the world of communicative invention for relationship formation and 'phatic' confirmation of connectedness (Jakobson 1960). Their stock-in-trade is semiosis: stories, movies, games, make-believe, day-dreaming, fantasy, fearful

---

[7] We are not saying that parents and children speak different languages, but that, since humans are born without speech, initial mother–infant communication is by contextual and non-verbal means that Lotman calls the 'language of smiles', within which, over time, speech plays an increasingly significant role. In other words, parent/infant communication establishes a semiosphere, where mutually untranslatable languages meet (or clash), resulting in intense productivity of meaningfulness (for the baby's survival and well-being) and sociality ('bonding'), albeit with minimal verbal 'content'.

anxiety (about survival, identity, sexuality, sociality and success) and projection of the self onto the environment (including negative experiments such as teasing, bullying, sexting, hooning, etc.).

We know this because many adult inventors and innovators mention childhood or childish insights and experiences as the spur to their creative careers. Picasso was one, as recorded by advertising and art entrepreneur Charles Saatchi: 'Picasso consistently pointed out that it took him four years to learn to paint like Raphael and the rest of his life to learn to paint like a child. "All children are artists. Our problem is how to remain an artist when we grow up."' (Saatchi 2013: 255).

Someone whose adult life was driven by a childhood nightmare rather than dream was the man who 'initiated' (his word) Esperanto, the world's most successful constructed language. L. L. Zamenhof describes how 'the idea, to which I have really given my whole life, appeared to me, ridiculous though it may seem, when I was only an infant, and since then it has never left me'. What was that idea? Nothing less than an entirely new language, specifically designed to overcome the demic adversarialism (inter-group enmity) that blighted the city in which he grew up:

> The place where I was born and spent my childhood gave direction to all my future struggles. In Białystok the inhabitants were divided into four distinct elements: Russians, Poles, Germans and Jews; each of these spoke their own language and looked on all the others as enemies. In such a town a sensitive nature feels more acutely than elsewhere the misery caused by language division and sees at every step that the diversity of languages is the first, or at least the most influential, basis for the separation of the human family into groups of enemies. I was brought up as an idealist; I was taught that all people were brothers, while outside in the street at every step I felt that there were no people, only Russians, Poles, Germans, Jews and so on. This was always a great torment to my infant mind, although many people may smile at such an 'anguish for the world' in a child.[8]

Zamenhof wasted no time: by the time he left school he had invented what in 1887 became Esperanto. It has survived to become by far the world's largest

---

[8]   L. Zamenhof, *Originala Verkaro*, ed. J. Dietterle, Leipzig 1929, 417–8. Accessible at: www.u-matthias. de/latino/latin_en.htm. Zamenhof's 'torment' was well founded. Białystok has changed hands many times, among Lithuanian, Polish, Prussian/ German and Russian lords or conquerors. Under Russian rule it endured a pogrom (1906), under the Nazis a Ghetto and deportations to death camps (1941–44). Such was the feared future to which Esperanto was intended to provide an alternative: idealistic, perhaps, but all too realistically motivated, in Zamenhof's early childhood.

constructed or auxiliary language, now claiming 2 million speakers and a place in the top 100 languages of the world. Zamenhof was doubtless an unusual child, but perhaps many more children than we normally allow are motivated by insightful observations and the will to see an insight through to implementation. Dismissed as a class, for inconsequential play, irrational irresponsibility, and impotent powers, children and their insights are simply wasted when it comes to finding solutions for today's problems. However, out of analytic sight, they are busy inventing the future, by growing their own knowledge networks; their own deme.

Wasted words?

Children are inveterate *talkers*, not only to parents and carers but also to siblings, family, kin and demic peers or 'honorary relatives' (Konner 2010: 506), in which context they create and share the crazes, in-jokes, songs, enthusiasms and other identity-markers that craft the 'we'-group of the future, and pick up all kinds of folklore – that is, cultural knowledge and repertoire.[9] Children are active two-way or 'bottom-up' parties in the process of 'kin communication', and their interests are not necessarily the same as (or blindly imitative of) those of their parents. Further, they actively make the extension from kin to deme, as they develop sociality with non-kin through child care, schooling and informal leisure or 'unproductive' activities from attending religious ceremonies or theatrical performances to encounters in the street or on the playing field. As Nobel laureate writer Albert Camus famously remarked: 'What little I know on morality, I learned it on football pitches and theatre stages. Those were my true universities'.[10] The sporting team is not just a rehearsal or metaphor for the political deme; it *enacts* players' developing knowledge of a 'we' community beyond kin.

As we've mentioned, our argument uses waste as a way of thinking through some of the issues involved in understanding how cultures evolve and survive. Among the most wasteful systems you can think of, it is hard to beat language. It is 'low cost' and unlimited – not a scarce resource but a superabundant

---

[9] Pioneers of the systematic study of what children say and hear in playgrounds were Iona and Peter Opie. See: www.indiana.edu/~liblilly/shorttitle/opie.html; and hear: http://sounds.bl.uk/Oral-history/Opie-collection-of-children-s-games-and-songs-.

[10] Quotation and discussion at: http://frenchfootballweekly.com/2013/11/07/goalkeeper-philosopher-outsider-albert-camus/.

one, available equally to all undamaged specimens of our species, at no charge to anyone apart from the time taken and proximity required to acquire it from kin, 'honorary relatives' and others including mediated interlocutors (stars, celebrities, teachers, priests, shamans, fantasy and fictional characters); and with no restrictive distinction relating to gender, intelligence, social hierarchy, historical period or relative affluence. Barring accidents or illness, everyone talks.

Languages are however naturally 'demic'. While they offer universal access to meaningfulness to all native speakers, they entail adversarial exclusion to all those who speak a foreign tongue. Such demic difference can spawn the prejudicial enmity experienced by Zamenhof as a child, but it can also be bridged by bilingualism and translation among languages, enriching both sides. It is possible that language difference itself evolved as a kind of 'copyright protection' among early tribal groups, who sought to protect their intellectual property against competitive predation by outsider groups. Thus language difference is itself wasteful, in the sense that it requires inventive profligacy at the *system* level. There are thousands of languages (currently, 7000 known) and many thousands more that are now extinct. Whole languages are routinely snuffed out, along with their unique corpus of embedded knowledge, metaphor and contextual traces, their peculiar ways of dividing up the continua of sense impressions into meaningful units (Leach 1964: 328–9), and their function as the number-one marker of a 'we' community. They disappear, die out, or evolve into something else.

Evolutionary biologist Mark Pagel in *Wired for Culture* (2012) addresses the puzzle of why there are so many languages. Pagel comes at this problem by way of social learning, noting that 'Humans, unique among animals, are capable of cultural or social learning' (2010: 38). True enough, and two key features follow: (1) the capability of sophisticated copying of novel behaviour merely by watching. We can transmit a certain 'behaviour' to others, and they have mechanism to understand it; and (2) we know what we are copying and can infer motive, intention, and can choose to copy the best (i.e. theory of mind, plus mirror neurons capabilities). No other animal can do these things. Yet from a design perspective, this huge proliferation of languages looks enormously wasteful. Wouldn't just one language be enough?

The puzzle of the huge proliferation of language groups in human cultural evolution can be understood as an adaptive mechanism to facilitate in-group social cooperation. Language is a cultural marker for recognizing others 'of your group' with whom to extend cooperation as a way of dealing with the problem of 'visual theft'. Pagel explains that: 'We have different languages because our ancestors used language to draw rings around their own cooperative groups, identifying those who are part of our own group and our knowledge from eavesdroppers in competing groups'. In sum:

> To make our societies work, . . . natural selection found ways for individuals to align their interests with those of their group. . . . Humans seem to be equipped with emotions that encourage us to treat others in our societies [who speak the same language] as if they were 'honorary relatives'. Taking this option would mean a vastly greater fund of accumulated wisdom and talent would become available than any one individual or family could ever hope to produce. This is the option we followed, and our cultural survival vehicles that we travelled around the world in were the result. (Pagel 2012: 72, 81)

The corollary is that this mechanism works by continuous creation of new language groups. This not only occurs at the level of natural languages, but more so at the level of registers, idioms, accents and ways of speaking, and via other forms of social signalling and cultural text. The production of novelty and newness can therefore be understood as a mechanism to maintain or regenerate spheres or webs of in-group cooperation. The 'product' of language, then, is not wastefulness but demic identity.

As a species, we seem to be 'irrationally enthusiastic' about *producing* language, but much less adept at 'consuming' it. As quickly as oratorical, narrative, musical and other forms of communicative 'costly signalling' are evolved within a community of language users, it seems that observers are just as quick evolve an equal and opposite capacity to discount, ignore or suppress them. There are thousands of courses on 'creative writing', 'public speaking' and the like, and entire disciplines devoted to communicative persuasion (rhetoric, marketing), but none that we know of on 'listening' or 'understanding'; or even 'reading'.[11] Listening is only valued as a component of security (human hearing is more acute at night), and in sinister appropriations of that function such as eavesdropping, spying, surveillance and data-mining. Language *reception* as a social practice is typically untutored in daily life, ignored in disciplinary research and unimproved in cultural or economic investment.

Inevitably, communication is highly asymmetric; much more is said than heard. Small wonder that systems theorists like Niklas Luhmann have

---

[11] Literary education retains a commitment to astute or critical reading, but typically assumes that skill, focusing on what to read, rather than how or why, and on texts, not readers.

concluded that communication cannot be understood as a linear conveyance of meaning from one individual into another. Communication is better grasped as the means by which individuals process information relating to their proximate environment, which is replete with semiotic as well as other meaningful signals (potential food; danger; mate). Most of information received goes unprocessed by any given organism, which may be presumed to be pursuing their own purposes, otherwise not paying attention to the external environment except to monitor the integrity of their boundary with it. Much of what is processed as incoming information never reaches the level of consciousness (i.e. meaningfulness), as recent brain science continuously demonstrates.

What Luhmann calls perception precedes reason, but 'perception' itself is already a radically filtered *representation* before we perceive it. Perhaps this is why languages and utterances alike are so redundant, verbally and grammatically, where repetition (the phone always rings twice) seems to concede in advance that no one's listening, therefore that most of what is uttered, and not just by advertisers, is wasted; and the enunciator – not to mention the system – knows it will be. Efficiency would be fatal here. We are left with a species that is wilfully profligate in the *production* of language (it's all 'me, me, me!'), but radically selective in its *reception*, both intuitive and deliberate (Kahneman 2011), because only a small part of what's heard is needed or heeded for most operational purposes. Productivity, then, relies on 'successful reproduction' of meaningfulness, not just on utterance.

As the very mechanism of externalism (linked brains and knowledge) and deme formation, language unites individualism (utterance) with sociality (awareness of others) as the foundation for the 'use' of culture. This feature allows for what counts as 'individual' to be scaled, such that abstractions and institutions may take the place of natural persons (individuals) and operate socially (as communicators), so much so that we personalize abstract forces and ascribe human characteristics to firms, which produce yet more language. Thus, utterance is produced independently of human agency and context, adding to the sheer quantity of unused semiosis in the 'universe of the mind'.

Language is also structurally wasteful at the semiotic or textual level. Language is 'lies, all lies'. Anything that can be used to tell the truth can also be used to lie (Eco 1976); and therefore every propositional utterance must have at least two potential *meanings*: 'this is the case' (Wittgenstein 1922), or 'I am deceiving you' (Hyde 2008), doubling its productivity, but making it yet more wasteful in use, because half or more of its potential meaningfulness is not realized. But this kind of wastefulness is not mere inefficiency. It is built into the earliest use to which interpersonal communication is put. The *first* 'utterance' of a newborn infant may be pure expression ('I can't breathe'. . . . I'm hungry . . . uncomfortable', etc.). This generally elicits a response from the mother or carer (the breast, comforting attention, etc.). But what about the *next* cry of the infant? It *says* 'I'm hungry', but it might *mean* 'I want that agreeable and anxiety-reducing attention that my previous cry elicited, and therefore I shall repeat the cry, even though my physical condition is not the same'. Such is the first *communication* of the human infant, directed towards creating a desired response in the interlocutor-carer. It's the first 'expression' of sociality, but it's not completely honest; in fact it's a lie. Pretty soon – perhaps right away – the attentive mother will learn to distinguish 'hungry', 'tired' or 'uncomfortable' from 'attention-seeking' cries, and the infant will learn that faking it won't always make it. Mutual learning and give-and-take characterize the process of language acquisition, from the get-go. Trust is tried and tested and slowly built up in communicative action, precisely because truth is not inherent in language.

Language's duplicity enables groups to deal with truth's fugitive nature, by linking speech to community via demic 'universal-adversarial' or 'we' versus 'they' boundary-formation. It means that all propositional content needs to be heard twice, as it were: once as if it is true (hopeful, inclusive, familial, 'we'); and once as if it's a lie (fearful, external, competitive 'they'). Each speaker must monitor every utterance to check on the trustworthiness of other speakers, and assess propositions accordingly. Our inner journalist must ask the famous 'Jeremy Paxman' question: 'Why is this lying bastard lying to me?'[12] More subtly, we must learn how to distinguish what is 'the case' from whatever is not, without rejecting all of the latter: we're hostile to lies, delusion and illusion (discovery of which converts a 'we' interlocutor to 'they'); but we love them when they are used *within* a deme for the purposes of creative imagination (fiction, religion, etc.). The trick is to tell which is which; but the reality is that language mixes them up indiscriminately.

The childish invention of culture

Melvin Konner, in his monumental study *The Evolution of Childhood*, lumps play into a chapter with 'social learning and teaching' (2010: 500–17), pointing

---

[12] A famous question; but not in fact Paxman's – it has been reattributed to Louis Heren, long-term foreign correspondent at *The Times*: www.theguardian.com/media/2005/jan/31/mondaymediasection. politicsandthemedia.

out that in hunter-gatherer playgroups, 'teaching, observational learning and play are combined and, in effect, become one process' (p. 517).

> Whatever the age structure of juvenile groups, play is one of their main activities. Play is a biological puzzle . . . it is generally defined as inefficient, partly repetitive movements . . . with no apparent purpose. This behaviour, combining as it does great energy expenditure and risk with apparent pointlessness, is a central paradox of evolutionary biology. (Melvin Konner 2010: 500)

More generally, he concludes that 'children socialize and enculturate each other . . . but it is not just culturally mandated behavior and knowledge that is transmitted: child groups may transmit what adults see as undesirable behavior, and they can become agents of change' (Konner 2010: 661). This squares with recent research on 'natural pedagogy' as an evolutionary adaptation (Csibra and Gergely 2011: 1150). They say:

> Our proposal is that the [evolutionary] adaptation for natural pedagogy was made necessary by the cognitively opaque knowledge and skills required by technological inventions during early human evolution. This technology, including its materialization as artefacts and its know-how as expertise, was inherently cultural in nature. . . . Conventions, rituals and novel symbol systems could also be transmitted to the next generation by natural pedagogy, and the operation of modern social institutions is unimaginable without communicative knowledge transfer. In this sense, natural pedagogy is not just the product but also one of the sources of the rich cultural heritage of our species.

Culture – knowledge, technology, symbol systems, institutions – is 'transmitted to the next generation' by 'natural pedagogy', of which children are both agents (source) and product. In other words, one of the 'main activities' of children is to teach themselves and each other in pleasurable/competitive company, growing knowledge and how to use it in an intersubjective, autonomous setting (without assigned tasks). Making it up as they go along, children's purposeless interactions with kin, peers, objects, symbols, pretend and environment teach them, inter alia:

- The *content* of language, including meaningfulness, rules, skills and customs;
- *Sociality* in cooperation, copying, competition and conflict, including both play-fighting and play sex (Konner 2010: 288);
- *Enterprise* in risk, iteration and reward, including testing boundaries;

- *Technology,* including *institutional* rules and forms; and
- *Recursive knowledge or epistemology*, including 'theory of mind', ability to alter rules, interpretation, 'collaborative learning' and thence 'enculturation' (Konner 2010: 283–5; ch. 26).

They do not passively receive language, culture, knowledge or meaningfulness; they remake them anew, and they can be 'agents of change'. In short, *what* children are 'making up' as they play is the *deme of the future*. Its value is 'paradoxical' to evolutionary biology because the 'body' in which it evolves is culture.

Language is the most complex system humanity has invented (although cities might also begin to stake a claim to that title). It is co-extensive with the species (we know of no human group or time without it), and yet it follows its own evolutionary path, whatever individuals think, do or say. There is no 'rational choice' involved in deciding which word follows another in a spontaneous utterance. Those decisions are made by the rules of the game, in this case, grammar, which is not in the gift of the speaker; and by the exigencies and immediate circumstance of utterance, to which individuals respond intuitively and emotionally, not rationally or deliberately (Kahneman 2011). Other 'general technologies' invented by humans, which use us even as we use them, include culture (Pagel 2012), technology (Arthur 2009), cities (Jacobs 1961, 1984), writing (including mathematical and musical notation) (Goody 1986; Ong 2012), and the internet (Benkler 2006; Barabási 2002). They too exert their own systemic causal force on individual actions, even as individuals create them. Although language is not a technology in the usual sense (it's not made of materials external to the human body), it does seem to have been 'invented' at a certain point during the early evolution of *H. sapiens*, in the way that Brian Arthur describes for technology; by *combinatorial evolution*, taking existing components of the human sound-making machinery (larynx, tongue, teeth, etc.), a set of components that is itself evolutionarily distinct from that of other great apes, and using the same for new purposes, possibly based on the interactions of mothers and infants (Fitch 2005).

As with biological species, most of the languages that have ever been spoken are now extinct. But new languages are coming into existence, as we speak. As the *New York Times* reported in 2013 (and see O'Shannessy 2005):

O'Shannessy, a linguist at the University of Michigan, has been studying the young people's speech for more than a decade and has concluded that they speak neither a dialect nor the mixture of languages called a creole, but a new language with unique grammatical rules. The language, called Warlpiri rampaku, or Light

Warlpiri, is spoken only by people under 35 in Lajamanu, an isolated village of about 700 people in Australia's Northern Territory. In all, about 350 people speak the language as their native tongue.[13]

Notice here that the new language appears 'from below', as it were – out of the mouths of youngsters under 35, not 'elders' whose cultural function is to preserve received knowledge; those who must adapt to new circumstances. Light Warlpiri is not the only new language to emerge in these circumstances. Australian field linguist Felicity Meakins has documented another, called Gurindji Kriol (Figure 8.1). She points out: 'In many remote areas of northern Australia, language loss has also been accompanied by language genesis. New Indigenous languages have emerged as a modern expression of Indigeneity'.[14]

Figure 8.1 The childish invention of culture: Gurindji children of the Kalkaringi community, Becky Peter, Chloe Algy-King and Nathaniel Morris, tell Felicity Meakins in Gurindji Kriol where to find a blue-tongue lizard. Photo: Peggy Macqueen © 2010. Used with permission.

---

[13] 'A Village Invents a Language All Its Own'. By Nicholas Bakalar. *New York Times* (14 July 2013): www. nytimes.com/2013/07/16/science/linguist-finds-a-language-in-its-infancy.html?pagewanted=1&_ r=0&hp. Lajamanu's *Wikipedia* entry suggests that the invention of the new language may be related to a Northern Territory government ban on children speaking Warlpiri at school: *Wikipedia*: Lajamanu, Northern Territory. See also: www.nytimes.com/imagepages/2013/07/16/science/16LANG.html.

[14] See: http://cccs.uq.edu.au/meakins-lecture.

None of this can be explained by recourse to methodological individualism. Other than a desire to connect with peers, no personal motivation or choice can produce such an outcome; only the mutuality of linked brains in conditions of sociality, in short, culture, motivated by a 'desire' for the survival of the group. The same sort of rule applies also to the development of a national accent – the Australian accent, for instance, and with that, national identity. Children *must* have invented these valued components of culture, because mature speakers would have come to Australia with their own regional accent (Cockney and Irish figuring prominently). It was their children who developed the new accent from the linguistic and social mixture and interactions of the new colony, including contact with other languages, indigenous or regional; and only this explains why so many British-English derived societies have developed distinct and sometimes mutually unintelligible accents, which may themselves be evolving into new language 'species', for example, Singapore Singlish (Ansaldo 2009).

There is an important rule here that methodological individualism misses because of its focus on rational or autonomous choice. That is, that allegiance to the group forms a large part of the social learning programme that is conventionally subsumed under the heading of 'childhood', restricting it to inconsequentiality and 'play' – that is, allowing it no causal or generative force – when in fact mother–infant communication and children's peer-to-peer interactions produce and create the sociality and networks within which adult individuals operate and have their identity. Rationality and autonomy are the very properties of the adult individual that are thought not to apply to children, who are therefore, methodologically, irrational dependants, and thus are left out of account in law as well as scientific analysis.

Unfortunately, such an approach cannot account for the impact that infants, toddlers, children, tweens, teens and youth may have on the dynamics of *group* formation and survival; indeed, as the coming generation, they *are* the generative force for future survival. As Konner remarks: 'Some "evil" tendencies – idleness, fantasy, risk taking, sexuality, selfishness and violence – are vital evolutionary adaptations' (2010: 669). Furthermore, children sustain and control an 'independent' *child culture* that Konner finds to be universal among humans but unknown among animals: 'games, jokes, superstitions, chants, songs and ditties, spoken formulas, symbolic hand-signals, and homemade toys . . . riddles, jeers, curses, oaths, pranks, tricks, and pacts' (2010: 662). By these means – which include 'exercises of power through humiliation' (bullying) – children 'enculturate' themselves.

Thus, even though they should not be left out of analytic account, youngsters are not exactly the same as everyone else in a given 'we'-group. Importantly, in relation to general economic activity, they are defined by practices of *consumption* and *communication* rather than *production* and *purpose*. They don't generally make the kind of decisions that are typically analysed in economics; nor do many of them (child actors and models aside) make the performances, productions, designs and networks that are typically analysed in cultural and media studies, although they do make some of the most devoted fans and audiences. As a result, those who study both decisions (economy) and productions (culture) simply omit children and young people from their frameworks of analysis, except as consumers. But in this context 'consumption' doesn't mean what it might do in relation to a packet of crisps: 'consumption' is not the 'end-use' of a product. Instead, cultural and media consumption by children and teens is the opening move in a turn-taking sequence; consumption here is *productive* – of group identity, individual identity and communicative sociality.

Observers are familiar enough with the passionate attachment to group identities that certain schools foster in relation to sports, debating, and other competitive activities that bond 'we'-groups, and exclude 'they'-groups. It is also well known that these activities model 'adult' allegiances such as patriotism and bonding in the workplace (the 'old school tie'; the 'playing fields of Eton', etc.); and that quite a few such activities, especially sport, survive into adulthood as lifelong markers of distinction. But the obvious conclusion has not been followed through – that childishness and tribalism are *productive* and creative; not just facing the future in 'we'-groups, but actively making 'we'-groups for the *purpose* of facing the future.

'Tribal' allegiance to sport, ceremony and competition may be mercilessly critiqued as 'arrested development' (where transition from the childish to the rational state is not effected successfully), as for example in Thorstein Veblen's wonderfully acerbic *The Higher Learning in America* (1918). But it is clear that 'adult' concerns penetrate childish or youthful subcultures, crazes and loyalties; and that 'childish' activities and affinities persist for a lifetime, colouring nations as much as persons. A common feature is 'tribalism', or devoted loyalty to a 'we'-group with attendant rituals, secret language, devotion to the egalitarian peer group (celebrated in Hollywood 'buddy movies' and Australian 'mateship') and aggression to outsiders (however defined – by gender, race, nation, age, region or competitor status). One might also note that as far as individuals go, there's a downside to arrested development – narcissism, 'mean girl' cliques, lack of empathy for difference and pride in ignorance.[15] The point here is that such 'tribalism', 'childishness', 'youth culture', 'arrested development' and its attendant playful inventiveness and crazes are all telling us something: children, not rational individuals, *invent* the future; and they do it with greater devotion to 'groupishness' than to self-interest.

As they play with each other via digital devices and online games, children may also be making up and shaping the kind of polity, and thus the kind of citizenship, we will experience in future (Hartley 2012: ch. 6). Common sense tells us that adult citizens – those who vote and pay taxes – are the makers and shapers of modern democracy, using some version of methodological individualism and rational choice to do it. However, we contend, on the contrary, that children exert a formally unnoticed but growing influence as they engage with one another and the wider society, both socially and online. Children are, by definition, not citizens . . . and yet they must *become* citizens if the reproduction of the system is to continue. Thus, the actual process of citizenship-formation is 'carried' by children who – individually, collectively and differentially – *produce* citizenship in their actions, forms of association, and thence identities. It follows that children are, at one and the same time, the least important component of institutionalized citizenship, since they remain non-citizens and non-voters; and its most important subjects, since they creatively undertake the practice of citizenship formation for the future. They are the inventors of new languages, including in-group slang, argot or subcultural style, new group dynamics, and new uses for available technological affordances and components. With the growth in digital media and communication, children are in fact becoming prime agents of *change* for citizenship, in that their unconsidered actions, preferences and unselfconscious associations may create the models for new modes of do-it-yourself (DIY) citizenship.

There's a tacit or unwitting recognition of the potential creative energy of youthful inventiveness, which can be discerned in the attempt by adult agencies to take it over. On the one hand, cultural production is infantilized in mainstream popular culture, where the ideal demographic seems to be the peripubescent consumer, whose predilections crowd out other audience segments. Youthful day-dreaming and time-wasting are commodified into narrative or play as

---

[15] For instance the statement attributed to the United States' first elected woman governor, Miriam 'Ma' Ferguson of Texas, who was said to have opposed bilingualism in schools in the 1920s with the (probably apocryphal) quip: 'If English was good enough for Jesus Christ, it ought to be good enough for the children of Texas'. *Wikipedia*: Miriam A. Ferguson.

action and rom-com (boy meets girl) in cinema, in-group competition in reality TV and first-person shooters. Young people are the prize in this game. But on the other hand, youthfulness is increasingly treated as a *disorder*, psychological or social. Individual youthful behaviour is pathologized, resulting in the clinical surveillance and mass medication of children with 'too much' energy and inventiveness (ADHD; Ritalin). Instead, children are trained to present as docile but aspirational (like adults) by puberty; submissive to biopolitical self-administrative processes and achievements. Groups of young people exercising their right of assembly are routinely criminalized as 'they'-groups, gangs and mobs, assumed to be high on drink or drugs or novel ideas, or as irrational fans in need of correction. If in addition to their age they display subcultural, migrant, colour or class/gender indicators, or if they are boisterous, unruly or unrespectable, apparently they pose a moral risk to the control culture (Skeggs 2005). Local media collaborate with law enforcement agencies to produce narratives of threat to 'our' community by 'they' identities that may be made up of our own children. The governing discourses are about 'protection and correction', and the boundary of the social, which can be discerned simply by observing young people's transgression of it. There are few countervailing discursive forays (except in fantasy fiction) into the role of children and young people as *creators* of the social, extending its boundaries or adapting to change. This kind of boundary-policing is demic, of course, making sure that the future is cut off from the present, but in the meantime it sustains a growing surveillance and security industry that impinges mainly on adult culture and society as a conservative force. Dick Hebdige, pioneer of 'subcultural' studies, spells out the lesson for culture generally:

> Instead of the idea that human culture is a negotiated situation, an intersubjective negotiation of difference, it's as if there's some bureau dictating that this is the metabolism that the world must have. Everybody's got to be happy so you get this dream about homogenizing the human race, to get rid of turbulent character traits and metabolisms which used to produce art and conflict and happiness. (interview in Dugdale 2004)

Playful, childish, mischievous DIY-citizenship, like other experimental forms such as art and entrepreneurship, is 'turbulent', potentially offensive, dangerous or risky, especially to established rules and rights. But that is its strength, to provide the 'turbulent character traits' associated with 'art and conflict', and thus to provoke not offence but renewal. It is arguably more democratic, certainly more productive, than formal versions of citizenship, because it is participatory, future-facing, peer-to-peer and generated within self-organizing 'bottom-up' networks. Thus, control mechanisms that seek to 'homogenize the human race' through bland cultural products and pacified groups may be doing it serious damage, leading to another, much less productive kind of wastefulness: a waste of future openness and potential.

The extension of 'new' digital online media into the space and time of childhood, including computer-based social networks, mobile devices and globally dispersed entertainment formats, has given children's actions and choices *as a group* far more significance and influence than scholarship has hitherto recognized. For example, children's online actions are already being closely tracked by business to determine their preferences in order to satisfy their demands for various products – and thus influence the course of industry. But these preferences extend more widely than commerce, to the kind of society and association children prefer, which governments and others are starting to pick up on. In the light of this, it is of some concern that some latter-day 'child savers' are trying to restrict and exclude children's access to and participation in the online world. The future is the invention of those who are going to live in it. What's new in these developments is not that they are new, but that so much of this informal social learning from peers and group formation among child-aged communities is now conducted online, and is therefore open to investigation – and surveillance.

9

Extinction

Resilience and Ossification

And what if she had seen those glories fade,
  Those titles vanish, and that strength decay, –
Yet shall some tribute of regret be paid
  When her long life hath reach'd its final day:
Men are we, and must grieve when even the shade
  Of that which once was great has pass'd away.
                    William Wordsworth, 'On the Extinction of the Venetian Republic'[1]

Culture is 'we'-group knowledge. Discussion of groups in the context of cultural studies or sociocultural anthropology is usually the underpinning for analysis of *social identity*, wherein social identity = the groups you self-identify with (Tajfel 1974), which then becomes *social constructivist* (an individual = the social groups they are made of). But that is not our angle here. Instead we want to focus on the way culture exists as group knowledge, rather than as a form of group identity. An individual can't have culture. Only a group can have culture, although an individual can obviously be part of a group, or many groups; culture is a property of the group, not of the individual. This is in the same sense as Luhmann's (1991) claim that an individual does not communicate, 'only communication communicates'.

Culture makes groups and groups make knowledge. Cultural dynamics therefore are changes in groups and changes in knowledge. This is a very different abstract conception to the standard evolutionary model of culture and cultural dynamics, in which culture exists in each mind and replicates through *social learning*, such that cultural dynamics are explained through differential social

---

[1] Palgrave's *Golden Treasury* (1875: 331): www.gasl.org/refbib/Golden_Treasury.pdf.

learning[2] (Cavalli-Sforza and Feldman 1981; Boyd and Richerson 1985, 2009; Mesoudi 2011). Note that 'social' here refers to the target of learning (someone else who is in some way socially connected) in contrast to *individual learning*, where the agent acquires knowledge by figuring it out themselves, for instance, through experimentation. Social learning is the acquisition of knowledge through the mechanism of recognizing that someone else already has that knowledge, and that it can be acquired by copying. The 'social' in social learning is not social as in group interactions, but social as a placeholder for some target 'other' from whom an individual can learn. There are individual and social referents, but no meaningful groups in this approach. It is usually implicit that the target is from within a 'we'-group, not from an outside 'they'-group. Copying does not fully capture what goes on in this manner of cultural dynamics because it misses this aspect of what we might recognize as a form of *gerrymandering*: redefining the boundary of the 'we' to include a new idea.

From the cultural science perspective, the growth of knowledge – and therefore the dynamics of culture, as group knowledge – occurs as 'they'-knowledge is adopted into 'we'-knowledge. This boundary-crossing process occurs at the level of groups not individuals, and is largely about communication groups – where a group is the effective range of communication over the full gamut of choices over 'information, utterance and understanding' (Luhmann 1991: 254) – and the re-formation of group boundaries, rather than being about differential imitation (Luhmann 2013). The social learning model of cultural dynamics therefore leads to some elementary misclassifications. A key one is the phenomenon of cultural extinction.

Cultural extinction is the risk or actuality of complete loss of a culture, which in anthropology is understood as a failure of copying or social learning to replicate a culture. This, in turn, is the model for interventions to replicate a culture artificially, in order to protect it from extinction. But the cultural science model offers a different perspective on cultural extinction by viewing it through the lens of externalism, demic concentration, meaningfulness and waste. In this view, the proximate cause of extinction is not failure of social learning and replication, but a consequence of ossification that comes from the very act of protecting culture and constraining its use as knowledge.

---

[2]   *Social learning* (Hoppitt and Laland 2013) is a process that occurs through various individual-to-individual mechanisms, including vertical (parent to child) and horizontal (peer-to-peer) transfer. Education and learning theory emphasizes the social context of learning and a hierarchical flow (adults teach children). The evolutionary model is bottom-up, as learners (including children) seek targets (see Chapter 8).

This can be observed in the rise and fall of cities, a prime demic group in which culture is carried. Cities grow when they are open to knowledge, and they fall when they overly protect their knowledge or culture. Sometimes this is being closed to people or trade, more generally it is being closed to new ideas; not necessarily from hermetic enclosure, but from the over-protection of existing ways of doing things, often manifest in proliferation of regulation and sanctioned rent-seeking (Olson 1982).

Interestingly, cultural growth by which 'they'-knowledge is transformed into 'we'-knowledge can indeed look like extinction, because of the seeming disappearance of meaningful identity with a cultural knowledge set, along with the weakening of associated resources and institutions following political overthrow, sociocultural swamping, invasion, war, conquest or imperialism. But from the cultural science perspective, what may be happening is closer to what economists call *unbundling*, where the cultural knowledge content is transformed by reintegration into a different group. This is not creation but *regrouping* of knowledge, requiring that ideas be abstracted for re-use. This, to a first approximation, is our model of cultural dynamics: culture grows as ideas are integrated into the 'we'-group, which is to say as the 'we'-group expands from the perspective of knowledge. Extinction is what happens when ideas are unable to be re-integrated, which can have multiple causes, including rigidity that is induced by protection. Extinction is not a failure to replicate, but rather a failure to re-integrate.

A prosocial groupish animal, honed by conflict and extinction

The foundations of our argument rest upon a model of the human being as a pro-social groupish animal. Specifically, humans, like other animals, have suites of evolved cognitive and behavioural responses, commonly known as *instincts* (Tooby and Cosmides 1992). For evolutionary cultural anthropologists, the capacity for social learning is the instinct that defines human nature (Mesoudi and O'Brien 2008; see also Darwin 1871), an observation that naturalizes culture. Indeed, as Pierre van den Berghe (1990: 428) explains: 'culture is the unique human way of adapting, but culture, too, evolved biologically'.

One example of such instincts is *pro-social preference*, or the tendency of humans to trust and cooperate with non-kin (Bowles and Gintis 2011; Morgan et al. 2011). Pro-social preferences underpin social learning, which is generally superior to individual learning. Interestingly, humans have these pro-social preferences because of *group selection* (Henrich 2004) in consequence of *group conflict*. Bowles and Gintis (2011: 17) explain that:

> The emergence, proliferation and biological or cultural extinction of collections of individuals such as foraging bands, ethno-linguistic units, and nations, and the consequent evolutionary success and failure of distinct group level institutions is an essential, sometimes preeminent influence on human evolutionary processes. The maintenance of group boundaries (through hostility toward outsiders, for example) and lethal conflict among groups are essential aspects of this process.

This gave rise to a complex evolved relationship between instinctual paro-chialism and instinctual altruism. (Parochialism = hostile to out-groups; altruism = preference for pro-social behaviours.) Furthermore, in the ancestral environment:

> Most altruists were parochial and most parochials were altruists, most of the parochial altruists were in groups with other parochial altruists, and ancestors lived in environments in which competition for resources favoured groups with significant numbers of parochial altruists willing to engage in hostile conflict with outsiders on behalf of their fellow group members. (Bowles and Gintis 2011: 134, 146)

Human nature is both altruistic (pro-social) and parochial (adversarially groupish). We are highly cooperative within a social group, and we are highly social within a cooperative group.[3] But we can be vicious to out-groups. This was demonstrated in a series of disturbing experiments by social psychologist Henri Tajfel (1970), who developed the concept of the minimal group paradigm as the point at which discrimination (or demic effectiveness, in our language) emerges. The human animal is both social and cooperative, but targeted to those within our deme. In consequence, in human evolutionary history, the primary punishment mechanism is ejection from a group, or *ostracism*, which in the Pleistocene age would be often fatal.[4]

Translated to knowledge, this groupishness explains the *'universal-adversarialism'* we noted in Chapter 3 and elsewhere: within a 'we'-group all

---

[3] Frijters and Foster (2013) argue that there are only five archetypal groups: reciprocal groups (large and small), hierarchical groups (large and small) and networks.

[4] In experimental laboratory studies artificially constructed so that being ostracized from a group has a higher pay-off than being included in a group, subjects that received the higher material pay-off still reported significant negative subjective well-being (van Beest and Williams 2006).

knowledge is knowable and universally accessible; but it is opposed to the knowledge of 'they'-groups. In social science, groups tend to be defined by function and interests (class in sociology, or interest group, coalitions or organizations in economics). In cultural science a group is defined by its span of integrative knowledge: groups can be cities, bands, nations or languages. It is 'we'-knowledge that is identified with a deme, as distinct from individual or abstract knowledge that does not have specific demic origin. In this view, it is not social learning (observation, imitation, replication) that is the central part of inquiry into evolutionary cultural dynamics, but rather the process of bringing knowledge within a deme (*despite* adversarial hostility to outsider-knowledge).

This is a shift in the standard logic for analysis of groups, which is functional or goal directed. A group has a common interest or goal and comes together in order to achieve that. Groups are by definition cooperative in pursuit of that goal, even when this cooperation is achieved through voluntary submission to an organization. But the line of argument that we make here seeks to shift attention to the communicative aspect of a group as a self-communicating system, rather than the cooperative aspect per se.

Cultural science focuses on the boundaries of groups and the processes by which ideas and knowledge move across those boundaries, or fail to. Consider two cases: first, culture 'at risk' that seeks protection; and second, cities and how they grow, thrive and collapse. In both cases, cultural dynamics are illuminated by the way in which groups work as self-communicating demic systems. We explain why ossification precedes extinction, and how cultural resilience arises from expanded 'we'-group boundaries.

How to protect valuable things

The UNESCO Intangible Cultural Heritage List of Humanity contains 298 'elements' – including the performance of the Armenian epic of 'Daredevils of Sassoun', 'Baul Songs' from Bangladesh, the practice of Falconry, the oral and graphic expressions of the Aajapi from Brazil, and Chinese shadow puppetry.[5] UNESCO's list is gathered, in their words, as 'a celebration of proclaimed cultural masterpieces'. But really it is a watch-list, as these 'cultural elements' are understood to be the analogue of endangered species 'at risk' of cultural extinction.

---

[5] http://www.unesco.org/culture/ich/index.php?pg=00011.

The list is manifestly a high-level contribution to cataloguing and indexing the product of human creativity and the finest artefacts of human culture. Ascension to this list marks the first stage in a process that culminates in global protection of the 'element'. This manner of official recognition and beatification has accelerated since the mid-twentieth century. It is widely regarded as a triumph of the bureaucratic arts, but its practical consequences are not always as intended. Cultural objects that achieve elevated status and protection tend to ossify beyond the point of working knowledge, becoming purely ceremonial; once judged to be 'at risk', they're subjected to interventions to protect them from extinction, but this process bleeds them of lively interaction with the rest of culture, society and economy, wrapping them in layers of protection, thereby producing only knowledge *about* them (tourism, etc.).

The general problem here is how to protect anything of value – natural, material or cultural – that is judged to be at risk of escalating harm attributed to some large-scale 'inevitable' process – for instance imperialism, globalization or environmental change. Protection is achieved through collective action to ameliorate the harm. Various forms of cultural 'loss' are subject to this type of concern, including that resulting from unsuccessful competition with stronger or dominating cultural forms. The first step (and human instinct) in protecting something valuable and vulnerable is to shield it. This typically results in new governance rules that delimit ownership, extend protective custody, and constrain use. If strong enough, these rules will shield the 'at risk' culture, protecting it from external depredations by limiting its unconstrained interaction. The second step is to artificially sustain it by subsidizing production and performance, say, or creating artificial demand. In this way 'at risk' culture is protected by regulation and/or transferal to public custodianship. We 'raise awareness' that a particular cultural element is now 'protected'. We regulate its use; buffer it against outside forces. But this solution often leads to an ossified 'ceremonial' culture that, while preserved and protected, no longer thrives.

How then can an endangered culture be protected without killing it? Many countries proceed through bureaucratic efforts (e.g. cultural ministries). France, for example, has government organizations to protect its language, along with its media and film industry, all of which are considered at risk of the depredations of globalization and market capitalism. In Australia, concern to protect Australia's indigenous visual arts industry has seen the growth of arts administration and bureaucratization.

To protect valuable things, economists tend towards property rights as a solution. Environmental resources subject to collective action dilemmas are a standard example. Economists argue that protection works best when it gets the incentives right, which begins with clear ownership to internalize the externalities associated with risk of loss. The best way to protect something is to ensure there is a market for it. But when this valuable thing is living culture, that can be an inefficiently indirect approach, requiring extensive creation of intellectual property that is difficult and costly to define and enforce. The cultural science perspective hews neither to the bureaucratic instinct to protect at-risk culture, nor to the economist's instinct to property rights, assuming culture to be discrete, robust and marketable. We think the way to approach this problem is to treat it not as one of cultural continuity (or maintained rates of cultural replication) but rather as a problem of *what happens when two groups meet*.

In the general language of game theory, this triggers the decision to *cooperate* or *defect* (Bowles and Gintis 2011). Further, it is usually abstracted to the simpler problem of what happens when two *agents* meet. Agents play strategies: either cooperating (trading, partnering), or defecting (fighting, stealing). But while individual agents may stand in for groups (such as tribes, organizations, nations), two groups meeting invokes a somewhat different context that additionally includes the significance of a boundary between them: a 'we' and a 'they' – and also a sense of differing knowledge and culture on either side of that boundary (*viz.* not only differing resources). When two groups meet there will be a border, and across this border resources will move from one group to the other (Malvoisine, war, conquest) or different resources may move from each group (trade, exchange).

But when two groups meet there are further possibilities that are not present when two individuals meet. People, ideas, knowledge, culture and language may also move across these borders, and not necessarily in the same direction and for the same reasons as the movement of resources. Second, the border itself may shift, changing the definition of a group, possibly without resources shifting. In this scenario, social or economic conquest, which would be normally understood as a species of defection, may actually be a form of cultural cooperation. What looks like extinction may actually be boundary-shifting integration.

What is cultural extinction?

Extinction – meaning to have no living members – is etymologically related to *extinguish*, to 'quench, wipe out, obliterate'. As a metaphor in evolutionary theory, extinction was applied to the end of a biological species (a *taxon*). What death is to an individual, extinction is to a species. Building on that metaphor, the concept extends to cultural theory: to speak of cultural evolution is also to speak of the prospect or risk of cultural extinction.

Extinction is the great stylized-fact of evolution. Something like 99.9 per cent of all species that have ever lived are now extinct. The average species 'lifetime' is 10 million years; beginning with speciation, ending with extinction. Most extinction occurs gradually as the population of a species falls below a critical reproductive threshold, usually well before the last individual of the species dies. Causes vary, but extinction is usually in consequence of *niche competition* coupled with inability to adapt to a changed habitat. However, it can also be due to the effects of predation, pathogens or some external shock. Very rarely, the external shock is sufficiently large to cause mass extinctions – also known as an 'extinction event'. In general, extinctions follow a power-law distribution (Ormerod 2005).

The species analogy to individual death suggests the manifest tragedy of extinction (such that the slogan 'extinction is forever' is now a marketing cliché) and therefore conditions our thinking in terms of risk of permanent loss. This sentiment carries from the natural to the cultural realm, to arrive at the value judgement that cultural extinction is also forever, and that this is tragic. But it is worth considering why 'evolution itself', so to say, doesn't seem to think this way, given her enormous (and seemingly wasteful) propensity to kill off species. Modern evolutionary thinking is built about the gene-centric view (Dawkins 1976) and the extinction of a species is the end of some particular combinations of genes, but many of these genes will also be in other species, possibly the very ones that outcompeted the now extinct species. The point is that evolution doesn't care about species. Evolution cares about genes. A species, in other words, is a set of 'we' genes, as distinct from all the other 'they' genes.

A similar understanding should extend to culture. We worry about cultural extinction – and extinction events, with globalization the prime contemporary risk factor. But we often fail to notice that elements of culture may continue, even if the particular aggregate pattern and its associated carriers do not. For instance, is Classical Greek culture extinct? Certainly yes if we refer to the particular constellation of practices and behaviours and technologies as carried by a particular group: it is completely extinct. But it is also apparent that many of its elements are extant in numerous cultural practices and mores. Indeed, given the population growth between 500 BCE and now, and the extent to which these elements enter into Western culture (in art, politics, philosophy, even sport), then there may be more Classical Greek culture now than there was in Classical

Greece, a culture that is now extinct. Historian William Durant (1939) wrote: 'excepting machinery, there is hardly anything secular in [Western] culture that does not come from Greece'. A Eurocentric overstatement, no doubt; but one that makes our point. In order to talk meaningfully about cultural extinction we need to talk carefully about groups and the many forms of differential replication and selection that shape cultural evolution.

The standard analytical view of cultural dynamics is as a differential information replication process, which is the metaphor borrowed from biological/gene-centric evolution, in which a unit of culture is copied from one 'carrier' to the next, and in which cultural extinction is a large-scale failure of this replication process. From the cultural science perspective, however, cultural dynamics is about the integration of knowledge into a group (the externalized demic generation of knowledge), which includes the prospect of bringing knowledge across a boundary, from 'they-knowledge' to 'we-knowledge'. This changes or reconstructs its meaning (that is, knowledge is *demically situated*).

This change in meaning can appear as loss and even extinction because the meaning of the knowledge has shifted from its previous demic associations and contexts. But this is also how knowledge is renewed as culture, which enables it to be carried by a group. Meaning changes when knowledge is integrated from a 'they'-group to a 'we'-group. This can look like extinction from the out-group perspective, while at the same time appearing as novelty or discovery from the in-group perspective. Cultural extinction is thus *demically relativistic*. What looks like cultural extinction from one reference point can simultaneously be seen as a cultural explosion from another.

What then is cultural extinction? It is a loss of meaningfulness of demic knowledge, not simply a failure to replicate. For Yuri Lotman (1990, 2005), extinction in culture is different from extinction in nature because cultural knowledge can be stored and then rediscovered, re-animated, for example, when Classical Greek culture was rediscovered in the Renaissance. But observe how this classic account of culture lost and found actually refers to two modes: (1) to a textual loss of information, the sign system – the particular manuscripts and the wherewithal to translate them; and (2) to the semantic meaning of these texts and the connection into a system of other concepts in the semiosphere. Lotman (2005: 212) explains:

> The boundary has another function in the semiosphere: it is the area of accelerated semiotic processes, which always flow more actively on the periphery of cultural environments, seeking to affix them to the core structures, with a

view to displacing them. For example, the history of ancient Rome illustrates well a more general conformity to natural laws: a cultural area, growing rapidly, incorporates into its orbit external collectives (structures) and transforms them into its own periphery. This stimulates strong cultural semiotic and economic growth of the periphery, which translates its semiotic structures through to the centre, setting cultural precedents and, in the long run, literally conquers the cultural sphere of the centre.

For Lotman (1990) new ideas are bought into existence only at the boundary of groups that are partially overlapping semiotic systems of language, texts, or cultures. He continues (Lotman 2005: 212):

> Antiquity constructs its 'barbarians', and it is irrelevant that these barbarians, firstly, might possess a significantly more ancient culture, or secondly, that they might form a cultural gamut ranging from the high civilisations of antiquity to tribes in hugely primitive stages of development. Nevertheless, antique civilisation may only regard itself as culturally intact through the construction of this allegedly unitary barbarian world, the main sign of which was the lack of a common language with the culture of antique civilisation. External structures, distributed on that side of the semiotic boundary, are presumed to be non-structures.

We can build on Lotman's insights into the evolutionary dynamics of culture arising from the clashes of semiotic systems to arrive at a new understanding of socio-political and economic forms of conquest and their effect on culture.

Conquest as cooperation

Since the end of the Pleistocene age 15,000 years ago, an era known as the Holocene, a central shaping force on cultural dynamics has been the role of *conquest* – of clashes of groups and civilizations, where one takes over and absorbs or destroys another. As we have documented in previous chapters, these clashes accelerated with the rise of the state following the development of weapons of mass destruction (metals and horses), that is, the Bronze Age (Gintis 2012). They are usually understood to be equivalent to war, or hostile intent in competition for territory and resources. But a cultural science approach to cultural dynamics suggests that such conquest – nominally about the capture and control of territory and resources – can also be understood as a deeper form of cooperation when we focus on what is happening to knowledge and culture.

Consider two models of cultural dynamics: (1) individual interactions, where one person (carrier) acquires cultural information from another; or (2) as group interactions, meaning that one culture is pitting itself against another. In the first instance, the prime mechanism is *social learning*. In the second, a prime mechanism is *conquest* and *war* (another is trade). With individual inheritance, cultural dynamics are predominantly differential replication. This proceeds through localized conformity and social learning via a number of parallel mechanisms: punishment of deviance; positive pay-off externality; conformity preferences; and communication. There are no groups or conquest in this story, just differential replication, or differential individual adoption of cultural information.

In an alternative (and more imperialistic) story, knowledge is contained in groups. This demic knowledge – this culture – affords these groups capabilities, and these groups periodically test each other to determine the effectiveness of their knowledge. The winner will often obtain some of the resources of the defeated (known as 'geras' in Homeric Greece, 'spoils of war' were the main currency of personal honour). They will also tend to impose their culture/knowledge. In short term this can be and usually is destructive; think of the aftermath of any civil war. Yet over longer periods, such conquest, as Thomas Sowell (1998) has documented, can benefit the conquered:

> Striking changes in productivity among peoples can often be traced to transfers of cultural capital from others – from the English to the Scots, from Western Europeans to Eastern Europeans, from China to Japan in an earlier era, or from the Islamic world to Europe in medieval times. Such transfers do not represent mutually cancelling gains and losses, for knowledge is not diminished at its source when it spreads to others.

We follow this apparently Whiggish but more accurately Lotmanian line, but seek to make a different point. Groups clash at *boundaries*, and resources then move from conquered to conqueror. But what happens to *culture* is often more complex, and rarely as simple as an imposition of the ways and institutions of the victors, as Sowell implies, indicating that conquest necessarily implies a form of cultural extinction, even if this leads to subsequent cultural improvement or benefit. This 'boundary-crossing' is not always an act of war, but can be pre-emptively invited or even sought by a group that may already be aware of the perceived weaknesses of its own culture or the relative strengths of others. Group expansion can be shaped by sympathy or empathy, what Adam Smith (1759) called 'moral sentiments'. Nationalism, group pride and identity are not always positively valued, and a self-aware negative assessment can be a powerful force for cultural change. Conversely, a proud identity can be a powerful inhibitor of change or adaptation.

To understand conquest as a model of cultural evolution we need to focus on what occurs at these boundaries, whether as hostilities or as a kind of surrender. The standard model is that resources flow to the victors (these 'spoils' are the pay-off, as it were, to successful conquest) and that the conquered will be forced to adopt the rules and culture of the victors (this is submission, or the cost of losing). Following successful conquest, resources and culture therefore move in opposite directions. But in the cultural science model of conquest, what happens is a redrawing of the boundaries of 'we'-group and 'they'-group. Institutional rules may be imposed – to come under a new protectorate, say – but what happens in a redrawing of such boundaries is that knowledge that used to belong to one group is now integrated into a larger 'we'-group. In the process meaning is changed, shifted to new referents, and elaborated. This is conquest as cooperation, increasing complexity in a process that can be easily observed in technologies and languages, and in trade. In this model, culture is an evolved communicative group. Cultural dynamics are the outcome of the interactions between groups as communication systems, resulting in in-group or 'we'-group expansion of those communication systems as new elements are absorbed into the deme with a redefined boundary. The outsider is transformed into the insider through a cultural integration process. As a self-communicative group, culture is an autopoietic system (Luhmann 2013) requiring that the knowledge within the boundary must be able to reproduce itself.

Cultural extinction is not the result of population-scale failure to achieve individual replication. Nor is it the result of conquest per se. Cultural extinction occurs when a group no longer works as an autopoietic communicative system. This is not a failure to replicate; it is a failure to self-communicate (or, in Lotman's terms, a failure of *auto-communication* – self-description, reflexivity and recursiveness). This, in turn, can be understood as a process of ossification. In other words, it is ossification (from within) that causes extinction, not conquest (from without).

Rules and ossification

In cultural science, the question of why something stops growing is closely related to the question of how it stops communicating. What happens is that it ossifies ('ossify' means for a living tissue turning to bone, hence metaphorically for something flexible to become rigid), which is a process that occurs as rules proliferate throughout a system, gradually freezing the system as the proliferation of rules inhibits change and adaptation. Such rules make it easier to veto or block new information rather than to enable it. A system becomes automated, and loses the ability to communicate organically with itself. Growth stops when communication closes down, and communication closes down – ossifies – when rules proliferate to protect the system from outsiders (or to create rents, in economic terminology).

For example, the accretion of class structure, constraining mobility, stifles adaptation in a social system. The accretion of regulation, by constraining entrepreneurship, stifles innovation in an economic system. Mobility and entrepreneurship are both mechanisms by which a social or economic system communicates with itself. A further example: a business or organization can ossify. An organization is a structure of knowledge and ways of doing things that, once entrepreneurially configured, will tend quickly to bureaucratic managerial rules. The logic of this is informational efficiency, where rules stand in for discretion and potentially carry a substantial amount of knowledge and even wisdom – for example, the operating manual of a franchise business required to run a standardized operation with high throughput of staff. The same rules that create informational and decision efficiency within the organization also protect the organization from the effects of outside information and knowledge. Indeed, that is precisely their intention, to constrain outside communication unless passed through specific protocols. But the trade-off is that an organization can ossify and fail to adapt to changed local circumstances. Universities are another clear example of the proliferation of rules as a mechanism designed to increase efficiency and professionalize operations, but which has the effect, intended or not, of ossifying adaption by shutting off many lines of communication with outside knowledge. Another example: copyright, which is a legal right expressly intended to prohibit subsequent use (as the mechanism by which to generate a rent). It has the effect of ossifying the creative re-use of ideas by tying it up in rules (known as licencing agreements) (Hargreaves 2011).

Ossification caused by rule-proliferation is the condition of cultural collapse. It is, indeed, what makes a group conquerable. But this also explains why it is not the same as a direct test of culture and why what matters in conquest, at least in the long term, is the removal of the ossified rules that had grown up and weakened the culture by reducing its ability to function as a communication system. This process can be observed in nation-states. Political economist Mancur Olson (1982) explained how market democracies tend to accumulate rent-seeking rules at points where information asymmetries enable small, organized groups (e.g. industry lobbyists) to defeat large disorganized groups (e.g. citizens). The economic order becomes ossified, leading to periodic collapse. It can no longer effectively self-communicate, which means that entrepreneurial ideas cannot integrate into and regenerate 'we'-groups. Such protecting rules become the agents of economic extinction.

For a knowledge-based group to remain resilient and avoid collapse, it needs to remain open and capable of autopoiesis as a communication system. Communication (not information) is moved closer to the centre of cultural evolutionary theory. As a model of extinction, when a system can no longer resolve communication, it then begins to ossify as a semantically productive system. This can be observed in the life and death of cities (in the language of Jane Jacobs). Cities are a further form of 'we'-group, where ideas from elsewhere can be integrated within the boundary of a knowledge system, enabling these ideas to be reused and repurposed, a demic crucible where meaning evolves at the intersecting and contested boundaries of multivalent demes.

Great cities as generators of semiosis

Joel Kotkin (2005) quotes Descartes, writing about seventeenth-century Amsterdam, who said that a great city should be 'an inventory of the possible'. Our own team has developed a new *Creative City Index* (Hartley et al. 2012), which required us to identify the causes of city greatness and to proxy these factors. The central insight from that study is a new way of understanding the role of culture in shaping why some cities are *creative* global cities and others are not. The answer, in short, is the extent to which a city is *semiotically productive*.

This is not how we normally understand city greatness, which conventionally turns on measures of imperial or economic power (Hall 1998), or more recently on measures of institutional quality and human capital (Florida 2002; Glaeser 2011). Cities are great to the extent that they are centres of productive valuable resources. These arguments shade into the knowledge-based accounts of externalities, spill-overs and technology clusters in which a city is a mechanism for bringing knowledge into a group to create a 'sustainable competitive advantage' (Saxenian 1994; Porter 1990). 'Creative city' writers such as Charles Landry and Richard Florida emphasize the strategic need to develop *attractors* for these valuable globally mobile factors, and of course we agree with that overarching proposition: cities must compete.

But the cultural science perspective on cities differs in the detail of what composes the creative potential advantage. For instance, youth culture, experimental space and 'novelty-bundling' occasions (festivals, fairs, markets, Potts 2012) where people can mix indiscriminately, and in stylistic competition, have been under-emphasized in much of the extant literature on global cities, where five-star hotels, museums and aerospace industries have been somewhat over-emphasized. Culture is not an attractor for cities in the cultural science view, but rather a semiotically productive resource that enables a city to be an evolving, self-organizing and intensely productive mechanism for dealing with problems of complexity. Cities begin to die when that process is stopped by an accumulation of rules and regulations that, however well intended or politically mandated, stifle creative expression and chill generative semiotic productivity. Cities die in the same way that a culture goes extinct. It ossifies in its rules, driven by an urge to protect what is deemed important and valuable; it closes down experimentation, the semiosphere stops expanding and interacting with others and may begin to collapse. At this point a city as a collection of buildings and people may continue, but no longer as a productive city generative of new ideas, like the Venetian Republic – its 'extinction' was lamented by Wordsworth; but its 'stones' (Ruskin) remain for elegiac tourism.

City as deme

Globalization is a centuries-long process driving the increased interdependence of peoples' economic, cultural, social and political lives. It expands towards universalization of all 'we'-groups. Global cities are at the leading edge of this process. In cultural science, a city is a primary example of a deme. Global cities can seem alike in respect of per-capita measures of factors such as public spending on cultural amenities, or the number of hotels and restaurants. This is to be expected when people and capital are relatively free to move, and where economic and political institutions are broadly comparable. However, cities can register far larger differences at the level of consumer co-creation and especially digital creative 'microproductivity' (Hartley et al. 2012). The cultural science approach indicates that 'consumer' activities – the nonprofessional creative productivity of ordinary citizens in digitally linked social networks – should be regarded as part of the innovation system of complex cultural economies, and that the paradigm example of such systems is the contemporary world city. Cities are crucibles of everyday human inventiveness through the rapid experimentation, social-market feedback and social learning processes that drive creative endeavour. Some cities do this better than others, and those that do can become great creative cities.

What is a great city?

Not so long ago the answer to what makes a great city was a simple arithmetic of:

Population + Wealth + Empire = Power

New York, London and Paris were big trading cities, capitals of empire and rich: that made them powerful global cities without much further consideration of the specific causal components. There were certainly bigger cities (Mexico City or Jakarta, for example), but they were poorer, not global cities in the modern sense. Earlier European power-cities like Florence, Venice, Genoa, Lisbon, Amsterdam and Vienna would successively have figured on the list; as would capitals of non-Western empires, such as Istanbul. Going back further we would include Athens, Rome, Constantinople, Xi'an and Alexandria; further still, Damascus and Byblos. These were all great cities according to our arithmetic model. Others, equally great in their heyday, have been lost to history (Thebes, Babylon, Ur, Hattusa, Angkor), or have declined to local significance, for example, eleventh century Lübeck. City historians Peter Hall (1998) and Joel Kotkin (2005) emphasize a simple political-economic arithmetic of a locus of power combined with fertile plains and effective institutions. Great cities were capital cities, places where power resided. By the Middle Ages, cities became places where commerce resided too, as power began to shift to the secular world. Here global cities began to emerge about trading ports and network hubs (e.g. the Hanseatic League or the Cinque Ports), not about castles and palaces. Thus the world began to urbanize as people came to cities for reasons of enterprise, not for alms or rents. Cities became concentrations of people who choose to move there, away from rural domains, in pursuit of a better life to be made by themselves and with the others they might meet there.

For urban economist Ed Glaeser (2011), like urban sociologist Jane Jacobs (1961), great cities are grown, not planned, arising as the self-organized consequence of good institutions and effective market incentives, along with attractive amenities, a point emphasized by economic geographer Richard Florida (2002) in his 'creative class' model, which expresses the new economics of cities as emergent products or crucibles of new ideas and attractors for highly mobile smart and enterprising people. Globally mobile human capital, rather than given natural resources or accumulated physical capital or political power, is the touchstone of what makes a great city. In this view, cities are complexes of people, and the more entrepreneurial and capable those people are, the greater the city will be.

In the older definition, a great city was so because it was powerful and rich; it was the centre – indeed the storehouse – of past greatness. In the new definition, a great city is so because those that seek to become rich choose to move there. It is great because of the present and future potential it offers, not because of its past accumulations. This shift in focus from a romantic and mostly static view of great cities as a *capital consequence* of great empires, towards the modern globalized and entirely dynamic view of great cities as *zones of attraction to semiotic complexity,* shifts the analysis of city greatness. In the older model, a city's greatness was identical to whether the empire or monarch that supported the city was great. But as empires have crumbled since World War I, and nation-states have weakened as economic entities since globalization, cities have re-emerged (as they were prior to the 1700s) as the crucibles of commerce and the proper focus of development and growth economics.

The historical and theoretical literature on city growth[6] can be summarized in three overarching observations: (1) cities matter; (2) cities rise and fall; and (3) cities compete. Historians and economists have tended to see the competitive dynamics of cities as a natural evolutionary process and emphasize its dynamic benefits. They focus on the strategies and institutions that have enabled some cities to compete successfully. Urban sociologists and geographers, for the most part, focus on the problems and troubles caused by mobility-induced competition, emphasizing dislocation, social problems, destruction of community and the like. They look to city-level government intervention and planning to redress these problems.

A cultural science approach to great cities sides with the historians and economists. It favours policy that builds on openness and human capital, but for different reasons. Cultural science recognizes that dynamic evolutionary processes create disruptions and transition problems; including 'creative destruction' of city infrastructure, legacy cultural forms and their attendant occupations, but an entrepreneurial and strategic response is required.

A global city is not understood with respect to exogenous factors such as a given political power base, industrial base or even cultural base, but rather

---

[6] There is a substantial literature on the rise of global cities by historians, such as Peter Hall and Joel Kotkin, urban sociologists such as Saskia Sassen and Manuel Castells, and urban social geographers such as Paul Knox and Peter Taylor.

with respect to the endogenous question of what makes the people and other factors who reside there *more productive and effective* than they would be elsewhere (i.e. why do existing 'customers' stay?) and why do people and other factors who are not there want to migrate there (i.e. why do new 'customers' arrive?). Such an approach focuses on the creative productivity benefit that a city offers, and what makes a city great is its *semiotic productivity* – its ability to generate new signs and meaning, new information and references, to construct a new language of opportunities and representation. Planning and protection weaken semiotic productivity, which thrives on openness. Semiotic productivity is a measure constructed by relating the intensity of semiosis to population. Decay and extinction begins in cities with the weakening of the intensity of semiotic productivity, something we measured with the creative city index (Hartley et al. 2012).

The origin of creative cities

Creative cities of the past did not arise from pre-constructed plans, but emerged as self-organized solutions to problems of complexity. The difficulty of achieving creative status for planned cities is demonstrated in the relation between federal capitals and world cities in, for instance, the USA (Washington DC), Australia (Canberra), Brazil (Brasilia) or Nigeria (Abuja). In no case do these forgettable capitals outshine the organically nurtured world city of their respective countries – New York, Sydney, Rio or Lagos. Such ventures are nevertheless plentiful, from the proposed Charter City movement (Paul Romer), the new 'aerotropolizes' such as New Songdo City in Korea, to the many new cities currently underway in China.

Cities develop organically by continual infusion of new talent and ideas, and by the annealing and selection that produces. Great cities are the outcomes of clashes and conflict of systems of value and meaning as much as of harmony and community. These transplant with difficulty. Hong Kong and Singapore became global cities through the synergistic creative energy of expat immigrants (from Britain, the Mainland, and across SE and South Asia) and local citizens (themselves of different origins) faced with open spaces and of opportunity. Both cities grew from small beginnings in pursuit of trade and networks, but their dynamism and innovation came from individuals seeking to take advantage of these opportunities, not from being designed in advance. Great cities develop from within, but they do so by infusion from without. This is the seeming paradox of great city development, yet can be understood from a cultural science perspective. A great city is a *complex dissipative system*, as Jane Jacobs first described in 1961, turning energy into information, generating value and waste (Georgescu-Roegen 1971).

The standard objective measures of city greatness – of population, industry and market growth – are a necessary but not sufficient basis for assessing creative cities. To predict a creative city, we need also to know how it facilitates expression of new ideas and how well it can adapt to forms of meaning and value that point to the future not the past. How does a city perform as an experimental space for those of its own citizens whose lives centre about such experimentation? As a demographic cohort, these are both the young, who are seeking to start their productive lives and who have weak ties to existing arrangements, and also the entrepreneurs and immigrants who seek to reinvent or improve their lives. In a creative city, citizens must be open to change their values and preferences, to recast their assessments of meaning. Historically, the city is a coordinating mechanism for generalizing these values among otherwise diverse populations and heterogeneous institutions. To the extent that social learning happens – which is to say the extent that communication is semiotically generative – cities are productively creative.

Such cities where meaning and value are open to contestation (requiring freedom) and where social learning can occur (requiring order) will by definition be sites of turbulence and conflict. This is not necessarily in a warring sense but rather as spaces of experimentation, negotiation, dissonance and discovery (Popper 1963; Stark 2009). Such cities may or may not have great leaders, but they invariably have great citizens. Few could name the mayors of London or Paris through the eighteenth or nineteenth centuries, but many people know their great citizens through that time. Similarly, many people can name famous denizens of 'Silicon Valley' for example, but they would be hard-pressed to name the political leaders of that 'city', much less the real-estate developers of the garages, lofts and offices in which now-global corporations had their beginnings. Creative global cities are known by the achievements of their citizens, not their political leaders.

The *Financial Times*' architecture critic, Edwin Heathcote,[7] has made the case for what attracts people to cities – it isn't a 'liveability' index (routinely won by 'boring' cities) but 'complexity, friction and buzz'. He prefers 'places which are large and complex, where you don't know everyone and you don't always know what's going to happen next; places of opportunity but also of conflict, but where you can find safety in a crowd'. Heathcote asks, can *poor* people and *immigrants*

---

7   Heathcote, E. (2011) 'Livable v lovable'. *Financial Times* (UK), 6 May.

'improve themselves, reinvent themselves? Is there upward mobility?' He cites London and New York as 'magnets for immigrants precisely because they allow those kinds of new beginnings'. The significance of this point is to underscore the role of the creative citizen, and especially those from the margins, including the young, in recreating culture and the industries and economies that are built upon it (Hartley 2009a, 2012; Potts 2011). A creative city is invariably powered by the energy and entrepreneurial experimentation of the young, of the outsider, of those seeking to create new ideas and to challenge existing ideas. A creative city will invariably be complex and challenging, 'lovable' more than 'liveable', edgy rather than middle-of-the-road, often with a clash of cultures, demographics and ideas in its mix.

Complex culture

Cultural extinction happens when a group can no longer integrate new knowledge because rule ossification renders it unable to effectively communicate. Cultures die not because they fail to replicate and pass knowledge forward to a new generation of individuals, but because they can no longer integrate ideas from outside a 'we'-group or generate new ideas and connect them to others. Creative innovation and cultural extinction are usually understood to be opposites. Creative innovation causes cultural extinction by edging out existing culture. From this diagnosis, the proper way to protect culture at risk is to artificially replicate it: through compulsory education, or public action and expenditure, culture welfare and subsidy, or preferential treatment. Yet cultural science explains how we may have misunderstood this relation as not being oppositional at all, but complementary. The way to protect culture at risk is not to artificially isolate it so that it may replicate, for along that path lies ossification and extinction. The best way to protect something is to integrate it, to bring it within a 'we'-group, which is to feed it in to creative innovation, not to distance it from it.

Humanity is a groupish animal and our culture is groupish too. This is a solid and repeated finding of evolutionary and social psychology, evolutionary anthropology and history. It gives rise to tribalism and nationalism, but also to languages, families, organizations and civil societies. Groupishness should not therefore be understood as a weakness, a human stain to be eradicated through political institutions and social engineering, nor should it be uncritically valorized or disappear from analysis whenever inconvenient. Groupishness is key to cultural science. Indeed, it is useful to start with a definition of culture as 'groupish (demic) knowledge'. This perspective then enables a better starting place for the study of how culture grows and changes.

It is standard in the social sciences (including education theory) to model cultural dynamics through the micro unit of 'socially' replicated information. In the cultural science approach, cultural dynamics are understood as the autopoietic reproduction of a system of ideas – the regeneration of culture from within – coupled with integration of ideas from outside into the 'we'-group, a naturalization process of remaking something so that it is no longer of 'the other'.

A culture becomes resilient when it achieves effectiveness at this process of remaking and regenerating group knowledge. The social system needs to be open as a generative semiotic system, which requires that it have relatively few rules, be experimental in design, and tolerant of diversity and difference within the same generative group. Such a system will invariably be wasteful and inefficient (but see Chapter 8). It may be seen to be chaotic, or at risk. Yet putting our argument together, we must also appreciate that these are the same criteria that afford it adaptive capabilities. The very properties that enable a system to grow are the same properties that rationally one might seek to eliminate. What cultural science enables us to do is to get underneath this seeming contradiction and to appreciate that cultural growth and resilience would seem to be best understood as a form of *complexity*.

Evolved cultural systems are likely to be complex. We mean this in the technical sense of the word, with complexity understood as a window of state-space of a system balanced between order and chaos (Kauffman 2000; Barabási 2005). Complexity is adapted resilience that maintains and replicates existing knowledge within the group and maintains sufficient disorder so as to be open to new ideas. Cultural complexity is neither ordered culture (traditional, conservative), as entirely stable knowledge within a group, nor is it chaotic culture (experimental, critical), as wholly transgressive culture within a group. Rather, cultural complexity is a convex combination of both aspects: ordered and chaotic; closed and open; 'we'-group and 'they'-group, all at once. Systems theory and autopoietic models emphasize the existence of a boundary between systems that separates agent from environment. This is the separation between the high-quality order of the (dissipative) system from the low-quality order of the environment. That boundary is the *zone of complexity* (Potts 2000). Cultural dynamics can therefore be analytically modelled through a *micro-meso-macro* conception of individual-group-system (Dopfer and Potts 2008). In cultural science, this is where cultural evolution occurs.

Outro

10

A Natural History of Demic Concentration

It introduces a humanistic science of the economy – 'humanomics' – directing attention to meaning without abandoning behavior, using literary sources without ignoring numbers, combining the insights of the human and the mathematical sciences.

Deirdre McCloskey[1]

The use of culture in society

This book has sought to elucidate a fundamental re-conception of what culture actually does. Culture is plainly a mechanism for carrying past knowledge, identity and meaning, and therefore a societal form of capital and wealth. 'We' (our clan) seek to protect and reproduce that stock of cultural capital and wealth; this is the basic model of culture that runs through anthropology, sociology and cultural economics, and forms the standard approach to cultural policy.

But culture is also a mechanism for the *production of newness and the growth of knowledge*. In addition, culture is a mechanism for the production of newness from sources that *cannot be identified in advance*, but which may arise at any point throughout and among social and semiotic systems, in a dynamic process where newness includes new *sources and systems* of knowledge as well as new content.

The cultural science that we have proposed here is a hybrid of cultural studies (textual, historical) and evolutionary economics (analytic, complexity). Perhaps we should have called it culturology, as the Russians do,[2] rather than cultural science. But a 'culture-ology' – a scientific study of culture in a systematic anthropological or sociological sense: what it is made of, its functional

---

[1] Quotation at: www.deirdremccloskey.com/books/index.php#16; argument at: www.deirdremccloskey.com/docs/humanomics.pdf.

[2] *Wikipedia*: Culturology.

components, its micro-foundations and macro-ecology – has not been our primary purpose. Rather, we have conceived of cultural science as the study of *the use of culture* in society as, shall we say, an engine of the future for the growth of knowledge, newness and innovation.

From the start, we have been fundamentally concerned with a theme arising out of cultural studies – the study of ordinary culture in the Raymond Williams (1958, 'culture is ordinary') sense, and specifically of the uses of culture, or of culture as productive. The central theme of this book has been that culture makes groups, groups make knowledge, and that new ideas (contributions to knowledge) occur as the tensioned and conflicted boundary of a group changes. Newness and novelty are not 'the production of an idea, using labour and capital inputs' (as the economists formulate it), but the reformation of a *group boundary* such that an idea becomes meaningful. This is the evolutionary model of cultural dynamics through the mechanisms of demic concentration.

This is a different model of newness and innovation: a cultural science model. Culture, under particular conditions, is productive of newness as part of the growth-of-knowledge process. Cultural science is the study of *the growth of externalized knowledge* through this complex, evolutionary semiotic mechanism whereby culture produces groups within which ideas are meaningful and groups produce newness and knowledge. This is a wasteful and conflict-shaped process, but ultimately it is a mechanism by which knowledge grows. Cultural science is the study of culture as a source of change and dynamics.

It is useful to think of this not only as a new approach to *cultural studies*, with a focus on the agency of cultural dynamics, rather than the politics of cultural capital, but also as a new approach to the *economics of culture*, with a focus on culture as productive (a mechanism of newness and innovation), rather than culture as consumption (a segment of markets and industry). In the cultural science approach, culture is productive of newness and knowledge. The use of culture in society is less about the reproduction and consumption of cultural capital, and more about the production of novelty. In this sense, the cultural science model of externalized demic meaningfulness is actually an alternative theory, not to the anthropological/sociological or political-economy models of *culture*, but more accurately a competitor with the economic production function (or investment) model of *innovation*.

The investment model of innovation – in which new ideas and innovations are produced by combining resource inputs (capital, labour and so on) – is at the core of modern growth economics in the form of a production function for knowledge (Romer 1990). To increase the output of innovation, we increase the level of inputs. That, in essence, is the economic model of growth through innovation and new knowledge. It is also the economic model of science (Arrow 1962). But culture can also be proposed as another model of innovation, in the externalized, demic conception we have proposed, where culture is viewed as a species of economics-via-language-and-stories, 'we'-group formation and meaningfulness. This furnishes a new approach to the economics of *groups* (cf. Frijters and Foster 2012) and the economics of *identity* (cf. Akerlof and Kranton 2000), but in both cases as a knowledge construct, not as a strategic or political construct.

At the core of this 'new economics of culture', and 'new cultural studies', both of which we gather under the rubric of cultural science, is a theory of the use of culture in society in which culture is understood as a newness-making mechanism. We do not claim that this is the only function of culture. Other functions are cumulatively and variously co-present. Rather we seek to redirect emphasis in the *study* of culture towards this functional role in the production of newness and innovation. This is a broader point in studies of households, firms, and entire economies, in that analysis tends to be defined in terms of *production function* (i.e. input–output) and *efficiency*, such that each unit is defined as producing a particular thing. Increases in output or gains in efficiency will come from better technologies or more effective organization. The way to produce more output is to increase the level of inputs, or improve the technology of production. The implication that carries from the economics of firms and economies to the study of culture, whether neoclassical (cultural economics) or Marxian (cultural studies) in foundation, is that this same input–output model of production also applies to novelty and innovation. Newness, in other words, is just another good. However, this is not what cultural science argues. The production of newness, novelty and innovation has another class of explanation in *externalized demic concentration*. This is another important, yet much neglected and misunderstood, use of culture in society.

Implications

As a new approach to both cultural economics and cultural studies, cultural science has a number of specific implications.

1 Innovation is ordinary

If culture is ordinary, in the Raymond Williams (1958) sense – and as a founding principal of cultural studies – then *so too is innovation*. This is a statement about the causal distribution of innovation. In the standard economic model, innovation is proportional to investment in innovation, which is in turn a function of the institutional incentives for such creative and entrepreneurial, competitively driven and cooperatively organized economic action. In that respect, innovation is special. It is not the natural course of economic events, outside of some exceptional institutional conditions (that describe, in essence, institutional modernity and market economies). Innovation, in this investment-driven and institutionally conditioned model, is an endogenous dynamic force not at all ordinary, if for no other reason than a special class of agent – the entrepreneur – is tasked with this operation (Schumpeter 1942).

But from the perspective of cultural science, innovation and newness is ordinary in the simple sense that it is widely distributed (or externalized across subpopulations), and a product of demic (knowledge-making group) concentration and tensioned interaction.[3]

This suggests a reconsideration of the theory of innovation, to be formulated less in terms of exogenous shocks and high-powered incentives (the economic way of viewing the world), but broadly through a skein of considerations extending through economic, social, cultural, technological, institutional, legal and psychological systems. The cultural science conception of the ordinariness of innovation suggests a much more interdisciplinary approach to the study of innovation.

2 The aims of cultural policy might be reconsidered

Cultural policy is largely configured, in most countries, in what might be called a 'welfare mode', or 'health care' as opposed to 'racketeering' model (see Chapter 5: 'Citizens'). It protects against risk of loss; it seeks to correct market failures; it supports those parts it favours. The raison d'être of cultural policy, viewed from the perspective of cultural economics, is to correct market

---

[3] This reconceptualization of cultural productivity as widely distributed matches Thomas Paine's reconceptualization of political leadership in *Rights of Man* (1792), where he argued against hereditary government and in favour of representative democracy on exactly these grounds – a momentous example of *newness* trumping behavioural, structural or power-based modes of explanation.

failures in the positive externalities of 'good' culture. From the perspective of cultural studies however, cultural policy is a battleground for personal-political and socio-economic consequences. In both cases 'policy' is restricted to the agency of the state (it rarely addresses *business strategy* as an interlocutor, for instance).

But from the perspective of cultural science, things look somewhat different. Specifically, cultural policy might reconsider its aims, and its addressee. It might not necessarily be centred about the state protection of cultural forms for the sake of the preservation of a rich (multi-)cultural ecology, or as a policy-warranted collective action correction (within a nominally 'capitalist' system) to a manifest market failure in the production of culture. Rather, cultural policy might be reconsidered as instead a 'soft-power' version of innovation policy.

Perhaps the simpler point is that cultural policy and innovation policy are related, and more closely than is commonly admitted. Indeed, according to cultural science, cultural policy can serve as a form of innovation policy – a business strategy, indeed – using cultural mechanisms to shape the development of new ideas and the coordination of knowledge, and therefore to shape innovation outcomes. Bad cultural policy may show up (hitherto, unexpectedly) as bad innovation policy, and, obviously, vice versa.

3 Increased importance of theory of groups

Cultural science is built around a theory of human social groups as knowledge-making formations (demes), whose founding characteristic is that they are construed in opposition to other, external groups. It is therefore important to direct attention to the study of groups in terms of the theory of formation, stability, productivity, and so on, and the cultural mechanisms used to achieve this, including semiospheres, the noösphere, and social networks using digital or other technological affordances. Essentially, a cultural science requires a sub-domain, assembled from an interdisciplinary consilience of theories, which furnishes a theory of groups.

The cultural science mechanism of innovation is a shifting of group boundaries to integrate (i.e. make meaningful) new ideas. Culture is a group identity-making process that makes ideas meaningful into knowledge. This is the conception of a deme, as a culturally coordinated knowledge group. Examples of these groups are basic economic units such as firms and households, but also demic groups such as social network markets (Potts et al. 2008), commons (Ostrom 1990), audiences and festivals (Hartley 2009), sciences, genres, cities. With groups reconstructed as a culturally formed site of productivity-in-tension, it will become increasingly important to develop a theory of groups that can underpin and explain this.

There are of course numerous theories of groups in the sciences, broadly considered. For biologists and economists, groups are a collective-action cooperation problem. For mathematicians they are an identity and aggregation problem. For sociologists they're a unit of analysis, and for anthropologists, political scientists and behavioural individualists, they're a puzzle. For linguists, language makes groups. For evolutionary linguists, groups make language. Groups can be an emergent phenomenon, or a linear consequence. Groups are made of information and groups are made of things. The point is that cultural science must ultimately be based on a unified and generalized theory of human groups (or demes, which is our hunch). Where cultural science is innovative in this regard is in the formulation of demes as 'universal-adversarial': open to all knowledge among the 'we'-group, but in antagonistic competition with the knowledge of 'they'-groups. That such antagonism is productive of innovation and newness can readily be observed in wars, hot or cold, real and metaphorical.

4 Reconsider previous works in cultural studies and evolutionary economics

An important implication of the cultural science programme is that it adds value by integrating two otherwise distinct research programmes: cultural studies and evolutionary/complexity approaches to economics. We have sought to formulate some key arguments in the different chapters of this book.

But there remains much yet that might be developed, and the most obvious place to begin this is with what we might call a 'back-catalogue trawl' of cultural studies, and evolutionary economics too, to review particular works through the lens of cultural science.

This means classifying work that has sought to describe: externalized knowledge; group-formation mechanisms; emergence of meaningfulness; production of waste; construction of newness; 'we-group/they-group' interface, interaction, hostility and boundary redefinition; citizenship; extinction and protectionism. A mapping of previous work along these lines would be a most valuable first step. But a second step would be to seek particular points from which to build out. Students of cultural studies might in this way find cultural science a possible research direction (Ostrom 1990).

5 Reconsider the value of interdisciplinary collaboration

An immediate further consequence of the general model of cultural science is that it invites closer collaboration between cultural studies with evolutionary economics and complexity approaches to social science and policy. The reason is simply that these offer conceptual, theoretical and analytic frameworks for the translation of particular elements of cultural studies into cultural science.

6 What is postmodern after cultural science?

Postmodernism is normally represented as a movement in twentieth century arts and letters marked by various modes of rejection, criticism and ultimately 'deconstruction' of the modernist conceit of an objective, observer-free interpretation of reality. But cultural science suggests a new theory of postmodernism that emphasizes a different aspect, namely multiplicity of starting points and combinatorial possibilities, arriving at an interpretation that emphasizes not only its deconstructive tendencies, but also its creative, or competitively re-constructive tendencies. This proposes a new theory of postmodernism that is less focused on its critical aspect and more on the world of *multiple simultaneous choice*, or *consequential choice under abundance*. Postmodernism hasn't been 'completed' yet: it has applied the test of doubt to realism, but it has not sufficiently moved on to investigate the possibilities of distributed intellectual innovation. By emphasizing the multiple starting points that then compete in a marketplace for ideas, we suggest that postmodernism has been abandoned too early, and somewhat misconstrued as a critical movement. It may better be understood as a decentralized creative movement in a world of abundance. This presents both cultural studies and evolutionary economics as part of a 'philosophy of plenty' (Hartley 2003). It is *DIY Darwinism*.

The postmodern humanities and postmodern science are central to the cultural science project. Unifying consilient questions are: What makes a group? What happens at boundaries? How does knowledge grow? This revisits the 'boundary crossing' themes of postmodernism and cultural studies from the demic perspective.

7 Reconsidering the cultural value of openness

A final implication we can note is that *openness* is a major and perhaps central principle of cultural productivity. Openness implies an adaptive rather than a planning strategic perspective. Planning requires standardized inputs and centralized control of agents and resources. This type of structured bureaucratic model works well in instances whether there is a known goal in mind, known methods by which it will be achieved, and an environment that is knowable or controllable. But such methods work much less well in more open (uncertain) environments.

An effective cultural system is in many ways an adaptation to an open environment. But this isn't at all the same as laissez-faire, for such adaptive capabilities require complex organization. The point, rather, is to guard against too much detailed planning and endeavours to enforce such plans: looser and more adaptive approaches are better because they make better use of distributed and continuously changing information and opportunities among multivalent agents.

Openness implies the tolerance of conflict and tension; indeed, an active search for it, inviting it, and then managing it as a mechanism of knowledge testing, variety creation, and opportunity discovery (Stark 2009). This idea has been expressed in the theory of 'novelty bundling markets' (Potts 2012). In these models harmony and consensus is not always an unalloyed good because it limits the ability to test and regenerate knowledge and to discover newness. Without it, it's a bit like accountability run by public relations (PR) rather than by criticism or adversarial argumentation – which is itself the foundation of both legal and scientific testing. In the same spirit, conflict, tension and complexity are not the enemies of knowledge systems. These are features, not bugs.

A natural history of demic concentration

Demic or cultural evolution enables the *reproduction of knowledge*, not of individuals or even cultural groups as such. But knowledge cannot simply be reproduced unchanged (that way extinction lies). It has to be reproduced with *growth*: added newness. The continuous productivity of that process over the extreme long term can hardly be overstated.

Indeed, over the time since *H. sapiens* emerged, we can see a correlation between knowledge technologies and economic transformations. That correlation is schematized on the logarithmic horizontal and right-hand vertical axis of Figure 10.1.

But we can also see that this process corresponds with continuous growth in a stylized measure we call demes-per-person (on the logarithmic left-hand vertical axis). We suggest this as a model of the evolution – the natural history – of culture, knowledge technology, and economy.

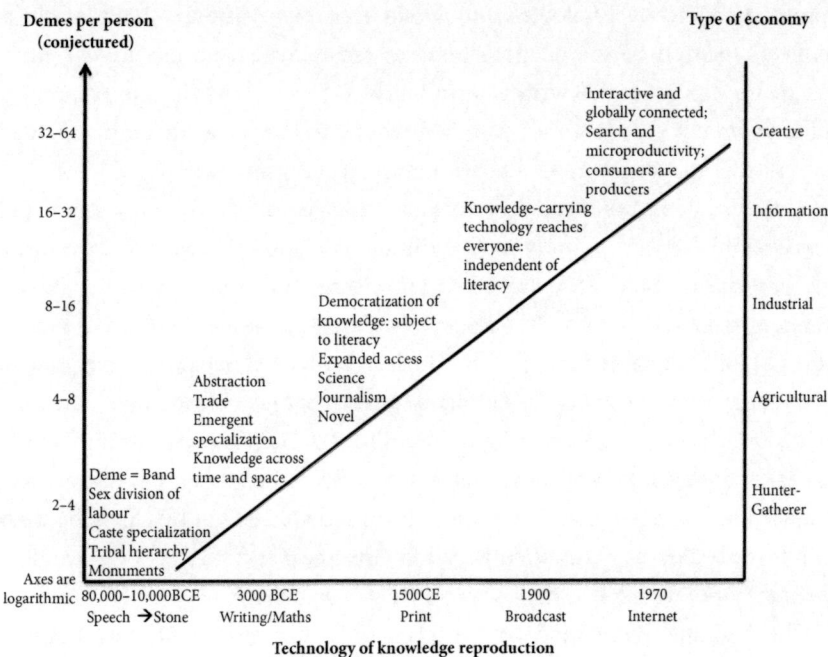

Figure 10.1 Demic concentration in relation to technologies of knowledge reproduction.

The horizontal axis of Figure 10.1 runs on a logarithmic scale from Paleo/ Mesolithic humans to the present. The first event in that timeline is the so-called Neolithic 'revolution' (but see Chapter 3: 'Demes'), when bands of *H. sapiens* began to switch from hunter-gatherer subsistence to early settlements. This period was increasingly complex and technologically equipped, but it was still an oral culture, with most semiotic expressions of knowledge in sound (and, later, a few special ones in stone).[4] Following that axis, we track the successive, 'explosive' changes in knowledge that have been associated with particular technological inventions – writing/maths, print, broadcasting, internet – and the cultural reordering that followed their widespread adoption. Each step enabled a broader social base to use *knowledge stocks* (access) and saw rapid, game changing increases in *knowledge flows* (detached from ethno-territorial descent).

In developing this logic we acknowledge Marshall McLuhan (1962) and Walter J. Ong (1958, 2012). We are interested here in the relationship between

---

[4] 'Stone' includes megaliths, stone-carving and painting on stone.

communications technologies and *group formation*, whereas both of these pioneers focused on the relations between technologies and the *human mind*. We are not confident that writing, printing, broadcasting and the internet impact quite so directly on 'the mind', especially when literacy in any medium remained a minority capability among humans until very recently.

However, it is not necessary to posit changes in 'the human mind' (an irrecoverable object of study at this distance of time) in order to investigate the relationship between culture and knowledge. Instead, we have hit upon a different metric, based on the number of different demes – actual social groups plus virtual or imagined groups – to which an individual person could belong in different epochs. We think the familiar sequence of oral, chirographic (writing), print, and electronic cultures proposed by Ong (2012) is still significant, but not as part of the 'evolution of consciousness' directly; rather as part of the growth of knowledge, which we conjecture impacts on individuals not by changing their minds (or brains, as neuroscientist Susan Greenfield asserts), but by expanding the number of demes to which any individual can belong.

The McLuhan-Ong model in précis is that 'the medium is the message', meaning that the medium of knowledge reproduction (oral, writing, print . . .) shapes particular modes of thought and therefore communicative and production possibilities, which we connect here to 'types of economy' (right-hand vertical axis of Figure 10.1). These types of economy are cumulative, such that an agricultural economy is built on top of and retains subsistence economy forms, just as an industrial economy is built on agricultural economy, and so on. The 'type of economy' designation characterizes its *expanding* frontier.

We can note two immediate points. First, these epochs are a *process*. They are cumulative and sequential, separated from one another by an 'explosion' (in Lotman's sense). Each epoch begins when an elite (e.g. priests, rulers, poets) adopts a 'new media technology', which diffuses through the population (both within a deme and across demes) before stabilizing as the dominant communicative knowledge reproduction institutions of an era. Each such era is associated with a particular type of economy. Second, this process is plotted logarithmically, meaning that it is *accelerating* (see also Hartley 2008: ch. 3, for an account of the increased frequency of 'public writing' across this range of media, from 'low frequency' stone to 'high frequency' social media).

Our novel contribution to this scenario is to track what is happening to *demic concentration* through these accelerating phases of technological revolution in knowledge reproduction and transformation of types of economy. We conjecture that the number of '*demes per person*' is also cumulatively rising.

We are not interested in the total number of demes in a culture or society or economy, just as a linguist need not count the number or words in a language or number of sentences uttered each day. Instead we believe it is possible to estimate (without needing fine precision) the number of demes that each individual inhabits in the course of ordinary activity; or, more important, the accelerating *growth* in that number across the *longue durée*. Obviously the number will differ from person to person, so we are referring here in our measure to a 'representative' individual. Equally obviously, the identification of a deme is not precise, and a great amount of work may be required to refine these concepts to the point of accuracy. Even so, some measures readily suggest themselves, such as belonging to groups organized around ethnicity, kin, gender, language, age-group, tribe (later; class), place (later; nation), specialism (later; occupation) and associative groups (later; citizenship). Conceptually, we suggest that while the dimensions of any one deme are fuzzy, the logic is distinctly monotonic (in ordered sequence), in that the number of demes per person rises cumulatively as time moves through successive 'explosions' in knowledge reproduction. An internet culture will have much higher demic concentrations (number of demes per person) than broadcast culture, where they are higher again than in print culture, and so on. Further, the later array of demic choice, compared to earlier epochs, includes many more 'virtual' demes (carried for instance in story, imagination, social network or audiencehood), as well as 'abstract' ones (nation rather than city, say; or 'human' rather than *our clan*).

In conceptualizing demes for the purpose of estimating changes in the number of demes-per-person over time, we follow Lotman's model of the semiosphere, which does not seek to over-specify their content. We have not sought to restrict what a deme contains, or even to decide whether it is 'empirical' or 'imaginary' (because it is both, from the point of view of individual members). As Ibrus and Torop (2014) put it:

> The semiosphere is presented by Lotman as an infinitely heterogeneous reservoir of dynamic processes with explosive potential. He emphasises the importance of space, interconnectivity and the multidimensionality of sign systems as well as foregrounding the relational and interactional elements of culture.

Thus, we cannot say with certainty how many demes or semiospheres were recognized in the Holocene, when the main technology of knowledge reproduction was oral communication – speech and song. We're guessing that the number of demes-per-person was small, perhaps just two or three associated with the band (of extended kin, mostly) and the language group. There would have come into play further demic concentration associated with specialized knowledge: men's/women's business, for example; or sacred knowledge particular to one's place in the tribal hierarchy or specialization (tracker, healer, hunter, gatherer, seer, etc.). Each individual person would occupy perhaps fewer than ten demes, depending on how many languages they retained in use and groups they interacted with over time: which 'knowledges' they could access. The archaeological record (e.g. grave goods) suggests that by the Neolithic era, the development of specializations associated with the 'domestic mode of production' bespoke increased social complexity and therefore demic concentration, which Marshall Sahlins, in *Stone Age Economics* (1974), characterized as *semiotic affluence*. In the same period, demic knowledge began to *externalize* further, communicated via stone and other sacred sites that 'broadcast' or mediated the stories and identity of the culture (as we described in Chapter 3). At this time, inter-demic communication occurred via trade, 'songlines' and boundary contact, friendly or otherwise, so each person's demic concentration may have been increased by such traffic, while 'imagined' demes – in play, story or expansionist and aspirational pressures ('promised lands' or 'greener grass over the hill', if you like) – were also available at an unknown scale.

The invention of writing (and mathematics) is associated with the surpluses created from the division of labour in social and political organization that was required for settled agricultural production, especially in the Fertile Crescent. But writing was revolutionary or 'explosive' because it enabled knowledge to travel across time and space unchanged. Writing enabled record keeping, and thus made trade, contract, money and law possible at greater scale and complexity, connecting communities separated in time and space. Mathematics and numeracy – abstraction carried much further – enabled knowledge to be created and used in a new way. The number of demes a person could connect to expanded beyond the compass of those within earshot. One could form demic concentrations with people from the past, and far away, or imagined. One could *project* demic groups, if powerful enough.

Print revolutionized demic associations further by its democratizing effects, breaking the ability of elites to maintain power and control by limiting demic concentrations (for example, the Protestant Reformation sought to do away with priestly intermediation in religion by putting a particular book into the hands of every family). Print enabled the three great textual systems of modernity – science, journalism and the novel (Hartley 1996) – to emerge, but only among those who acquired print literacy, which was initially confined to a limited and mostly elite fraction of the population; the democratic potential of print culture took several centuries to flow through to the population at large. But the net effect of this expansion of the print form of knowledge reproduction was to increase the number of demes per person: the creation of a 'reading public' allowed individuals to align with groups whose members they may never meet (nations, fans, associations). This knowledge commons – and the exponential growth of specialized knowledge that could nevertheless be generalized across cultures using print – created the conditions for education and inquiry-driven discovery, for entrepreneurship and industry, indeed an industrial economy became possible, as did a representative democracy, and therefore the modern nation state.

Broadcast technology greatly expanded the process through a range of media (film and radio at first, then television from the second half of the twentieth century). The difference between print and broadcasting is that broadcast communication is no longer constrained by literacy-requirements, such that this technology of knowledge reproduction can reach everyone with a receiver. Electronic communication also hastened the development of information-based economic production. The number of demes per person again rises because of this expanded diffusion effect, and further virtualization or abstraction of groups.

The internet dates from the 1970s, although it only becomes a mass phenomenon in the late 1990s. From the start it had one major property that distinguished it from the previous era of broadcast forms of knowledge reproduction, namely that it is two-way by design: ordinary users can be content-producers as easily as receivers.[5] It is participatory and searchable, and thus creative. Here, the demic space can be substantially large (multi-demic) and highly reticulated.

How culture works

The natural history of knowledge reproduction has evolved through several distinct phases, or Lotmanesque 'explosions', as above: from oral to writing

---

[5] User-created content and participatory interaction were nascent in broadcast media, for example community radio (Rennie 2006), illustrating a more general rule, which is that many 'new' features of 'new media' have been thoroughly rehearsed, as it were, prior to the 'explosive' reordering of the system as a whole.

to print, broadcast and now internet. With each explosion, or jump in the capabilities of technologies of knowledge reproduction, the number of demes per person rises (we hypothesize that this rises exponentially).

Consider some implications. First, as demes-per-person increase so does the extent of access, and the level of abstraction achieved. The new technologies of knowledge reproduction lower the cost of discovery and entry into demes, lowering barriers, and making it harder to exclude others, or to protect knowledge and culture by excluding outsiders. Economists would view this as lowering rents (and thus an efficiency gain), but it can also be seen as opening access and attention (which itself has an under-acknowledged economic value: Lanham 2006), and raising literacy, thence both the levels of consciousness and competence of everyone in the deme. That gain is achieved by increased abstraction through a process of releasing knowledge from situated to more general (from knowledge locked in the here and now to knowledge applicable across novel situations, times, places and users). This process of enlarging the size and citizenship in a deme is enabled by changes in the externalized technologies of knowledge reproduction.

Second, as demes-per-person increase, so do scale and 'wastefulness'. The scale of culture is now global, and the size of demes can be measured in the millions and billions. But demes can also be very small; and most people are citizens in a large (albeit indeterminate) and changing number of demes. We live in an extraordinarily rich and complex semiosphere. To flourish in such an environment requires wastefulness in connections in order to generate proximity (many 'hooks' to achieve few 'hook-ups'), which is required for adaptation (or newness). Demic geometry is increasingly network geometry.

Third, as demes-per-person increase, so does choice and imagination. In the oral (speech and stone) period of knowledge reproduction technologies there was relatively little choice over demic belonging. Demes were local, inherited vertically and apparently unchanging (handed down from the ancestors, and modified only unwittingly). Culture was static, but for occasional boundary events. But each revolution in the reproductive technology of knowledge opened this situation up, and accelerated its growth and evolution. Demic citizenship was literally dislocated in space and time, and multiplied. It became virtualized, and storied. It became imaginative and creative as people were able to access constructed ways of being: for example modelling heroism, stoicism, piety, revelry, honesty, passion, earnestness, gentlemanly conduct or entrepreneurial adventure in stories from afar.

Demic citizenship also makes connections that build the organizations and structures that induce further growth and development in economic and socio-political (institutional) systems. The emancipation of the deme drives the evolution of the economy. The result is not just semiotic but also material affluence – the tide lifts everyone.

Consider the forces that act directly on the demes-per-person axis. We can think of a representative person in a given culture (at a particular point in the sequence of technology of knowledge reproduction) as having a particular 'measure' of demes-per-person, say 20. Obviously, that's a population average: some people will have higher numbers and some lower. The relatively younger and wealthier will tend to amass higher numbers of deme-per-person measures by virtue of greater propensity and access.

Also, a person's total will change through a lifetime: rising rapidly through childhood, peaking, then declining through maturity, along a quasi-stochastic, contextually dependent path. We hazard a guess that the graph of lifetime changes in 'demes-per-person' for each individual might resemble the famous Gartner Hype Cycle, which plots the hype surrounding the emergence and adoption of new technologies.[6]

Gartner's evocatively named 'peak of inflated expectations', 'trough of disillusionment', 'slope of enlightenment' and 'plateau of productivity' (Figure 10.2) were designed to follow the 'hype cycle' of new technology adoption, but these stages may better describe a person's journey through deme-accumulation and change, from childhood and youth (peak), through the onset of family and work commitments (trough), to what is called in German *Mündigkeit* or coming of age into responsibility, caring, action (slope), and then maturity and age (plateau). In each stage the number of demes per person varies, reaching a peak as young people turn from peer-group formation to employment and family-building, when the number of demes may fall, recovering later as shown. This is our hunch – but it can be tested.

People build demes with stories, and those who make good stories can become very powerful and celebrated. But we also build demes with children, or, more accurately, children build new demes. Culture is not just the product of adult genius, it is also assembled by children as they venture out to accumulate and combine demes, old and new. Demic boundary-shifting is impelled by the yearning energy (longing for new experience and knowledge) of a highly

[6] See: www.gartner.com/technology/research/methodologies/hype-cycle.jsp.

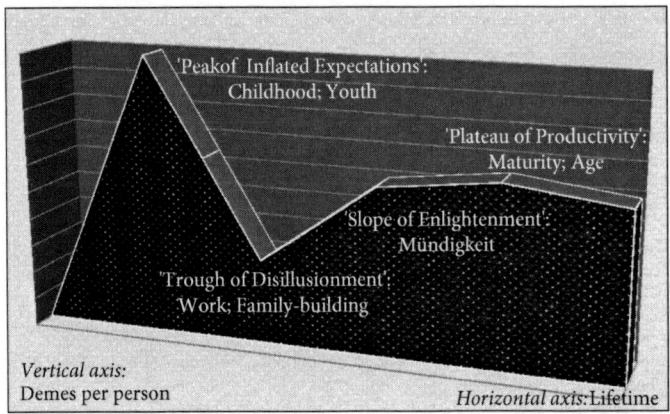

Figure 10.2 Plotting the number of Demes per person over a lifetime (conjectured as a 'hype-cycle' graph).

social and intensely semiotic childhood, which learns by copying, playing, experimenting, timewasting, mischief and adventure. It can appear chaotic and wasteful, seemingly requiring protection, or inconsequential, which is perhaps why children do not figure in economics, where the default individual is the rational adult. But, in both cases, the problem arises not from culture but from the act of observation: from not identifying the right 'problem of culture'. The 'problem' of culture is how to grow new knowledge, which is where children come into their own, scooping it up, sharing it round, making it new.

The purpose of a cultural science is to provide an analytic framework for a general reconceptualization of the theory of culture – in the original cultural studies 'ordinary uses' sense – one that is focused not on its political aspect but rather its evolutionary significance as a generator of newness and innovation. We sincerely hope that this book will serve to gather together some ideas and models from which that project might be advanced, to tell a new story about the nature of culture.

Acknowledgements

Cultural Science has been a long time in the making, undergoing radical metamorphosis along the way. None of it could have occurred without the support of the ARC Centre of Excellence for Creative Industries and Innovation (CCI), to which we owe our thanks. We want to single out John Banks of Queensland University of Technology (QUT). He contributed substantially to the formative discussions of the project and especially to Chapter 2. He wanted to call this book *The Nature of Culture*, which is probably still a good idea for another book: we look forward to that title, John!

We are grateful to Trent MacDonald of RMIT University, not only for providing a timely and decisive critique of the MS at a late stage, but also for contributing to the research on which part of Chapter 9 is based (see Hartley et al. 2012).

John Hartley's acknowledgements:

- I thank Michael Hutter for the invitation to visit WZB, the Social Science Research Centre, Berlin (Wissenschaftszentrum Berlin für Sozialforschung), as a Visiting Scholar, 2013. Thanks to Thomas Petzold and colleagues for their collegial hospitality.
- I am grateful to the 'merry throng' of scholars who have been active in the cultural science network and research workshops since 2008, especially Carsten Herrmann-Pillath (Frankfurt School of Finance & Management); Alex Bentley, Paul Ormerod, Alex Mesoudi, Richard E. Lee, Evelyn Welch and Pierpaolo Andriani. Their work has been a beacon for ours. As far as 'cultural science' goes, it is a pleasure to acknowledge that Carsten beat us to it, setting a formidable standard that augurs well for this nascent field (Herrmann-Pillath 2009, 2013).
- I am grateful to colleagues, postdocs and postgrads in the CCI at QUT: Jean Burgess, Lucy Montgomery, Burcu Şimşek, Axel Bruns and Michael Keane; and those in CCAT (Centre for Culture and Technology) at Curtin University, the late Niall Lucy, Tama Leaver, Eleanor Sandry, and Henry Siling Li.
- My greatest debt of gratitude (tinged with surprised amazement at how productive true proximity can be) goes, as ever, to Tina Horton.

Jason Potts' acknowledgements:

- I would like to acknowledge many of the same tribe in the CCI, and recognize the substantial support that the centre offered to the cultural science project. Cultural science is in some ways interdisciplinary catnip to a certain type of scholar, and we have benefitted enormously from generous support for research visits, seminars and discussions over the past few years.
- I would like to thank Ulrich Witt and colleagues at the Max Planck Institute in Jena, Germany, and Hans-Walter Lorenz at the Frege Centre for Structural Science, also in Jena.
- I thank Prateek Goorha and Sinclair Davidson in the School of Economics, Finance and Marketing at RMIT University, for useful discussion of parts of this project.
- Most important, I thank Ellie Rennie, who writes much better books than I do.

Acknowledgement of funding:

- John Hartley is the recipient of an Australian Research Council Federation Fellowship, *The Uses of Multimedia: Citizen Consumers, Creative Participation and Innovation in Australian Digital Content* (FF0561981), 2005–10.
- Jason Potts is the recipient of an Australian Research Council Future Fellowship, *The Innovation Commons: How Australian industries are pooling innovation resources and why this matters* (FT120100509), 2012–16.
- This research was conducted at the Australian Research Council Centre of Excellence for Creative Industries and Innovation (SR0590002), 2005–13. The views expressed herein are those of the authors and are not necessarily those of the Australian Research Council.

We acknowledge the support of FEAST (Forum for European-Australian Science & Technology Cooperation), and the State Library of Queensland, especially State Librarian Lea Giles-Peters, for the first international cultural science research workshop (Brisbane 2008). We are grateful to the Centre for the Coevolution of Biology and Culture at Durham University for support for the second workshop, held there at the Institute for Advanced Studies in 2010. We acknowledge the continuing support of QUT, Cardiff University, RMIT University and Curtin University for material assistance in the preparation of this book.

We thank the team at Bloomsbury, especially Frances Pinter, who allowed us to pitch the book when Bloomsbury Academic was but a gleam in her entrepreneurial eye; Emily Drewe for commissioning the title and Katie Gallof and Mary Al-Sayed for publishing the book.

John Hartley thanks Gianpietro Mazzoleni, Kevin Barnhurst, Indrek Ibrus, Peeter Torop, Wiley and Sage for the opportunity to try out some of the ideas (here revised, repurposed and extended), that have been rehearsed elsewhere:

- Part of Chapter 3: in G.-P. Mazzoleni (ed.), *The International Encyclopedia of Political Communication* ('Narrative, Political'), Wiley; and in Hartley, J. (2013) 'A Trojan Horse in the Citadel of Stories?' *Cultural Science Journal* 6(1): 71–105.
- Part of Chapter 5: in Hartley, J. (2015) 'Urban Semiosis: Creative Industries and the Clash of Systems'. *International Journal of Cultural Studies* 18(1).

References

Akerlof, G. and R. Kranton (2000), 'Economics and Idenity'. *Quarterly Journal of Economics* CXV(3), 715–53: http://public.econ.duke.edu/~rek8/economicsandidentity.pdf.

Ammerman, A. and L. Cavalli-Sforza (1984), *The Neolithic Transition and the Genetics of Populations in Europe*. Princeton, NJ: Princeton University Press.

Anderson, B. (1991), *Imagined Communities: Reflections on the Origins and Spread of Nationalism*, 2nd edn. London: Verso.

Anderson, C. (2008), *The Long Tail*, 2nd edn. New York: Hyperion.

—(2012), *Makers*. London: Random House Business.

Ansaldo, U. (2009), *Contact Languages: Ecology and Evolution in Asia*. Cambridge: Cambridge University Press.

Arnold, M. (1869), *Culture and Anarchy*. Accessible at: www.gutenberg.org/ebooks/4212.

Arrow, K. (1962), 'The Economic Implications of Learning by Doing'. *The Review of Economic Studies* 29(3): 155–73.

Arthur, W. B. (2009), *The Nature of Technology: What it is and How it Evolves*. New York: Free Press.

Aspers, P. (2010), *Orderly Fashion: A Sociology of Markets*. Princeton, NJ: Princeton University Press.

Austin, J. L. (1962), *How to do Things with Words*. Oxford: Clarendon Press.

Bakhshi, H., I. Hargreaves and J. Mateos-Garcia (2013), *A Manifesto for the Creative Economy*. London: NESTA: www.nesta.org.uk/sites/default/files/a-manifesto-for-the-creative-economy-april13.pdf.

Banet-Weiser, S. (2011), 'Convergence on the Street: Rethinking the Authentic/Commercial Binary'. *Cultural Studies* 27(4/5): 641–58.

Barabási, A.-L. (2002), *Linked: The New Science of Networks*. Cambridge, MA: Perseus Books.

—(2005), 'Network theory-the emergence of creative enterprise'. *Science* 308: 639–41: www.barabasilab.com/pubs/CCNR-ALB_Publications/200504-29_Science-NetworkTheory/200504-29_Science-NetworkTheory.pdf.

Barringer, J. (1999), *Reading the Pre-Raphaelites*. New Haven, CT: Yale University Press.

Barthes, R. (1972), *Mythologies*. Trans. A. Lavers. London: Paladin (first published 1957).

Baym, N. (2010), *Personal Connections in a Digital Age*. Cambridge: Polity Press.

Bednar, J. and S. Page (2007), 'Can Game(s) Theory Explain Culture? The Emergence of Cultural Behavior within Multiple Games'. *Rationality and Society* 19(1): 65–97.

Beinhocker, E. (2006), *The Origin of Wealth: Evolution, Complexity, and the Radical Remaking of Economics*. New York: Random House.

Benkler, Y. (2006), *The Wealth of Networks: How Social Production Transforms Markets and Freedom*. New Haven, CT: Yale University Press.

—(2011), *The Penguin and the Leviathan: How Cooperation Triumphs over Self-Interest*. New York: Crown Business.

Bentley, R. A., M. Earls and M. O'Brien (2011), *I'll Have What She's Having: Mapping Social Behavior*. Cambridge, MA: MIT Press.

Bergstrom, T. (2003), *An Evolutionary View of Family Conflict and Cooperation*. University of California at Santa Barbara, Economics Working Paper Series. Online: http://escholarship.org/uc/item/4qc0q1gh.

Blacking, J. (1984), 'Dance as Cultural System and Human Capability: An Anthropological Perspective'. In J. Adshead-Lansdale (ed.), *Dance, A Multicultural Perspective*. Guildford: University of Surrey, 4–21.

Bloom, H. (1998), *Shakespeare: The Invention of the Human*. New York: Riverhead Press.

Boden, M. (1990), *The Creative Mind*. London: Weidenfeld & Nicholson.

—(ed.) (1994), *Dimensions of Creativity*. Cambridge, MA: MIT Press.

Bollier, D. (2008), *Viral Spiral: How the Commoners Built a Digital Republic of Their Own*. New York: The New Press.

Boltanski, L. and L. Thévenot (2006), *On Justification: The Economies of Worth*. Princeton, NJ: Princeton University Press.

Bono, E. de (1985), *Six Thinking Hats: An Essential Approach to Business Management*. New York: Little, Brown.

Booker, C. (2004), *Seven Basic Plots: Why We Tell Stories*. London: Bloomsbury.

Boulding, K. E. (1977), 'Economic Development as an Evolutionary System', *Fifth World Congress of the International Economic Association*. Tokyo: International Economic Association.

Bowles, S. and H. Gintis (2011), *A Cooperative Species: Human Reciprocity and its Evolution*. Princeton, NJ: Princeton University Press.

Boyd, B. (2008), 'The Art of Literature and the Science of Literature'. *American Scholar*, Spring. Online: http://theamericanscholar.org/the-art-of-literature-and-the-science-of-literature/#.UvwOO_aCbPA.

—(2009), *On the Origin of Stories: Evolution, Cognition, and Fiction*. Cambridge, MA: Harvard University Press.

Boyd, R. and P. Richerson (1985), *Culture and the Evolutionary Process*. Chicago: University of Chicago Press.

—(2005), *The Origin and Evolution of Cultures*. Oxford: Oxford University Press.

—(2009), 'Culture and the Evolution of Human Cooperation'. *Philosophical Transactions of the Royal Society B* 364: 3281–88.

Boyd, B., J. Carroll, and J. Gottschall (eds) (2010), *Evolution, Literature and Film*. New York: Columbia University Press.

Boyd, R., H. Gintis, S. Bowles and P. Richerson (2003), 'The evolution of altruistic punishment'. *Proceedings of the National Academy of Sciences of the USA (PNAS)* 110(6): 3531–35: www.pnas.org/content/100/6/3531.long.

Bruns, A. (2008), *Blogs, Wikipedia, Second Life, and Beyond: From Production to Produsage*. New York: Peter Lang.

Buchanan, J. (1965), 'An Economic Theory of Clubs'. *Economica* 32: 1–14.

Buchanan, J. and G. Tullock (1962), *The Calculus of Consent: Logical Foundations of Constitutional Democracy*. Ann Arbor, MI: University of Michigan Press.

Buonanno, M. (2005), 'The "Sailor" and the "Peasant": The Italian Police Series between Foreign and Domestic'. *Media International Australia* 115: 48–59.

Burke, E. (1790), *Reflections on the French Revolution*. Accessible at: Bartleby.com (2001): www.bartleby.com/24/3/.

Campbell, D. (1960), 'Blind variation and selective retention in creative thought as in other knowledge processes'. *Psychological Review* 67: 380–400.

Carroll (2011), *Reading Human Nature: Literary Darwinism in Theory and Practice*. New York: SUNY Press.

Cavalli-Sforza, L. (2000), *Genes, Peoples, and Languages*. New York: North Point Press.

Cavalli-Sforza, L. and M. Feldman (1981), *Cultural Transmission and Evolution: A Quantitative Approach*. Princeton, NJ: Princeton University Press.

Caves, R. (2000), *Creative Industries: Contracts between Art and Commerce*. Cambridge, MA: Harvard University Press.

Cheshire, T. (2013), 'Talent Tube: how Britain's new YouTube superstars built a global fanbase'. www.wired.co.uk/magazine/archive/2013/02/features/talent-tube.

Chevedden, P. (2000), 'The Invention of the Counterweight Trebuchet: A Study in Cultural Diffusion'. Washington DC: Dumbarton Oaks Papers, No. 54. Accessible at: www.doaks.org/resources/publications/dumbarton-oaks-papers/dop54/dp54ch4.pdf.

Childe, V. G. (1925), *The Dawn of European Civilization*. London: Kegan Paul, Trench, Trubner.

—(1936), *Man Makes Himself*. London: Watts, rev. edn 1951.

Chouliaraki, L. (ed.) (2012), *Self-Mediation: New Media, Citizenship and Civil Selves*. London: Routledge.

Clark, G. (2007), *A Farewell to Alms: A Brief Economic History of the World*. Princeton, NJ: Princeton University Press.

Clemens, M. (2011), 'Economics and emigration: Trillion dollar bills on the sidewalk'. *Journal of Economic Perspectives* 25(3): 83–106.

Coleman, S. (2003), *A Tale of Two Houses: The House of Commons, the Big Brother House and the People at Home*. London: Hansard Society. www.clubpublic.net/eve/030708/Hansardb_b.pdf.

Coleman, S. (2005), *Direct Representation: Towards a Conversational Democracy.* London: Institute for Public Policy Research (ippr exchange). Available online: www.ippr.org.uk/ecomm/files/Stephen_Coleman_Pamphlet.pdf.

Cooke, P. and L. Lazzeretti (eds) (2008), *Creative Cities, Cultural Clusters and Local Economic Development.* Cheltenham: Edward Elgar.

Cowen, T. (1998), *In Praise of Commercial Culture.* Cambridge, MA: Harvard University Press.

—(2004), *Creative Destruction: How Globalization is Changing the World's Cultures.* Princeton, NJ: Princeton University Press.

Csibra, G. and G. Gergely (2011), 'Natural pedagogy as evolutionary adaptation'. *Philosophical Transactions of the Royal Society B* 366: 1149–57.

Csikszentmihalyi, M. (1996), *Creativity.* New York: Harper.

Currid, E. (2007), *The Warhol Economy: How Fashion, Art, and Music Drive New York City.* Princeton, NJ: Princeton University Press.

Dardanelles Commission (1917–19), *The Final Report of the Dardanelles Commission.* London, HMSO. Online: http://nla.gov.au/nla.aus-vn2035864.

Darwin, C. (1859), *On the Origin of Species by Means of Natural Selection.* London: John Murray. Accessible at: http://darwin-online.org.uk/converted/pdf/1859_Origin_F373.pdf.

—(1871), *The Descent of Man.* Accessible at: www.gutenberg.org/ebooks/2300; and at: http://darwin-online.org.uk/content/frameset?viewtype=text&itemID=F955&pageseq=157.

Davidson, D. (1973), 'Radical Interpretation'. *Dialectica* 27(3): 14–28.

Dawes, R. (1980), 'Social dilemmas'. *Annual Review of Psychology* 31: 163–93.

Dawkins, R. (1976), *The Selfish Gene. 30th Anniversary Edition* (2006). Oxford: Oxford University Press.

—(1982), *The Extended Phenotype: The Long Reach of the Gene.* Oxford: Oxford University Press.

Deacon, T. (1999), 'The Trouble with Memes (and what to do about it)'. *The Semiotic Review of Books.* 10(3): http://projects.chass.utoronto.ca/semiotics/srb/10-3edit.html.

Derrida, J. (1976), *Of Grammatology.* Baltimore, MD: Johns Hopkins University Press.

Diderot, D., J. D'Alembert and J. Le Rond (eds) (1753), *Encyclopédie, ou Dictionnaire raisonné des sciences, des arts et des metiers,* Tome 3. Paris: chez Briasson.

Dopfer, K. and J. Potts (2008), *The General Theory of Economic Evolution.* London: Routledge.

Dugdale, T. (2004 Spring), 'Dick Hebdige: Unplugged and Greased Back'. *Post-Identity.* 4(1). Online: http://hdl.handle.net/2027/spo.pid9999.0004.102.

Dunbar, R. (1998), *Grooming, Gossip, and the Evolution of Language.* Cambridge, MA: Harvard University Press.

Durant, W. (1939), *The Life of Greece.* New York: Simon & Schuster.

Dutton, D. (2009), *The Art Instinct: Beauty, Pleasure and Human Evolution*. London: Bloomsbury.

Dworkin, D. (1997), *Cultural Marxism in Post-War Britain: History, the New Left, and the Origins of Cultural Studies*. Durham, NC: Duke University Press.

Earls, M. (2009), *Herd: How to Change Mass Behaviour by Harnessing Our True Nature*. London: Wiley.

Eco, U. (1976), *A Theory of Semiotics*. Bloomington: Indiana University Press.

Edelman, G. (1987), *Neural Darwinism: The Theory of Neuronal Group Selection*. New York: Basic Books.

Edgerton, D. (2006), *Warfare State: Britain, 1920–1970*. Cambridge: Cambridge University Press.

Elias, N. (1939), *The Civilising Process: Sociogenetic and Psychogenetic Investigations*. Oxford: Blackwell, this edn 2000.

Eliot, T. S. (1920), *The Sacred Wood*. London: Methuen.

Ellis, L. (1991), 'A synthesized (biosocial) theory of rape'. *Journal of Consulting and Clinical Psychology* 59: 631–42.

Elyot, T. (1531), *The Boke Named the Governour*. Online (Dutton/Dent edn): http://darkwing.uoregon.edu/~rbear/gov/gov1.htm.

Fehr, E. and U. Fischbacher (2003), 'The nature of human altruism'. *Nature* 425: 785–91.

Fewster, K. (1982), 'Ellis Ashmead Bartlett and the making of the Anzac legend'. *Journal of Australian Studies* 6(10): 17–30.

Findlay, C. S. (1992), 'Phenotypic evolution under gene-culture transmission in structured populations'. *Journal of Theoretical Biology* 156(3): 387–400.

Fisher, W. (1984), 'Narration as a Human Communication Paradigm: The case of Public Moral Argument'. *Communication Monographs* 51(1): unpaginated.

Fitch, W. T. (2005), 'Language Evolution: A Comparative Review'. *Biology and Philosophy* 20: 193–230.

Flew, T. (2012), 'Michel Foucault's *The Birth of Biopolitics* and contemporary neo-liberalism debates'. *Thesis Eleven* 108(1): 44–65.

Florida, R. (2002), *The Rise of the Creative Class*. New York: Basic Books.

—(2005), *Cities and the Creative Class*. New York: Basic Books.

Flowers, S. (2008), *The New Inventors: How users are changing the rules of innovation*. London: NESTA. www.nesta.org.uk/library/documents/Report%2015%20-%20New%20Inventors%20v6.pdf.

Foster, K., T. Wenseleers and F. Ratnieks (2006), 'Kin selection is the key to altruism'. *Trends in Ecology and Evolution* 21(2): 57–60.

Foucault, M. (2008), *The Birth of Biopolitics: Lectures at the Collège de France 1978–1979*. Basingstoke: Palgrave.

Frank, R., T. Gilovich and T. Regan (1996), 'Do economists make bad citizens?' *Journal of Economic Perspectives* 10(1): 183–92.

Frazer, N. (1992), 'Sea Turtle Conservation and Halfway Technology'. *Conservation Biology* 6: 179–84.

Frijters, P. with G. Foster (2012), *An Economic Theory of Greed, Love, Groups and Networks*. Cambridge: Cambridge University Press.

Fromm, H. (2003), 'The New Darwinism in the Humanities, Part I: From Plato to Pinker', and 'Part II: Back to Nature, Again'. *The Hudson Review* Spring (Vol. LVI, No. 1) and Summer (Vol. LVI, No. 2): unpaginated.

Gans, J. (2012), *Information Wants to be Shared*. Cambridge, MA: Harvard Business Review Press.

Garnham, N. (1987), 'Concepts of culture: Public policy and the cultural industries'. *Cultural Studies* 1(1): 21–36.

Georgescu-Roegen, N. (1971), *The Entropy Law and the Economic Process*. Cambridge, MA: Harvard University Press.

Geyer, F. (1994), 'The Challenge of Sociocybernetics'. Accessible at: http://uwacadweb. uwyo.edu/Red_Feather/chaos/006challenges.html.

Gillies, M. (2013), 'City state'. *Times Higher Education*, 18 July.

Gintis, H. (2012), *Human Evolution: A Behavioral Synthesis*. New Mexico: Santa Fe Institute. http://tuvalu.santafe.edu/~bowles/HumanEvolution.pdf.

Gintis, H. and S. Bowles (2011), *A Cooperative Species: Human Reciprocity and Its Evolution*. Princeton, NJ: Princeton University Press.

Gintis, H., E. A. Smith and S. Bowles (2001), 'Costly Signaling and Cooperation'. *Journal of Theoretical Biology* 213: 103–19.

Gitlin, T. (1983), *Inside Prime Time*. New York: Pantheon Books (Revised edn, Routledge, 1994).

Glaeser, E. (2011), *The Triumph of the City*. London: Pan Macmillan.

Goggin, G. (2008), 'Regulating Mobile Content: Convergences, Commons, Citizenship'. *International Journal of Communications Law and Policy* 12: www.ijclp.net/12_2008/ pdf/goggin.pdf.

Goggin, G. and J. Clark (2009), 'Mobile phones and community development: a contact zone between media and citizenship'. *Development in Practice* 19(4/5): 585–97.

Goody, J. (1986), *The Logic of Writing and the Organization of Society*. Cambridge: Cambridge University Press.

Gottschall, J. (2012), 'Why Storytelling is the Ultimate Weapon'. *Fastcocreate*. Online: http://www.fastcocreate.com/1680581/why-storytelling-is-the-ultimate-weapon.

Gray, J., J. Jones and E. Thompson (eds) (2009), *Satire TV*. New York: NYU Press.

Greene, J. (2013), *Moral Tribes: Emotion, Reason, and the Gap Between Us and Them*. New York: Penguin Books.

Gregory, A. (2006), 'The State We Are In: Insights from Autopoiesis and Complexity Theory'. *Management Decision* 44(7): 962–72.

Hacking I. (2000), *The Social Construction of What?* Cambridge, MA: Harvard University Press.

Hall, P. (1998), *Cities in Civilization*. New York: Pantheon.

Hamilton, W. D. (1964), 'The Genetical Evolution of Social Behaviour. I/II'. *Journal of Theoretical Biology* 7: 1–52.

Hardy, T. (1915), 'The Convergence of the Twain: Lines on the loss of the "Titanic"'. *Collected Poems of Thomas Hardy*. London: Macmillan, this edition 1932.

Hargreaves, I. (2011), *Digital Opportunity: A Review of Intellectual Property and Growth*. London: Intellectual Property Office: www.ipo.gov.uk/ipreview.htm.

Harris, A., J. Wyn and S. Younes (2010), 'Beyond apathetic or activist youth: "Ordinary" young people and contemporary forms of participation'. *Young: Nordic Journal of Youth Research* 18(1): 9–32.

Hartley, J. (1992a), *The Politics of Pictures: The Creation of the Public in the Era of Popular Media*. London & New York: Routledge.

—(1992b), *Tele-ology: Studies in Television*. London & New York: Routledge.

—(1996), *Popular Reality: Journalism, Modernity, Popular Culture*. London: Edward Arnold [Bloomsbury].

—(1999), *Uses of Television*. London & New York: Routledge.

—(2003), *A Short History of Cultural Studies*. London: Sage Publications.

—(2006), 'The Best Propaganda: Humphrey Jennings' *The Silent Village* (1943)'. In A. McKee (ed.), *Beautiful Things in Popular Culture*. Malden MA and Oxford: Wiley-Blackwell, 144–63.

—(2008), *Television Truths: Forms of Knowledge in Popular Culture*. Malden, MA and Oxford: Wiley-Blackwell.

—(2009a), *The Uses of Digital Literacy*. St. Lucia: UQP; New Brunswick, NJ: Transaction Publishers (2010).

—(2009b), 'TV Stories: From Representation to Productivity'. In J. Hartley and K. McWilliam (eds), *Story Circle: Digital Storytelling Around the World*. Malden, MA and Oxford: Wiley-Blackwell, Chapter 2.

—(2012), *Digital Futures for Cultural and Media Studies*. Malden, MA and Oxford: Wiley-Blackwell.

—(2013), 'Authorship and the Narrative of the Self'. In J. Gray and D. Johnson (eds), *A Companion to Media Authorship*. Malden, MA and Oxford: Wiley-Blackwell, 23–47.

Hartley, J., J. Burgess and A. Bruns (eds) (2013), *A Companion to New Media Dynamics*. Malden, MA and Oxford: Wiley-Blackwell.

Hartley, J. and J. Green (2006), 'The Public Sphere on the Beach'. *European Journal of Cultural Studies* 9(3): 341–62.

Hartley, J. and K. McWilliam (eds) (2009), *Story Circle: Digital Storytelling around the World*. Malden, MA and Oxford: Wiley-Blackwell.

Hartley, J., J. Potts, S. Cunningham, T. Flew, M. Keane and J. Banks (2013), *Key Concepts in Creative Industries*. London: Sage Publications.

Hartley, J., J. Potts and T. MacDonald, with C. Erkunt and C. Kufleitner (2012), *Creative City Index. Cultural Science* 5(1): 110.

Hayek, F. A. (1945), 'The Use of Knowledge in Society'. *American Economic Review* 35(4): 519–30. www.econlib.org/library/Essays/hykKnw1.html.

—(1952), *The Sensory Order: An Inquiry into the Foundations of Theoretical Psychology.* Chicago, IL: University of Chicago Press.

—(1973), *Law, Legislation, and Liberty, Vol. 1: Rules and Order.* Chicago, IL: University of Chicago Press.

Henrich, J. (2004), 'Cultural group selection, coevolutionary processes and large-scale cooperation'. *Journal of Economic Behavior & Organization* 53(1): 3–35.

Herrmann-Pillath, C. (2009), *The Economics Of Identity And Creativity: A Cultural Science Approach.* St Lucia: University of Queensland Press/New Brunswick, NJ: Transaction Publishers (2010).

—(2013), *Foundations of Economic Evolution: A Treatise on the Natural Philosophy of Economics.* Cheltenham: Edward Elgar.

Hobbes, T. (1651), *Leviathan.* Edited with an introduction by C. B. Macpherson. Harmondsworth: Penguin (1968).

Hodgson, G. and T. Knudsen (2010), *Darwin's Conjecture: The Search for General Principles of Social and Economic Evolution.* Chicago, IL: University of Chicago Press.

Hoffmeyer, J. (1996), *Signs of Meaning in the Universe.* Bloomington, IN: Indiana University Press, 61.

Hofstadter, R. (1944), *Social Darwinism in American Thought.* Philadelphia, PA: University of Pennsylvania Press.

Hoggart, R. (1957), *The Uses of Literacy.* London: Chatto & Windus.

—(2004), *Mass Media in a Mass Society: Myth & Reality.* London: Continuum.

Hoppitt, W. and K. Laland (2013), *Social Learning: An Introduction to Mechanisms, Methods and Models.* Princeton, NJ: Princeton University Press.

Hornblower, S. and A. Spawforth (2005), *The Oxford Classical Dictionary,* 3rd edn. Oxford: Oxford University Press.

Howkins, J. (2009) *Creative Ecologies: Where Thinking Is A Proper Job.* St. Lucia: University of Queensland Press.

Hughes, R. (1991), *The Shock of the New: Art and the Century of Change* (updated and enlarged edn). London: Thames and Hudson.

Hutter, M. (2008), 'Creating Artistic from Economic Value: Changing Input Prices and New Art'. In M. Hutter and D. Throsby (eds), *Beyond Price.* Cambridge: Cambridge University Press, 60–74.

—(2010), 'Familiar Surprises: Creating Value in the Creative Industries'. In P. Aspers and J. Beckert (eds), *The Worth of Goods.* Cambridge: Cambridge University Press.

—(2012), 'Experience goods'. In R. Towse (ed.), *Handbook of Cultural Economics,* 2nd edn. Cheltenham: Edward Elgar.

Hutter, M., A. Berthoin Antal, I. Farías, L. Marz, J. Merkel, S. Mützel, M. Oppen, N. Schulte-Römer and H. Straßheim (2010), 'Research Program of the Research Unit: "Cultural sources of newness"'. *WZB Discussion Paper* (SP III 2010–405): http://bibliothek.wzb.eu/pdf/2010/iii10–405.pdf.

Huxley, J. (1942), *Evolution: The Modern Synthesis.* London: Allen & Unwin.

—(1955), 'Guest Editorial: Evolution, Cultural and Biological'. *Yearbook of Anthropology* 2–5.

Hyde, L. (2008), *Trickster Makes This World: How Disruptive Imagination Creates Culture*. Edinburgh: Canongate Books (first published 1998).

Ibrus, I. and P. Torop (2014), 'Remembering and Reinventing Juri Lotman for the Digital Age'. *International Journal of Cultural Studies* 18(1).

Jablonka, E. and M. Lamb (2005), *Evolution in Four Dimensions: Genetic, Epigenetic, Behavioral, and Symbolic Variation in the History of Life*. Cambridge, MA: MIT Press.

Jacobs, J. (1961), *The Death and Life of Great American Cities*. New York: Random House, new edn 1993.

—(1984), *Cities and the Wealth of Nations: Principles of Economic Life*. New York: Random House.

Jakobson, R. (1960), 'Closing Statement: Linguistics and Poetics'. In T. Sebeok (ed.), *Style in Language*. Cambridge MA: MIT Press.

Jenkins, H., S. Ford and J. Green (2013), *Spreadable Media: Creating Value and Meaning in a Networked Culture*. New York: NYU Press.

Kahneman, D. (2011), *Thinking, Fast and Slow*. New York: Farrar, Straus and Giroux; London: Macmillan.

Kauffman, S. (1995), *At Home in the Universe: The Search for Laws of Self-Organization and Complexity*. Oxford: Oxford University Press.

—(2000), *Investigations*. Oxford: Oxford University Press.

Keane, M. (2013), *Creative Industries in China: Art, Design and Media*. Cambridge: Polity Press.

Kelly, G. (1955), *The Psychology of Personal Constructs*, Volume 1: *A Theory of Personality*; Volume 2: *Clinical Diagnosis and Psychotherapy*. New York: W. W. Norton & Co.

Kelly, K. (2010), *What Technology Wants*. New York: Viking.

Kirzner, I. (1973), *Competition and Entrepreneurship*. Chicago, IL: University of Chicago Press.

Knightley, P. (1975), *The First Casualty – from Crimea to Vietnam: The War Correspondent as Hero, Propagandist, and Mythmaker*. New York: Harcourt Brace Jovanovich.

Konner, M. (2010), *The Evolution of Childhood: Relationships, Emotion, Mind*. Cambridge, MA: Harvard University Press.

Kotkin, J. (2005), *The City: A Global History*. New York: Modern Library.

Krueger, A. (1974), 'The political economy of the rent-seeking society'. *American Economic Review* 64(3): 291–303.

Kuhn, T. (1962), *The Structure of Scientific Revolutions*. Chicago: University of Chicago Press.

Kull, K. (1999), 'Biosemiotics in the 20th Century: A view from biology'. *Semiotica* 127(1): 385–414.

—(2000), 'Copy versus translate, meme versus sign: development of biological textuality'. *European Journal for Semiotic Studies* 12(1): 101–20.

Kull, K., T. Deacon, C. Emmeche, J. Hoffemeyer and F. Stjernfelt (2010), 'Theses on Biosemiotics: Prolegomena to a Theoretical Biology'. *Biological Theory* 4(2): 167–73.

Kurzweil, R. (2005), *The Singularity is Near*. New York: Viking.

Lakatos, I, (2001), *The Methodology of Scientific Research Programmes*. Cambridge: Cambridge University Press.

Laland, K., J. Kumm and M. Feldman (1995), 'Gene-culture Coevolutionary Theory: A Test Case'. *Current Anthropology* 36(1): 131–56.

Lambert, J. (2006), *Digital Storytelling*, 2nd edn. Berkeley, CA: Digital Diner Press.

Lanham, R. (2006), *The Economics of Attention: Style and Substance in the Age of Information*. Chicago: Chicago University Press.

Larsson, M. (2009), *Shattered Anzacs: Living with the Scars of War*. Sydney: UNSW Press.

Lash, S. (2007), 'Power after Hegemony: Cultural Studies in Mutation?'. *Theory, Culture & Society* 24(3): 55–78.

Latour, B. (2005), *Reassembling the Social: An Introduction to Actor-Network Theory*. Oxford: Oxford University Press.

Laycock, S. (2012), *All the Countries We've Ever Invaded: And the Few We Never Got Round To*. UK: The History Press.

Leach, E. (1964), 'Animal Categories and Verbal Abuse'. In S. Hugh-Jones and J. Laidlaw (eds) (2000) *The Essential Edmund Leach*. New Haven, CT: Yale University Press, 322–43.

—(1965), 'The Nature of War'. In S. Hugh-Jones and J. Laidlaw (eds) (2000) *The Essential Edmund Leach*. New Haven, CT: Yale University Press, 343–57.

Leadbeater, C. (2008), *We Think: Mass Innovation not Mass Production*. London: Profile Books.

—(2010), *Cloud Culture: The Future of Global Cultural Relations*. London: Counterpoint.

Leadbeater, C. and P. Miller (2004), *The Pro-Am Revolution*. London: Demos.

Leadbeater, C. and A. Wong (2010), *Learning from the Extremes*. Online: Cisco: www.cisco.com/web/about/citizenship/socio-economic/docs/Learningfrom Extremes_WhitePaper.pdf.

Leavis, F. R. and D. Thompson (1933), *Culture and Environment: The Training of Critical Awareness*. London: Chatto & Windus.

Lee, R. E. (2003), *Life and Times of Cultural Studies: The Politics and Transformation of the Structures of Knowledge*. Durham, NC: Duke University Press.

—(2010), *Knowledge Matters: The Structures of Knowledge and the Crisis of the Modern World-System*. St. Lucia: UQP; New Brunswick, NJ: Transaction Books (2011).

Lemke, J. (1999), 'Typological and Topological Meaning in Diagnostic Discourse'. *Discourse Processes* 27(2): 173–85: http://academic.brooklyn.cuny.edu/education/jlemke/papers/topomed.htm.

Lepenies, W. (2006), *The Seduction of Culture in German History*. Princeton, NJ: Princeton University Press.

Lewis, J. (2002), *Cultural studies: The Basics*. London: Sage Publications.

Liu, H., F. Prugnollea, A. Manicab and F. Ballouxa (2006), 'A Geographically Explicit Genetic Model of Worldwide Human-Settlement History'. *American Journal of Human Genetics* 79(2): 230–7.

Lord, A. (1960), *The Singer of Tales*. Cambridge, MA: Harvard University Press.

Lotman, Y. (1990), *Universe of the Mind: A Semiotic Theory of Culture*. Bloomington and Indianapolis: University of Indiana Press.

—(2005), 'On the Semiosphere'. *Sign Systems Studies* 33(1): (first published 1985). www.ut.ee/SOSE/sss/Lotman331.pdf.

Lotman, Y. [J.] (2009), *Culture and Explosion*. Berlin: Mouton De Gruyter.

Lotman, Y. and A. Shukman (1982), 'The Text and the Structure of Its Audience'. *New Literary History* 14(1): 81–7.

Lucy, N. (2004), *A Derrida Dictionary*. Malden, MA and Oxford: Wiley-Blackwell.

Luhmann, N. (1986), 'The Autopoeisis of Social Systems'. In F. Geyer and J. van der Zouwen (eds), *Sociocybernetic Paradoxes – Observation, Control and Evolution of Self-steering Systems*. London: Sage Publications, 172–92.

—(1991), 'What is Communication?' *Communication Theory* X: 251–9.

—(2000), *Art as a Social System*. Stanford, CA: Stanford University Press.

—(2013), *Theory of Society, Volume 1*. Stanford, CA: Stanford University Press.

Lundby, K. (ed.) (2009), *Digital Storytelling, Mediatized Stories*. New York: Peter Lang.

Lyell, C. (1863), *The Antiquity of Man*. Online: http://en.wikisource.org/wiki/The_Antiquity_of_Man.

MacGregor, N. (2011), *A History of the World in 100 Objects*. London: Viking.

Malešević, S. and K. Ryan (2013), 'The Disfigured Ontology of Figurational Sociology: Norbert Elias and the Question of Violence'. *Critical Sociology* 39(2): 165–81.

Mandela, N. (1994), *Long Walk to Freedom*. London: Little, Brown.

Maturana, H. and F. Varela (1980), *Autopoiesis and Cognition: The Realization of the Living*. Dordrecht/Boston: Reidel.

Mazower, M. (2012), *Governing the World: The History of an Idea*. New York: Penguin.

McCloskey, D. (2006), *The Bourgeois Virtues: Ethics for an Age of Commerce*. Chicago, IL: University of Chicago Press.

—(2010), *Bourgeois Dignity: Why Economics can't Explain the Modern World*. Chicago, IL: University of Chicago Press.

McLellan, D. (2006), *Karl Marx: His Life and Thought*, 4th edn (first published 1973). London. Palgrave Macmillan.

McLuhan, M. (1962), *The Gutenberg Galaxy: The Making of Typographic Man*. Toronto: University of Toronto Press.

McNair, B. (2006), *Cultural Chaos: Journalism, News and Power in a Globalised World*. London: Routledge.

Meadows, D. and J. Kidd (2009), '"Capture Wales." The BBC Digital Storytelling project'. In J. Hartley and K. McWilliam (eds), *Story Circle: Digital Storytelling around the World*. Malden, MA and Oxford: Wiley-Blackwell, 91–117.

Meadows, D., L. Heledd and C. Evans (2006), 'How public broadcasting serves the public interest in the digital age'. *First Person: International Digital Storytelling Conference*, Australian Centre for the Moving Image, 5 February: www.acmi.net.au/global/docs/first_person_meadows.pdf.

Mendelberg, T. (2002), 'The deliberative citizen: Theory and evidence'. *Political Decision Making, Deliberation and Participation* 6: 151–93.

Mesoudi, A. (2010), 'Evolutionary Synthesis in the Social Sciences and Humanities'. *Cultural Science* 3(1).

—(2011), *Cultural Evolution: How Darwinian Theory can Explain Human Diversity and Synthesize the Social Sciences*. Chicago: University of Chicago Press.

Mesoudi, A. and M. O'Brien (2008), 'The Cultural Transmission of Great Basin Projectile-point Technology: An Experimental Simulation'. *American Antiquity* 73: 3–28.

Miller, G. (2009), *Spent: Sex, Evolution, and Consumer Behavior*. New York: Penguin Books.

Miller, T. (2006), *Cultural Citizenship*. Philadelphia, PA: Temple University Press.

Mokyr, J. (2009), *The Enlightened Economy: Britain and the Industrial Revolution 1700–1850*. London: Penguin.

Morgan, T., L. Rendell, M. Ehn, W. Hoppitt and K. Laland (2011), 'The Evolutionary Basis of Human Social Learning'. *Proceedings of Royal Society B* 279: 653–72.

Myers, F. (1991), *Pintupi Country, Pintupi Self: Sentiment, Place, and Politics Among Western Desert Aborigines*. Berkeley, CA: University of California Press.

—(2002), *Painting Culture: The Making of an Aboriginal High Art*. Raleigh, NC: Duke University Press.

Nelson, O. (2013), 'Dark undercurrents of teenage girls' selfies'. *Sydney Morning Herald*, 11 July. Online: www.smh.com.au/comment/dark-undercurrents-of-teenage-girls-selfies-20130710-2pqbl.html.

Nowak, M. (2011), *Supercooperators: The Mathematics of Evolution, Altruism and Human Behaviour (Or, Why We Need Each Other to Succeed)*. With R. Highfield. Edinburgh: Canongate Books.

Oakeshott, M. (1975), *On Human Conduct*. Oxford: Clarendon Press.

O'Connor, J. (2010), *The Cultural and Creative Industries: A Literature Review*. 2nd edn. Newcastle: Creativity, Culture and Education: http://www.creativitycultureeducation.org/the-cultural-and-creative-industries-a-literature-review.

Olson, M. (1965), *The Logic of Collective Action*. Harvard: Harvard University Press.

—(1982), *The Rise and Decline of Nations: Economic Growth, Stagflation, and Social Rigidities*. New Haven, CT: Yale University Press.

Ong, W. (1958), *Ramus and the Decay of Dialogue: From the Art of Discourse to the Art of Reason*. Cambridge, MA: Harvard University Press.

—(2012), *Orality and Literacy: Technologizing the Word; 30th Anniversary Edition with Additional Chapters by John Hartley*. London: Routledge (first published 1982).

Ormerod, P. (2005), *Why Most Things Fail: Evolution, Extinction and Economics*. London: Faber & Faber.

—(2012), *Positive Linking: How Networks and Incentives Can Revolutionise the World*. London: Faber & Faber.

O'Shannessy, C. (2005), 'Light Warlpiri: A New Language'. *Australian Journal of Linguistics* 25(1): 31–57.

Ostrom, E. (1990), *Governing the Commons: The Evolution of Institutions for Collective Action*. Cambridge: Cambridge University Press.

Ostrom, E. and C. Hess (2011), *Understanding Knowledge as a Commons: From Theory to Practice*. Cambridge, MA: MIT Press.

Page, S. (2011), *Diversity and Complexity*. Princeton, NJ: Princeton University Press.

Pagel, M. (2012), *Wired for Culture: The Natural History of Human Cooperation*. London: Allen Lane.

—(2012b), 'The Culture Bandwagon'. *New Humanist*. Accessible at: www.eurozine.com/articles/2012-02-21-pagel-en.html.

Paine, T. (1792), *Rights of Man*. Online: http://ebooks.adelaide.edu.au/p/paine/thomas/p147r/.

Papacharissi, Z. (2010), *A Private Sphere: Democracy in a Digital Age*. Cambridge: Polity Press.

Parker Pearson, M. (2012), *Stonehenge: Exploring the Greatest Stone Age Mystery*. Great Britain: Simon & Schuster.

Patai, D. and W. Corral (2005), *Theory's Empire: An Anthology of Dissent*. New York: Columbia University Press.

Peirce, C. S. (1868/1977), *Semiotics and Significs*. Ed. C. Hardwick. Bloomington: Indiana University Press.

Pieterse, J. (2003), *Globalization and Culture*. New York: Rowman & Littlefield.

Pinker, S. (2011), *The Better Angels of our Nature: Why Violence has Declined*. New York: Viking.

Pocklington, R. and M. Best (1997), 'Cultural Evolution and Units of Selection in Replicating Text'. *Journal of Theoretical Biology* 188(1): 79–87.

Popper, K. (1945), *The Open Society and its Enemies Vol 1: The Poverty of Historicism*. London: Routledge.

—(1963), *Conjectures and Refutations: The Growth of Scientific Knowledge*, 2nd edn. London: Routledge, this edn 2002.

—(1972), *Objective Knowledge: An Evolutionary Approach*. Oxford: Clarendon Press.

—(2002), *The Logic of Scientific Discovery*. London: Routledge.

Porter, M. (1990), 'The Competitive Advantage of Nations'. *Harvard Business Review*, March–April: 73–91. Accessible at: http://kkozak.wz.cz/Porter.pdf.

Potts, J. (2000), *The New Evolutionary Microeconomics: Complexity, Competence and Adaptive Behaviour*. Cheltenham: Edward Elgar.

—(2010), 'Review of C. Shirky *Here comes everybody* and C. Leadbeater *We think*'. *Innovation: Management, Practice and Policy* 12(1): 118–20.

—(2010), 'Can behavioural biases in choice under novelty explain innovation failures?' *Prometheus* 28(2): 133–48.

—(2011), *Creative Industries and Economic Evolution*. Cheltenham: Edward Elgar.

Potts, J. (2012), 'Novelty-Bundling Markets'. In D. Andersson (ed.), *The Spatial Market Process (Advances in Austrian Economics, Volume 16)*. UK: Emerald Group Publishing, 291–312.

—(2013), 'Rules of spontaneous order'. *Taxis + Cosmos* 1(1): 30–41: http://cosmosandtaxis.files.wordpress.com/2013/11/cosmostaxis_nov18_r1.pdf.

Potts, J., S. Cunningham, J. Hartley and P. Ormerod (2008), 'Social network markets: a new definition of the creative industries'. *Journal of Cultural Economics* 32(3): 166–85.

Potts, J., J. Hartley, J. Banks, J. Burgess, R. Cobcroft, S. Cunningham and L. Montgomery (2008), 'Consumer co-creation and situated creativity'. *Industry & Innovation* 15(5): 459–74.

Pultar, G. (ed.) (2014), *Imagined Identities: Identity Formation in the Age of Globalization*. Syracuse, NY: Syracuse University Press.

Quiggin, J. (2006), 'Blogs, wikis and creative innovation'. *International Journal of Cultural Studies* 9(4): 481–96.

Rabinow, P. and N. Rose (2006), 'Biopower Today'. *BioSocieties* 1: 195–217.

Rennie, E. (2006), *Community Media: A Global Introduction*. Lanham, MD: Rowman and Littlefield.

Richards, I. A. (1936), *The Philosophy of Rhetoric*. Oxford: Oxford University Press.

Richards, T. (1993), *The Imperial Archive: Knowledge and the Fantasy of Empire*. London: Verso.

Richey, S. (2013), *The Social Basis of the Rational Citizen: How Political Communication in Social Networks Improves Civic Competence*. New York: Lexington Books.

Ritchie, D. (1896), 'Social Evolution'. *International Journal of Ethics* 6(2): 165–81.

Roberts, M. D. (2008), *Does Meaning Evolve?* Accessible in ArXiv: http://arxiv.org/pdf/cs/9811004.pdf.

Romer, J. (2012), *A History of Ancient Egypt: From the First Farmers to the Great Pyramid*. London: Penguin.

Romer, P. (1990), 'Endogenous technological change. *Journal of Political Economy* 98(5): 71–102.

Rose, F. (2012), *The Art of Immersion. How the Digital Generation is Remaking Hollywood, Madison Avenue, and the Way We Tell Stories*. New York, NY: W. W. Norton.

Rose, N. (2006), *The Politics of Life Itself: Biomedicine, Power, and Subjectivity in the Twenty-First Century*. Princeton, NJ: Princeton University Press.

Rossi, A. (1977), 'A Biosocial Perspective on Parenting'. *Daedalus* 106(2): 1–31.

Rothstein, E. (2009), 'Darwin's Wake Splashed Artists, Too'. *New York Times*, 2 March: www.nytimes.com/2009/03/03/arts/design/03muse.html.

Runciman, W. G. (2009), *The Theory of Cultural and Social Selection*. Cambridge: Cambridge University Press.

Ruskin, J. (1862), *Unto This Last: Four Essays on the First Principles of Political Economy*. Accessible at: http://web.archive.org/web/20081025033653/http://etext.lib.virginia. edu/toc/modeng/public/RusLast.html.

Saada, E. (2012), *Empire's Children: Race, Filiation, and Citizenship in the French Colonies*. Chicago: University of Chicago Press.

Saatchi, C. (2013), *Babble*. London: Booth-Clibborn Editions.

Saussure, F. de (1974), *Course in General Linguistics*. London: Fontana.

Saxenian, A. (1994), *Regional Advantage*. Boston, MA: MIT Press.

Scammell, M. (2000), 'The Internet and Civic Engagement: The Age of the Citizen Consumer'. *Political Communication* 17: 351–5.

Schmidt, K. (2010), 'Göbekli Tepe – the Stone Age Sanctuaries. New results of ongoing excavations with a special focus on sculptures and high reliefs'. *Documenta Praehistorica* XXXVII: 239–56: http://arheologija.ff.uni-lj.si/documenta/ authors37/37_21.pdf.

Schumpeter, J. (1942), *Capitalism, Socialism and Democracy*. New York: HarperPerennial, this edn 1975.

Seal, G. (2004), *Inventing Anzac: The Digger and National Mythology*. St Lucia: University of Queensland Press.

—(2013), *Great Anzac Stories: The Men and Women who Created the Digger Legend*. Sydney: Allen & Unwin.

Shackle, G. (1972), *Epistemics & Economics: A Critique of Economic Doctrines*. Cambridge: Cambridge University Press.

Shaw, G. B. (1937), *The Intelligent Woman's Guide to Socialism, Capitalism, Sovietism and Fascism*. 2 vols. London: Pelican Books [A1 and A2].

Shirky, C. (2008), *Here Comes Everybody: The Power of Organizing without Organizations*. New York: Penguin Press.

Şimşek, B. (2012), *Using Digital Storytellign as a Change Agent for Women's Participation in the Turkish Public Sphere*. PhD Thesis, Queensland University of Technology: http://eprints.qut.edu.au/50894/1/Burcu_Simsek_Thesis.pdf.

Simon, H. (1962), 'The architecture of complexity'. *Proceedings of the American Philosophical Society* 106(6): 467–82: http://ecoplexity.org/files/uploads/ Simon.pdf.

Simonton, D. (1999), *Origins of Genius*. Oxford: Oxford University Press.

Skeggs, B. (2005), 'The Making of Class and Gender through Visualizing Moral Subject Formation'. *Sociology* 39(5): 965–82.

Smiles, S. (1859), *Self Help; with Illustrations of Conduct and Perseverance*. Project Gutenberg: www.gutenberg.org/ebooks/935.

Smith, A. (1759), *The Theory of Moral Sentiments.* Accessible at: www.excellentfuture. ca/sites/default/files/Theory%20of%20Moral%20Sentiments%20Adam%20Smith. pdf.

Smith, E. A. (2010), 'Communication and collective action: language and the evolution of human cooperation'. *Evolution and Human Behavior* 31: 231–45.

Sober, E. and D. S. Wilson (1998), *Unto Others: The Evolution and Psychology of Unselfish Behavior.* Cambridge, MA: Harvard University Press.

Sokal, R., N. Oden and C. Wilson (1991), 'Genetic evidence for the spread of agriculture in Europe by demic diffusion'. *Nature* 351: 143–5.

Sowell, T. (1998), *Conquests and Cultures: An International History.* New York: Basic Books.

Sparrow, J. (2011), *Warfare State: World War II Americans and the Age of Big Government.* Oxford: Oxford University Press.

Spence, M. (1973), 'Job Market Signaling'. *Quarterly Journal of Economics* 87(3): 355–74.

Stano, P. and P-L. Luisi (2010), 'Achievements and open questions in the self-reproduction of vesicles and synthetic minimal cells'. *Chemical Communications* 46(21): 3639–53.

Stark, D. (2009), *The Sense of Dissonance: Accounts of Worth in Economic Life.* Princeton, NJ: Princeton University Press.

Stephenson, W. (1967), *The Play Theory of Mass Communication.* Chicago: Chicago University Press.

Stordeur, D. (1999), 'New Discoveries in Architecture and Symbolism at Jerf el Ahmar (Syria), 1997-1999', *Neo-Lithics: A Newsletter of Southwest Asian Lithics Research* 1(00): 1–4: http://www.exoriente.org/docs/00018.pdf.

Storey, J. (1996), *Cultural Studies and the Study of Popular Culture: Theories and Methods.* Athens GA: University of Georgia Press.

Sunstein, C. (2002), 'The law of group polarization'. *Journal of Political Philosophy* 10(2): 175–95.

Swedberg, R. (2006), 'The Cultural Entrepreneur and the Creative Industries: Beginning in Vienna'. *Journal of Cultural Economics* 30: 243–61.

Tacchi, J. (2004), 'Creative Applications of New Information and Communication Technologies'. *International Journal of Cultural Studies* 7(1): 91–103.

Tajfel, H. (1970), 'Experiments in intergroup discrimination'. *Scientific American* 223: 96–102.

—(1974), 'Social Identity and Intergroup Behavior'. *Social Science Information* 13(2): 65–93.

Taleb, N. (2012), *Anti-Fragile: Things that Gain from Disorder.* New York: Random House.

Tallis, R. (2011), *Aping Mankind: Neuromania, Darwinitis, and the Misrepresentation of Mankind.* Durham: Acumen.

Taylor-Gooby, P. (2008), *Reframing Social Citizenship.* Oxford: Oxford University Press.

Thomas, D. and J. Seely Brown (2011), *A New Culture of Learning: Cultivating the Imagination for a World of Constant Change*. Online: CreateSpace Independent Publishing Platform. Accessible at: www.newcultureoflearning.com/.

Thumim, N. (2012), *Self-Representation and Digital Culture*. London: Palgrave.

Tomlinson, J. (1996), 'Cultural globalisation: Placing and displacing the west'. *European Journal of Development Research* 8(2): 22–35.

Tooby, J. and L. Cosmides (1992), 'The Psychological Foundations of Culture'. In J. Barkow, L. Cosmides and J. Tooby (eds), *The Adapted Mind: Evolutionary Psychology and the Generation of Culture*. Oxford: Oxford University Press, 19–136.

Twain, M. (1897), *Following the Equator*. Online: www.online-literature.com/twain/following-the-equator.

Tylor, E. (1871), *Primitive Culture: Researches Into the Development of Mythology, Philosophy, Religion, Art, and Custom*. 2 Vols. London: John Murray.

Uexkull, J. (1973), *Theoretische Biologie*. Frankfurt: Suhrkamp.

van Beest, I., Williams, K. (2006), 'When inclusion costs and ostracism pays; ostracism still hurts'. *Journal of Personality and Social Psychology* 91(5): 918–28.

van den Berghe, P. (1990), 'From the Popocatepetl to the Limpopo. In B. Berger (ed.), *Authors of Their Own Lives: Intellectual Autobiographies by Twenty American Sociologists*. Berkeley: University of California Press, 410–31.

Veblen, T. (1898), 'Why is economics not an evolutionary science?' *Quarterly Journal of Economics* 12. Accessible at: http://socserv.mcmaster.ca/econ/ugcm/3ll3/veblen/econevol.txt.

—(1899), *The Theory of the Leisure Class: An Economic Study of Institutions*. Accessible at: www.gutenberg.org/ebooks/833.

—(1918), *The Higher Learning in America*. New York: Cosimo Classics. First published 1918 by Hill and Wang; this edn 2006. Accessible at: http://socserv2.mcmaster.ca/~econ/ugcm/3ll3/veblen/higher.

Vedres, B. and D. Stark (2010), 'Structural folds: Generative disruption in overlapping groups'. *American Journal of Sociology* 115(4): 1150–90.

Vernadsky, V. I. (1938), 'The Transition from the Biosphere to the Noösphere'. Excerpts from *Scientific Thought as a Planetary Phenomenon*, trans. William Jones'. *21st Century*, Spring-Summer 2012/04: (published 2012). www.21stcenturysciencetech.com/Articles_2012/Spring-Summer_2012/04_Biospere_Noosphere.pdf.

—(1943), 'Some Words about the Noösphere'. *21st Century*, Spring 2005: 16–21. (published 2005). Online: https://www.21stcenturysciencetech.com/translations/The_Noosphere.pdf.

Vivienne, S. (2013), *Digital Storytelling as Everyday Activism: Queer Identity, Voice and Networked Publics*. PhD thesis, Queensland University of Technology: http://eprints.qut.edu.au/60660/.

Vološinov, V. (1929/1973), *Marxism and the Philosophy of Language*. New York: Seminar Press.

Warner, M. (2005), *Publics and Counterpublics*. New York: Zone Books.

Watson, P. (2010), *The German Genius: Europe's Third Renaissance, the Second Scientific Revolution, and the Twentieth Century*. London, etc.: Simon & Schuster.

Williams, R. (1958), 'Culture is Ordinary'. Reprinted in B. Highmore (ed.), (2002) *The Everyday Life Reader*. London: Routledge, 91–100.

—(1960), *Culture and Society: 1780–1950*. London: Penguin. Accessible at: http://archive.org/details/culturesociety17001850mbp.

—(1973), 'Base and Superstructure in Marxist Cultural Theory'. *New Left Review*, Series I, no. 82; reprinted in C. Mukerji and M. Schudson (eds) (1991) *Rethinking Popular Culture: Contemporary Perspectives in Cultural Studies*. Berkeley and LA, CA: California University Press, 407–23.

—(1977), *Marxism and Literature*. Oxford: Oxford University Press.

Willis, P. (1979), 'Shop Floor Culture, Masculinity and the Wage Form'. In J. Clarke, C. Critcher and R. Johnson (eds), *Working Class Culture: Studies in History and Theory*. London: Hutchinson, 185–98.

Wilson, E. O. (1975), *Sociobiology: The New Synthesis*, 2nd edn (2000). Cambridge, MA: The Belknap Press.

—(2012), *The Social Conquest of Earth*. New York: W. W. Norton & Co.

—(1998), *Consilience: The Unity of Knowledge*. New York: Vintage.

Wimsatt, W. (1999), 'Genes, memes and cultural heredity'. *Biology and Philosophy* 14: 279–310.

Wittgenstein, L. (1922), *Tractatus Logico-Philosophicus*. Online: Project Gutenberg: www.gutenberg.org/files/5740/5740-pdf.pdf.

Wolfe, C. (2009), *What Is Posthumanism?* Minneapolis MN: University of Minnesota Press.

Zahavi, A. (1977), 'The cost of honesty (further remarks on the handicap principle)'. *Journal of Theoretical Biology* 67(3): 603–5.

Ziman, J. (ed.) (2000), *Technological Innovation as an Evolutionary Process*. Cambridge: Cambridge University Press.

Zittrain, J. (2008), *The Future of the Internet – And How to Stop it*. New Haven, CT: Yale University Press; London: Penguin.

Index